Justice on Demand

Contemporary Approaches to Film and Media Series

A complete listing of the books in this series can be found
online at wsupress.wayne.edu

General Editor
Barry Keith Grant
Brock University

Dafna Lemish, 2010
Routledge, Abingdon
222pp (pbk), ISBN 978-0-415-48206-6

The journal reference style is <u>Chicago Author-Date</u>

- Submissions should be in English using American or British spelling and American punctuation (i.e. "with punctuation appearing within quotation marks.").
- All text should be double-spaced, 12-point Times New Roman.
- Use unjustified mode and align text to the left, leaving the right margin ragged.
- Use the underline function in Word to indicate text that you want to show up as being in italics in your published article.
- Do not hyphenate words at the ends of lines. Do not use soft returns (Shift-Enter).
- Insert hard returns only at the end of each paragraph and heading.
- Insert a tab at the start of each new paragraph at .5 inches.
- Set the margins at 1.25 inches on the left and 1.25 inches on the right. (Go to File/Page Setup to set the margins.)
- When using a word which is or is asserted to be a proprietary term or trade mark, authors must use the symbol ® or TM.
- Use double quotation marks, except where "a quotation is 'within' a quotation."
- Keep capitalization to a minimum.
- Be consistent in how you use verb tense throughout your article.

- Use three hyphens for an em dash, the long dash that sets off a phrase from the rest of a sentence.
- Use two hyphens to link number ranges, two items linked in a political context, and to link the names of joint authors.
- Use one hyphen wherever you would normally use a hyphen, as in compound words.
- Place the month before the day in full dates. Examples: July 8, 1999 and on July 8.
- Do not spell out years or use an apostrophe for decades. Examples: 1943 and 1990s.
- Spell out centuries. Example: twentieth century (not 20th century).
- Insert a hyphen when a century is used adjectivally (e.g. twentieth-century art).
- To make the origins of emphasis explicit, use italics mine (if the text was written) or emphasis mine (if the text was spoken).
- Post-feminism/post-feminist rather than postfeminism/postfeminist

First-time reviewers may also find the following link helpful:
http://writingcenter.unc.edu/handouts/book-reviews/

Feminist Media Studies

Book Review Guidelines

The Commentary and Criticism section of *Feminist Media Studies* aims to publish book reviews that go beyond a detailed description of content to provide productive critique and stimulate critical debate. We strive to find reviewers who have expertise in, or a good working knowledge of, the areas/themes of particular books. We hope that this will enable reviewers to contextualise the book in relation to what they perceive to be the most important/current debates in the wider field(s).

Book reviews should be no more than 1000 words (including references) and should be emailed directly to Melanie Kennedy (mjk29@le.ac.uk) and Safiya Noble (snoble@g.ucla.edu) within 10 weeks of receiving the book.

Please do not submit reviews via the ScholarOne system, as reviews submitted in this manner will not be processed properly.

Style guidelines

Format for book reviews:

Title
Author, year of publication
Publisher, place of publication
Page numbers (indicate if paperback or hardback), ISBN number

JUSTICE
ON DEMAND

True Crime in the Digital Streaming Era

Tanya Horeck

WAYNE STATE UNIVERSITY PRESS
Detroit

ISBN 978-0-8143-4063-9 (paperback); ISBN 978-0-8143-4720-1 (case);
ISBN 978-0-8143-4064-6 (ebook)

Library of Congress Control Number: 2019946658

Wayne State University Press
Leonard N. Simons Building
4809 Woodward Avenue
Detroit, Michigan 48201-1309

Visit us online at wsupress.wayne.edu

Contents

Acknowledgments

THIS BOOK WAS A long time in the making, and probably first began germinating in my youth in Sudbury, Ontario, Canada, the small mining town where I was born and raised. I was the daughter of a criminal defense lawyer, and there is no doubt that my father's career influenced my research interests. My first jobs as a young woman were as a runner for his law firm and then, slightly later, as an administrator for Legal Aid. It is important to note, however, that my mother's interest in celebrity culture was also significant in shaping my interests; the *People* magazines that were always readily available in my home no doubt intertwined with my interest in crime to create the particular constellation of academic interests that characterize my work today. I'm grateful to my parents for providing me with the security and freedom of a Northern Ontario childhood where I had the space to think, to read, and to watch old black-and-white movies on a Saturday night with Elwy Yost.

Life (and a Commonwealth Scholarship) brought me far away from my Northern Ontario roots to the UK, and it now seems deeply significant that my move to Brighton to study at the University of Sussex coincided with the announcement of the O. J. Simpson verdict in 1995. Landing at Heathrow, exhausted after my first solo transatlantic flight, I can still remember being stunned as I watched the announcement of the "not guilty" verdict on my hotel TV. Recently, watching the TV series *The People v. O.J. Simpson* and the ESPN documentary *O.J.: Made in America* strongly reminded me of the affective force of that moment and the enduring cultural significance of that trial in shaping my interests in crime, celebrity, and reality TV.

I would like first of all to thank Annie Martin of Wayne State University Press for seeing the promise of this book based on my Society for Cinema and Media Studies (SCMS) paper in Chicago in 2013. Thanks for your patience and your enthusiasm, Annie, as well as for the Bloody Marys (unpalatable house mix aside). It was you who first encouraged me to listen to *My Favorite Murder* and for that I am grateful too. While Karen and Georgia's incessant swearing poses some challenges in a house with children, I love the podcast and am always grateful for their company and for their love of murder. Thanks also to my editor, Marie Sweetman, who took over at a later stage and who has been so kind and helpful and to Barry Keith Grant for overseeing it all.

While this book was written over the course of several years and emerged out of various conference papers and keynotes, it could not have been completed without the help of a sabbatical and much-needed teaching relief, courtesy of Anglia Ruskin University (ARU). I would like to thank Farah Mendlesohn, my former head of department, for providing me with the time and financial support it takes to complete academic research. As much as books can be a labor of love, they are also considerably grueling and time consuming to write and it is important to acknowledge the material conditions of writing (especially in these neoliberal times).

Thanks to Sebastian Rasinger for his steady support at the English and Media helm and to Sarah Etchells and Annie Morgan James for their many kindnesses (and effortless glamour). I would also like to thank the support staff at ARU, especially Jolene Cushion, the best subject librarian out there, and my fellow Canadian Marlene Buick, who was always there for a chat and a cold one.

A previous version of chapter 1, "A film that will rock you to your core": Emotion and Affect in *Dear Zachary* and the True Crime Documentary, was published in the journal *Crime, Media, Culture: An International Journal* in 2014 and I would like to thank Sage for granting me the permission to include a reworked version of my essay in this book. I would also like to extend thanks to Kim Akass and *CST* online, where I first published a blog on *Making a Murderer*, which I eventually developed into the extended piece found in this book. Some of the insights on binge-watching found within the pages to follow are also adapted from a co-written piece (with Tina Kendall and Mareike Jenner) in *Critical Studies in Television*.

There are many other people I need to acknowledge and thank here. Special thanks to the Dions—Dan, Julie, and especially my Aunt Laura for always being there for me—I appreciate your support more than I can say. It has also been good to reconnect with Paul and Rose.

One thing I know for sure is that I would not have been able to complete this book without the love and support of my friends who have sustained me in all sorts of ways. Paul Fryer and Erin Fryer Chu have been there for me throughout the process of writing this book, and I am eternally grateful to them for their lifelong friendship. Tina Kendall is my colleague and academic twin but also a dear friend, and I am deeply indebted to her for reading various drafts of my work. Her fiercely intelligent feedback skills and constructive criticism are unparalleled in the biz. That, along with her sunny Southern Californian disposition and her love of a fine cocktail, has sustained me through the long, hard slog of academic writing. Thanks also to Mareike Jenner for being such a supportive and engaging colleague: it has been rejuvenating to have someone on site with a shared set of interests in binge-watching, Netflix, and true crime podcasts. Although he had the audacity to leave Anglia Ruskin, I would also like to thank Joss Hands, for being such a good friend. I would also like to extend thanks to Sarah Barrow, who is a constant source of inspiration and support, and to Vicky Lebeau for being such a longstanding and generous mentor.

Thanks, as well, to all the students who took my "Documentary Film Theory" course over the years at Anglia Ruskin and who watched true crime documentaries with me. Teaching documentary film continues to be immensely rewarding and inspiring for me.

I would also like to thank the people who have shown an interest in my research on true crime and digital violence and who have invited me to give talks along the way, including Sam McBean, Zara Dinnen, Michael Goddard, Deborah Jermyn, Kirsty Fairclough, Martin Goutte, Antoine Gaudin, Barbara Laborde, Thea Cronin, Feona Attwood, Alison Winch, and Jamie Hakim. This book is enriched because of the feedback provided by you and the audiences at your respective institutions in Birmingham, London, Salford, Paris, Middlesex, and Norwich.

Many of these chapters started out as Society for Cinema and Media Studies papers and I want like to thank SCMS for providing me with such a wonderful sense of professional belonging and collegiality over the past ten years. Incredible experiences of collaboration have emerged out of my SCMS membership. Deep thanks to Barbara Klinger and Kathleen McHugh for being such wonderful inspirations to me. My experience of collaborating with you and Lisa Coulthard has been a career highlight, and I am so grateful for your mentorship and for your friendship. Thanks also to Ina Rae Hark for her support and enthusiasm with all things crime TV and then some; it is a privilege to know all of you.

In 2017, I was awarded a Harry Ransom Fellowship that enabled me to conduct research in the Erle Stanley Gardner archives, some of which appears here in chapter 3. I would like to thank Bridget Gayle and all the folks at the Harry Ransom Center for their help and assistance during my brief—if wonderful—stay in Austin, Texas. Thanks also to fellow scholar Diletta De Cristofaro for being a friendly face and for taking me out for BBQ!

I consider myself very lucky to know an impossibly brilliant, witty, and glamorous crew of UK Film and TV scholars who have supported me in so many ways during this project. Caroline Bainbridge, Lucy Bolton, Sofia Bull, Shelley Cobb, Neil Ewen, Hannah Hamad, Deborah Jermyn, Lisa Purse, and Helen Wood—you are all amazing people and my life is so much the better for knowing you all. And to the Canadian crew that is Lisa Coulthard and Lindsay Steenberg—well, I could not ask for a better pair of friends or intellectual partners in crime—long may our adventures continue . . .

During some rocky times, many old (and some new) friends reached out and offered much-needed emotional sustenance and support. Special thanks in particular to Deirdre Kirkwood, Stacey Mitsopulos, Chrissie and Todd Hellstrom, Lisa Grassi Blais, Lorna Fryer, Jake Rupert, Anita Grassi Blais, Louise Tarini, D'Arcy Vachon, Judi Vachon, Lorna Fryer, and Jane Harper Agosta. This much I know for sure: you can take the girl out of Sudbury but there is no taking the Sudbury out of the girl.

Thanks to my network of friends, including Lorraine Chapman, Sharon Gruskin, and Gail Harrison. Very special thanks to Caroline and Andy Webb for being there for me and my children. Caz—you always buoyed me up when I needed it the most and I really could not have completed this book without your support.

Thanks also to Caetlin Benson-Allott, Siobhan Boakes, William Brown, Sean Campbell, Julia Chan, Deborah Curtis, Neal Curtis, Greg Elmer, Danielle Fuller, Kristin Fuhs, Sarah Gibson-Yates, James Harvey, Debbie Ging, Ronda Gougeon, Jessalyn Keller, Julia Leyda, Nikolaj Lubecker, Adele and Craig McMurrough, Kaity Mendes, Jason Middleton, Diane Negra, Una McCormack, Jussi Parikka, Agnieszka Piotrowska, Lisa Purse, Sean Redmond, Jessica Ringrose, Kate Saines, Deborah Shaw, Lesley Shaw, Eugenia Siapera, Robert Sinnerbrink, Daniel Smith, Will Smythe, Yvonne Tasker, Milla Tiainen, Ed Vollans, Johnny Walker, Elke Weissman, Catherine Wheatley,

Katie Worthington, and Lorraine York, all of whom have offered help and inspired me in ways they might not realize.

I am very grateful for the constructive and supportive comments I received from the two anonymous reviewers of this book, which pushed me, in the best possible way, to buck up some of my ideas.

Finally, thanks to my darling Grace and Edward for hanging in there with me. I love you both dearly and I'm looking forward to the next chapter (of life) with you . . .

Introduction

My Favorite Murder and the
Rise of "Murderino" Culture

IF THERE IS ONE program that captures the sea change in the status of true crime in mainstream culture over the last ten years, it is the female-fronted comedy podcast *My Favorite Murder* (2016–).[1] Hosted by self-identified feminists and "lifelong fans of true crime,"[2] Georgia Hardstack and Karen Kilgariff—or Georgia and Karen as they are more typically and affectionately known—*My Favorite Murder* is predicated on the unabashed assertion that stories of murder are deeply enjoyable, and especially so for women.[3] In fact, one of the central claims of the podcast is that women love to know all the terrible details of murder cases so that they can gain some sort of power over culturally endemic narratives in which girls and women are brutalized. With over ten million downloads every month, *My Favorite Murder,* or *MFM* as it is known, has become an unexpected cultural phenomenon, garnering a loyal and devoted set of fans that call themselves "murderinos,"[4] thousands of whom extend their engagement with the program on social media networks such as Facebook.[5] The participatory nature of the podcast[6] is further foregrounded through its additional feature of "hometown murders," in which listeners are invited to share their own stories of murders from the towns in which they grew up.

It is fitting to begin this book with a discussion of *MFM* because it openly reveals many of the key features associated with the capture and consumption of true crime in twenty-first-century digital culture, including the solicitation of audience interactivity across multiple media platforms, the mobilization of affective reaction and response, and the commodification of true crime as a multimodal entertainment "experience." Describing themselves as just "two girls who love murder," Karen and Georgia are forthright about the enjoyment that can be derived from true crime as a form of "clickable" entertainment in a 24/7 media culture.[7] Much of the charm of the podcast derives from the sense that the hosts are just like us—interested in the prurient details of murder cases, which are now readily available online (both hosts routinely pause to google information during the podcast)—but also ethically minded and appropriately outraged at gross social injustices as we click from source to source to source.

The emphasis on how women in particular need to be vigilant against crime builds on the work of popular female true crime authors such as Ann Rule (1931–2015), who envisioned her true crime writing as a way of preparing women, especially young women, for how to deal with potentially dangerous situations (Case Punnett 2018, 56–57; Browder 2010, 128–29).[8] MFM takes up this mission, and mines the new possibilities for engaging with true crime stories in the multiplatform era. "Stay Sexy, Don't Get Murdered" has become the podcast's catchphrase and encapsulates its central premise that talking (and joking) about murder helps to ward off anxieties about violence, and that women in particular need to "fuck politeness" (to quote another motto from the show) in order to protect themselves from toxic masculinity. Fan art created around the show's slogans abounds, and on sites such as Etsy you can find "merch" including T-shirts, key chains, fridge magnets, stickers, crochet stitching, badges, jewelry, crockery, candles, birthday cards, baseball caps, and mugs (for example). MFM thus feeds into a wider monetized convergence culture, which is characterized by the "flow of content across multiple media platforms," to borrow Henry Jenkins's widely cited phrase (2006).

Most significant, for the purposes of this book, is how explicitly MFM illustrates the affective power and resonance of true crime as a genre that invites viewer judgment on matters of justice. The format of the podcast, which is released on a weekly basis and which includes hour-long episodes as well as shorter "minisodes" and longer recordings of live broadcasts, consists of one of the female cohosts telling a story of a real-life murder (largely cribbed from Wikipedia pages) as the other one listens and shares her reactions of anger, sadness, horror, and—more often than not—laughter. To be very clear, Karen and Georgia are not laughing at the murders themselves; rather, the humor comes from their irreverent, foul-mouthed banter as they share their personal responses to crimes, and the wider issues they throw up regarding, for example, mental health, gender, victimhood, and survival. It is the friendly, conversational, and emotional *responses* of Karen and Georgia to the grue-some stories of murder they recount that are most relatable for audiences in a twenty-first-century media culture that revolves around the sharing of affec-tive reactions and judgments. Their sharp intakes of breath and their squeals of "oh no, sweet baby angel!" upon hearing the other host recount the story of the murder of a child, for example, lend themselves to online GIF-able meme culture, where a premium is placed upon the capture and commodification of legible emotions of happy, sad, angry, and the like.

This capturing of affective response—and the way in which digital true crime both shapes and manages audience attention—is the subject of this book. In focusing on what Barbara Klinger calls the "apparatus of capture" (2018a, 7) in a selection of contemporary true crime images and texts, *Justice on Demand: True Crime in the Digital Streaming Era* explores the affectivity of true crime images and their remediation across multiple media platforms. This book is deeply informed by the affect theory that has burgeoned in the humanities in the past two decades, especially that which has emerged in the field of internet research and digital media. My approach builds on the work of affect theorists such as Susanna Paasonen, Jodi Dean, Richard Grusin, and Steven Shaviro, who draw on "non-representational theory" in their attempts to explore "the things mediation *does* rather than what media mean or rep-resent" (Grusin 2010, 7, my emphasis). Such an approach is concerned with the kinds of affective sensations, intensities, and embodied responses that are generated through our engagement with media texts. Of particular impor-tance for my analysis of digital-era true crime is the notion of "networked affect," which, as Paasonen, Ken Hillis, and Michael Petit explain, refers to the connections and attachments forged through our affective encounters with a range of cultural objects and platforms—including TV shows, websites, GIFs, and apps—in a media convergence culture (2015, 1–3). In this account, affects are generated and mobilized within networks and cannot be attributable to the agency of individual actors.

This book, therefore, is neither a comprehensive study of representa-tions of true crime nor is it an empirical audience study, even though it offers reflections on certain recurring features of true crime texts and explores the kinds of audience responses that emerge through online sites. Rather, I am primarily interested in thinking about the role true crime has come to play as an exemplary genre for the digital, multiplatform era, especially in terms of how it constructs, hails, and interpellates its audiences. *Justice on Demand: True Crime in the Digital Streaming Era* offers a theoretical rumination on the question asked in countless blogs and opinion pieces of the last decade: why, at this particular cultural juncture, are we so obsessed with true crime? Or, to put the question slightly differently: why is true crime thought to be such a good vehicle for the new modes of viewer and listener engagement favored by online streaming-on-demand culture? This question, in turn, leads to another, which asks after the ethico-political dimensions of viewer engagement with real-life crime through the internet: what kind of audience responses are enabled—or disenabled—by the socio-technical platforms through which "users" now watch, listen, and engage with audiovisual true crime images? A key contention of this book is that it is only through close analysis of the kind of viewer interactivity and engagement solicited by the digital platforms and interfaces through which true crime images are now relayed that we can begin to understand the renewed popularity of the genre—and be in a position to contend with its ideological implications.

Internet Sleuthing and the Precariousness of Justice in the Digital Era

There has been an undeniable turn in contemporary digital culture toward what Mark Andrejevic calls a "culture of detection" (2007, 38). As Andrejevic suggests, "detection has become one of the watchwords of popular culture," as evident in the proliferation of media formats that promise to take us "behind the scenes" and "behind the public performance" in order "to prove that one isn't taken in by it" (2007, 38). For many of us, digital "sleuthing" is a part of our quotidian reality as we spend an untold number of hours each day searching for information online, googling and trawling through profiles on Facebook and other social media sites.[9] As journalist Michael Zelenko has noted, "in the age of Google, it is hard not to become an amateur detective" (2014).

The implications of this cultural turn to desktop detection are wide reaching and at times very troubling. In April 2013, for example, following the bombing during the Boston Marathon, the dangers of crowdsourcing crime solving were brought into disturbing relief when groups of people on Reddit mistakenly identified a number of individuals—many of them nonwhite—including missing Brown University student Sunil Tripathi, as being responsible for the bombing (Coscarelli 2013). These wrongly suspected individuals and their families were subjected to public abuse and attacks; Reddit's general manager, Erik Martin, issued a public apology in which he acknowledged that "some of the activity on reddit fueled online witch hunts and dangerous speculation which spiraled into very negative consequences for innocent parties" ("Reflections" 2013). As James Surowiecki wrote in the *New Yorker*, the design of the Reddit platform had a major role to play in the debacle:

> The way Reddit's comment threads work, with certain comments being promoted and featured more prominently than others, meant that some commenters exerted an inordinate influence over the group as a whole . . . instead of offering up lots of diverse, independent opinions, there was a tendency for Redditors to herd together, taking their cues from the conclusions that others before them had reached. . . . It was a process that ended up fostering groupthink more than collective intelligence. (2013)

Although Surowiecki reflects on some of the future ways in which the Reddit community might be able "to use the power of the crowd to help authorities" to solve crimes (2013), a sentiment that is echoed in the Reddit statement and its highlighting of the positive ways in which the site "served as a great clearinghouse for information" ("Reflections" 2013), the entire incident nevertheless foregrounds the dangers of the "digital witch hunt" and the porous line separating "an empowered crowd from a raging mob" (Wadhwa 2013).

A less sensational but still telling example of the uncertain line between digital information-seeking and criminalized activity—in this case, between sleuthing and stalking—is demonstrated in a 2013 feature from the world's largest men's magazine, *Men's Health,* titled: "Be an Internet Super-Sleuth: Everybody Stalks So You May as Well Do It Right. Here Are the Key Tactics You Can Use to Gather Intel on Others—and Yourself." Remarkably, the article that follows provides its core readership of men, aged twenty-one to forty, with information on how best to do "online stalking." That it does so through the allegedly benign notion that "we're really just a bunch of junior Dick Tracy wannabes at heart" does not diminish the unsettling nature of the piece, which, in effect, advocates—and provides training for—stalking. As Sarah Jacobsson Purewal, the author of the piece, writes, "there's more to online stalking than Googling someone's email address or finding their semi-public Facebook page. In fact, by using a few very simple techniques, you can discover tons of publicly available information about people—without paying a dime or breaking the law. We asked some crackerjack digital sleuths to show us how to gather information, from criminal records to online profiles to ancient news-group flame-wars" (2013). This example from *Men's Health* implicitly gestures toward the gendered nature of forms of digital violence,[10] and the kinds of toxic masculinity and misogyny that are both enabled and normalized by social media networks.

More often than not, however, the notion of internet sleuthing is inflected positively, as a way to become involved in "Neighborhood Watch" style activities online. On Facebook people share closed-circuit television (CCTV) footage of criminals stealing from local shops or information about missing young people in the spirit of being Good Samaritans. Police departments now post mug shots on their Facebook pages, where people are able to respond with emojis and comments.[11] On Twitter people tweet their personal judgments about crimes and criminals and follow court reporters as they live tweet about criminal cases; as one court reporter recounts: "I've been followed by judges and barristers and I get quite a bit of feedback from police officers. I tweeted that one defendant hadn't turned up for a court appearance and a police officer who follows me saw the tweet and then saw him in the street, and arrested him—that's happened a couple of times" (Banks 2012).[12] More strongly than ever before, perhaps, there is a sense of a collective "public" involved in what Erle Stanley Gardner, the creator of *Perry Mason* (CBS, 1957–66, 1973–74) and *The Court of Last Resort* (NBC, 1957–58), which I will discuss in chapter 2, referred to as the "administration of justice" (2017, 15). It is this sense of a networked public involvement in matters of crime and justice that provides a vital backdrop for the proliferation of true crime texts that have taken hold in the last two decades.[13]

What has become evident through the recent rise of true crime audiovisual texts, from *Buzzfeed Unsolved: True Crime* videos on YouTube (2016–), to podcasts such as *Serial* (2014–) and *My Favorite Murder* (2016–), to long-form true crime documentaries such as Netflix's *Making a Murderer Part 1* (2015), *Making a Murderer Part 2* (2018), *The Keepers* (2017), and *Evil Genius: The True Story of America's Most Diabolical Bank Heist* (2018), is the extent to which the true crime genre has come to epitomize participatory media culture and, in particular, an increasingly prevalent notion of the listener or viewer as a "desktop detective" or an "internet sleuth."[14]

If armchair detection has long been a central part of the appeal of true crime, a genre that has its roots in the nineteenth century and even earlier,[15] then the internet has thoroughly rebooted the notion of audiences' interactive engagement with crime for the contemporary era. One of the central arguments of this book is that true crime thrives and proliferates across the digital interfaces and platforms of Web 2.0 because of how it invigorates a notion of "armchair detection." It is not just that the internet rapidly spreads true crime stories but that true crime as a genre lends itself to the attention economies of 24/7 "platform capitalism" (Srnicek 2016) and its solicitation of "active" user or viewer engagement through participatory media technologies.

Defining True Crime

True crime scholars such as Jean Murley, Mark Seltzer, and Anita Biressi have defined true crime in various ways but tend to agree on the basic fact that its enduring popularity as a genre derives from its importance as a vehicle for articulating sociocultural issues of the time. Murley suggests that "true crime" is "more than a single popular literary genre or even a set of technical narrative conventions" and instead "has become a multi-faceted, multi-genre aesthetic formulation, a poetics of murder narration" (2008, 2). For Murley, what is most interesting is the "cultural work" of the genre and the host of ethical questions it raises, including the "easy acceptance of violence as entertainment," the sensational reification of images of violence against women, and its limited racial and class perspective (2). In this book I am also concerned with true crime's ethical purchase, but my interest is in how its digital updating raises significant new questions about audience participation in social justice through online media networks and the wider capacity of those networks to address structures of power.

For Mark Seltzer, true crime is the most popular genre of what he terms the "pathological public sphere" or "wound culture," in which people gather around the scene of the crime (2007, 10). Seltzer's work examines the close imbrication of true crime and media theory and systems and is therefore an important precursor for this book's thesis that true crime sheds significant light on the dynamics of digital media cultures. Seltzer, however, was writing in a time before social media networks had fully taken their hold, in which a discussion of true crime websites could still be referred to as a "sort of Internet-centered criminal justice cottage industry" (36), and in which digital culture was treated as a mere *part* of a wider theoretical discussion of what he calls the "violence-media complex" (7). By contrast, in a post-2010 socially networked world, internet discussions of true crime and social justice are much more than a "cottage industry." As my analysis of true crime entertainment will demonstrate, in a networked digital era, what is most significant is not the content of true crime per se but the specific media formats and platforms through which we are invited to affectively engage with it. As I will examine in chapter 3, for example, true crime trailers need to be understood as more than mere promotional objects or paratexts; rather, these short-form videos are central platforms for user interaction with true crime in the streaming era.

In *Crime, Fear and the Law in True Crime Stories*, Biressi suggests that true crime is not "a single, monolithic genre" (2001, 2), and this book does not treat it as such; rather, my aim is to consider audiovisual true crime in its digital formats and to explore the cultural stakes of its varied modes of affective address. Writing on true crime literature in Britain in the 1980s, Biressi observed that "true crime is promoted primarily and explicitly as a leisure pursuit," as with the true crime magazine summer specials that "invite viewers to put their feet up and relax" (1). However, as I will argue, true crime is no longer primarily promoted as a way to relax; in a digital network culture that puts a premium on the participatory involvement of audience members as "viewers with a job to do" (Clover 2000a, 246), true crime is now cast as a genre that performs more serious cultural work. While true crime is still also promoted as a form of entertainment, this book argues that twenty-first-century audiovisual true crime's intersection with the more culturally prestigious genre of documentary has led to its new credibility and branding as a media format that effects social change.

Examining the kinds of affective communities or publics (Papacharissi 2015, 8) that are constructed—however tenuously—by digital-era true crime, I deploy textual, audience, and social media network analysis, in order to focus attention on the imbrication of affective response and judgment that undergirds a notion of the viewer-as-detective. It is the way in which new forms of media produce community, or what Jodi Dean calls *"feelings* of community"

(2010b, 22, my emphasis), that is most significant in considering the relationship between affect and ideology in constructions of networked publics. My aim is to examine how true crime is repackaged and redefined for users and consumers in an era of "connected viewing" (Holt and Sanson 2014) in which content is designed to be distributed and shared across social media platforms and streaming services. As Barbara Klinger suggests, "this new century has seen streaming—the digital delivery of data in a continuous flow of audio and/ or video content—become an influential new norm in industrialized countries" (Klinger 2018b). The rise of Netflix, and other streaming services such as iTunes, Audible Books, and Hulu, "have not only created new business models, but have also resulted in the availability of more media content and different means of accessing it and experiencing it" (Klinger 2018b). True crime provides endless material for the streaming era and lends itself to participatory media culture through its solicitation of viewer involvement in crime solving.

Even though the interactive nature of digital true crime seems to open up the potential for closer public engagement with crime and legal processes, I interrogate how corporations such as Netflix exploit a notion of true crime's interactivity as a means of binding users more tightly to their commercial products, thus reinforcing what Andrejevic calls "the logic of commercially driven convergence" (2007, 26). This book's title, "Justice on Demand," refers to how, in contemporary digital culture, notions of social justice are commodified and bound up with the viewing habits of the streaming era, generating a powerful, if often illusory, sense that "justice" is something that can be accessed and produced through the practice of user-controlled listening and viewing, as with, for example, the "binge-watching" of a long-form true crime series such as *Making a Murderer*, discussed in chapter 4.

To gain a further sense of the popular definition of "true crime," it is helpful to turn to Wikipedia: "True crime is a non-fiction literary and film genre in which the author examines an actual crime and details the actions of real people."[16] As basic a definition as this is, it is undeniable that the authored "reality" of true crime comes with a strong affective charge and is a central part of the appeal of all the popular texts I examine in this book. However, it is worth pausing to consider the fact that dictionary definitions of true crime tend to define it primarily in relation to "reality," as with this definition from the Cambridge English Dictionary: "true crime: books and films about real crimes that involved real people." The "truth" of true crime tends to get sidelined in such definitions. It is important, however, to distinguish between terms such as "reality" and "truth," especially in a cultural moment where it is widely acknowledged that the borders between reality and fiction are entirely unstable and in which "truth" is increasingly put in scare quotes. Pointing to the "relays" between "fact and fiction" in true crime, Seltzer suggests that "true crime" is treated as "crime fact of a specific kind . . . a species of paperback sociology that, for the most part, retells real-life cases of crime" (2007, 16). I agree with Seltzer that the paradoxical distinction between "crime fiction and crime fact" (17) is constantly at play within true crime, but I posit that the "truth" of "true crime" is what gives the genre renewed resonance for these "post-truth" times. In a Trump era that revolves around "post truth," "fake news," and "alternative facts," strong questions have been raised about what truth is, "and our commitment to the idea of truth" (McIntyre 2018, 152). As *Time* magazine asked with its cover story on April 3, 2017: "Is Truth Dead?"

In its various digitized manifestation(s), true crime plays on the desire for truth that bubbles beneath the post-truth surface. True crime feeds into what television theorist Jason Mittell calls a "forensic fandom," which invites audiences "to try to crack each program's central enigmas," thereby converting viewers into "amateur narratologists, noting patterns and violations of convention, chronicling chronologies, and highlighting both inconsistencies and continuities across episodes and series" (2015, 52). The vision of the viewer-as-truth-seeker is indeed very powerful, as I will discuss in relation to a range of digital-era true crime formats. However, as I will also argue, many contemporary true crime texts are exercises in media manipulation. In persuading viewers to make judgments based on strong emotional reactions and responses generated from within the texts themselves, recent true crime texts appear to enact certain principles of a post-truth world in which "opinions and feelings" play a key role in "shaping what we think of as facts and truth" (McIntyre 2018, 172). While I want to keep a space open for thinking about ways in which digital true crime might also offer up the possibility for a more critically resistant engagement, this book explores the ways in which true crime's rhetorical modes of audience address often work to harness affective responses to dubious ideological and political ends.

Where many previous studies of true crime have tended to include a chapter about true crime and the internet at the end of the book (see Murley 2008)—or refer to online culture only in passing (see Seltzer 2007)—*Justice on*

Demand: True Crime in the Digital Streaming Era starts from the assumption that it is now impossible to discuss true crime outside of a discussion of digitality and online data flows, just as, in turn, any discussion of digital culture would be incomplete without a consideration of the violence that inheres in its networks. My assertion is that a major part of the appeal of true crime for the internet era derives from the way in which it lends itself to the operations of Google search culture and the circulation of information, judgments, and affects that govern interactions on Facebook and other forms of social media. This book is thus an exploration of the nature of our affective investment in true crime in a time of ever-expanding modes of "digital delivery" (Tryon 2013, 4). The animating question of all the chapters that follows is: Why has true crime emerged as such a vital cultural product in a postnetwork, post-cinematic media landscape in which viewing on demand now dominates? In what ways has true crime come to exemplify a "new" kind of viewer consumption, in which "access to entertainment is promoted as mobile, persistent and interactive" (Tryon 2013, 4)?

Feminist media studies scholar Deborah Jermyn has noted that the rise of real crime images in contemporary culture speaks to "our enduring cultural curiosity with seeing visual evidence of real victims and real criminals in crime stories" (2004, 87). And while it is true, as Jermyn notes, referring to Foucault, that this fascination "can be traced back to a time long preceding the emergence of photographic and video technologies" (87), it is nevertheless the argument of this book that the growth of digital culture and new media technologies has opened up new spaces of engagement for the user or spectator and has intensified the rhetoric around the idea of an involved and interactive true crime audience. Digital culture has revitalized true crime just as true crime has helped to inform and shape the new modes of storytelling practices that have come to characterize the digital era.

While it is important to take seriously the affective pleasures of contemporary true crime and explore its potential for opening up debates about social justice, I want to sound a cautionary note about the rhetoric of interactivity that infuses recent iterations of the genre. Though true crime blockbusters such as *Serial* and *Making a Murderer* have been packaged and sold to audiences as entertainment products that afford the unique opportunity to become involved in righting social wrongs, there are limitations to their attempts to position listeners and viewers as interactive digital "citizens." As I hope to demonstrate in the chapters that follow, true crime's overt solicitation of emotional responses from viewers does not necessarily equate to meaningful social involvement or "action." However, this is not to say that true crime is without its ethical and political merits: the key assertion of this book, after all, is that to explore the spread of true crime images in mainstream popular culture is to explore profoundly ethical questions regarding what it means to watch, listen, and "witness" in a digital era of accessibility, immediacy, and instantaneity.

The Ethics of Looking

The question of what it means to "witness" crime and violence has become an increasingly fraught one in an era in which user-generated videos of extreme violence are now readily accessible. In August 2015, for example, a vociferous public debate emerged about the implications of the "auto-play feature" on social media sites when a gunman, Vester Flanagan, opened fire during a live on-air TV interview in Virginia in the United States, murdering reporter Alison Parker and photographer Adam Ward. Debates about whether "to watch or not to watch" (McNamara 2015a) the murders were largely preempted by the automatic playback video feature on Facebook and Twitter, which "effectively forced legions of unsuspecting users to watch [the] grisly footage" (Covert 2015). Not only was the killing shown on live TV but the killer himself, who shot the victims with a gun in one hand and filmed the murders with his camera phone in the other, uploaded his first-person video of the killings to his social media accounts. Anyone who "followed" Flanagan on social media automatically saw the video, which was then shared widely on Twitter and Facebook in the minutes before it was taken down as a breach of "community guidelines."[17] As senior editor of the *Verge*, Tom Warren, tweeted at the time: "Twitter and Facebook autoplay videos made me witness the murder of someone from multiple angles today. Good job technology" (quoted in Covert 2015). Such a dark example of the inseparability of death, violence, and technology raises challenging questions about our role as "witnesses" to violent crimes.[18] Where the possibility of witnessing images of "real" murder—as with so-called snuff videos, for example—used to be the stuff of cultural mythology, it is now a disturbing and increasingly normalized part of our everyday digital lives (Kendall 2016a, 262). The rampant and unbridled circulation of real crime images in an online era—which no longer necessarily come to us through the reassuring frame of the "news" or the newscaster—brings us up against debates about the ethics of looking that have long preoccupied film and media theorists.

Even though it has not always been acknowledged as strongly as it might be, there is a history of real crime images playing an important role in how the disciplines of film and media studies have theorized the activity of looking and spectatorship. One of the most significant modern examples of this is the beating of black citizen Rodney King by a group of white police officers in Los Angeles in 1991. The beating was captured on videotape by amateur videographer George Holliday, distributed widely on television, and displayed prominently in the subsequent trials in Simi Valley, California, which resulted in the acquittal of the police officers involved. News of this acquittal was followed by one of the "worst riots in the United States in this century, with a toll of fifty-three people dead and $1 billion in damage" (Tomasulo 1996, 75). There have been many interesting articles on the Rodney King videotape, described by Holliday's attorney in the 1990s as "the most viewed and . . . most important videotape of the twentieth century" (quoted in Tomasulo 1996, 75) but what I want to draw attention to here is its significance for thinking about how documentary crime images bring film and media scholars up against fundamental questions about the nature of looking at, and interacting with, screen images.

As testament to the significance of the Rodney King incident for the discipline of film, the Society for Cinema Studies (SCS, now the Society for Cinema and Media Studies) drew up a petition in the wake of the "Not guilty" verdicts and distributed it at its annual conference in April 1992. Included in the SCS's political statement was the contention that "the verdict to acquit four white Los Angeles Police Department officers contradicts powerful visual evidence—video evidence of excessive police brutality seen globally" (quoted in Tomasulo 1996, 79). Taking particular issue with how the video was used in court by defense attorneys, who replayed it repeatedly in slow motion and subjected it to "close reading" techniques, Frank Tomasulo discusses how the statement expresses justifiable "outrage" on behalf of "media educators" at how, "even with visual evidence, blacks' experience of police brutality does not count" (79). As a political statement against the "outrageous Simi Valley verdict" (79), this petition was powerful—and necessary. However, it has been criticized for "succumb[ing] to the positivist fantasy that there are brute facts that speak for themselves" (Gooding-Williams 1993, 167). Robert Gooding-Williams, for example, argues that "no one should have been surprised by the Rodney King verdicts" because the act of looking at the tapes was framed through corporeal schemas that interpreted the video images according "to a received stock of already-interpreted images of black bodies" as inherently animalistic and dangerous (165).

Almost three decades later, in a media ecology of internet speed and accessibility, in which smartphone videos of racialized violence are transmitted "live" and can be instantaneously shared across social media platforms, new kinds of questions have emerged for film and media scholars regarding the relationship between racialized crime, spectator accountability, and "regimes of visibility" (Juhasz 2016). Writing on "viral black death" and the cultural significance of Diamond Reynolds' Facebook Live video of the aftermath of the murder of her boyfriend, Philando Castile, by a police officer in July 2016, documentary film scholar Alexandra Juhasz writes that "ethical viewing considers not just our own looking at viral videos but at the broader political-economic and technological structures that produce, hold, and frame the videos that we see and share" (2016). In other words, as with the Rodney King video, it is not just a matter of individual looking but of the technological structures and frameworks through which notions of both individual and collective "agency" and accountability now take form.[19]

Although the expansion of real crime images through social media networks has raised the cultural stakes of a genre that revolves around "claims to present reality in terms of crime, criminals and victims" (Cavender and Fishman 1998, 14), it is critical to distinguish between true crime as a constructed generic entertainment and user-generated videos of real-life violence. Indeed, there is a significant tension between culturally manufactured "true crime" and user-generated "real crime," and I want to argue that the troubling proliferation of videos of viral black death in which the murders of black people by police officers are captured on smartphones and spread via social media platforms such as Facebook and Twitter, renders visible the extent to which true crime is a racialized formation.

Viral videos of black people being murdered are simultaneously highly visible and ubiquitous and yet often strangely unseen and normalized. As Jennifer Malkowksi argues: "instances of Black male suffering consumed as spectacle have been such a consistent feature of U.S. media and public life—from the beating of Uncle Tom in nineteenth-century literature to the beating of Rodney King on twentieth-century TV news—that viewers may expect and even feel entitled to that graphic display when they click on a YouTube video purporting to show a Black man die on camera" (2017, 195). The rise in visibility of such videos has notably *not* led to an increase in prosecutions; the police officers responsible for the murder of black citizens are rarely held legally accountable for their crimes. It was in response to the murder of black youth Trayvon Martin and the acquittal of police officer George Zimmerman that the Black Lives Matter movement was founded, as a means of urgently bringing social attention to "state-sanctioned violence and anti-Black racism" (Black Lives n.d.). While the circulation of videos of black death through user-generated sites and social media networks may spread awareness—and encourage people to share responses of outrage through the use of emojis, comments, and shares—such outrage does not necessarily change the structures and systems of power that govern society (Benson-Allott 2017). What must therefore be interrogated, as Caetlin Benson-Allott argues, is the nature of an assumed "white gaze" and the issue of who benefits from the affective states initiated by social media platforms (2017).

The crucial issue, in other words, is how violence and suffering are *framed* and understood in the public domain. As Judith Butler argues, what matters is "the way in which suffering is presented to us, and how that presentation affects our responsiveness" (2009, 63). In chapter 2, when I turn my attention to elevator assault videos involving black celebrities, I think about the cultural framing of these videos and how they render the black male body as inherently criminalized, while simultaneously preventing the possibility of seeing the black female body as victimized. These elevator videos featuring black celebrities are not publicly framed or understood as "true crime," and do not feature the violent death or murder typically associated with the genre. Nonetheless, I argue that it is important to consider how these CCTV videos produce a similar kind of "participatory true crime infotainment experience" (Yardley et al. 2018, 103) through inviting people to analyze the videos, share their thoughts, and create their own memetic representations through networked spaces.

In thinking about the relationship between the rise in the mainstream popularity of true crime as a genre and the rise of endemic real-life violence on the internet, I want to ask: How does the appeal made to the viewer in more formally constructed long-form true crime texts such as *Serial* and *Making a Murderer*—to "actively" decide questions of guilt and innocence—relate, for example, to feelings of passivity in the face of a constant stream of images of violence on the internet? And why, given the increased accessibility of real crime images on the internet and a growing awareness of forms of racialized violence and police brutality, does true crime remain so persistently white in its focus?

In general, true crime has been viewed as a conspicuously white genre (Durham, Elrod, and Kinkade 1995; Murley 2008; Case Punnett 2018; Yardley, Kelly, and Robinson-Edwards 2018b). While there have been many excellent documentaries that explore the relationship between race and crime in America,[20] including, for example, *Who Killed Vincent Chin?* (Choy and Tajima-Pena, USA, 1987), *Murder on a Sunday Morning* (de Lestrade, France/USA, 2001), *The Trials of Daryll Hunt* (Stern and Sundberg, USA, 2006), *The Central Park Five* (Burns, Burns, and McMahon, USA, 2012), and, more recently, ESPN's *O.J.: Made in America*[21] (Edelman, USA, 2016), it is noticeable that historically, as Murley has suggested, true crime as a popular packaged entertainment has tended to center on white killers and white victims and to address itself to a white gaze (2008, 2).

While there is some racial diversity on long-running series such as *Forensic Files* (TLC, Court TV, NBC, truTV, 1996–2011), much schlocky cable-era true crime tends to be white-focused.[22] More recently, true crime blockbusters such as Netflix's *Making a Murderer* are also centered on whiteness. Those mainstream true crime texts that do deal with nonwhite participants, such as *Serial*, which I will discuss in chapter 4, have been strongly criticized for their lack of reflexive engagement with racial categories and for shoring up tired racial stereotypes. Running throughout this book, then, is a consideration of the gendered and racial discourses of true crime. Even when—or perhaps *especially* when—it is not flagged as important by the texts themselves, questions of gender and race are central to the affective mechanics of digital-era true crime as a popular cultural format. This book explores some of the most talked about recent mainstream true crime docuseries in relation to the construction of whiteness and reflects on their racial politics in a moment when violence against black people is more visible than ever before.[23] In chapter 4, I reflect on the politics of *Making a Murderer* as a blockbuster that provides members of a white middle-class audience with the opportunity to cast themselves in the role of "good" white citizens.[24]

Traditionally, true crime books and TV programs have tended to dress themselves up as serious exposés of the "unmitigated evil" (Murley 2008, 1) of the criminal mind, with the "killers . . . usually incarcerated or executed at the end of the story, reassuring us with good old-fashioned reordering of the chaos wrought by crime" (3). While this has now changed considerably, with many true crime programs reflecting a profound mistrust of authorities and the criminal justice system (Case Punnet 2018; Yardley et. al, 2018; Kennedy 2018), true crime still has its reassuring qualities, as I will demonstrate through the case studies that follow. Mistrustful or not, contemporary true crime finds a new set of heroes to valorize, whether it is in the form of the affable white female podcast host (*Serial*) who sets out to right a social wrong or the white defense attorneys (male and female) who fight for justice on behalf of the underprivileged (*Making a Murderer Part 1* and *Part 2*).

True Crime, Documentary, and Media Spectatorship

As much as it is an exploration of true crime's retooled multiplatform popularity in early twenty-first-century digital culture, this book is also an examination of the documentary modes deployed in the attempt to capture and commodify true crime images and stories. In the case studies that follow, I interrogate the relationship between images of true crime, modes of documentary, and forms of digital media audience engagement in an effort to grapple with the question of how the advent of digital technologies has impacted on our understanding of true crime and its relationship to documentary film and media. While true crime has been culturally elevated before, as, for example, with Truman Capote's *In Cold Blood* ([1966] 2000), a "non-fiction novel" that claimed to invent a new art form (Browder 2010, 121), I am interested in how the current vogue of *audiovisual* true crime relates to its relationship with documentary. Indeed, my assertion is that the current popularity of true crime documentaries provides a critical opportunity for film and media scholars to reflect upon the affective and political force assigned to the documentary form in our contemporary multimedia, multiplatform moment. While Laura Browder suggests that (traditional) true crime presents a "dystopian" version of documentary because of how it dislocates itself from the documentary drive to effect social change, and instead presents a "picture of problems that are insoluble because they are rooted in the individual"—in "the realm of the psychopath" or the sociopath (2010, 125)—recent true crime blockbusters tend to revolve around a more active sense of the genre and its potential, as I discuss below.

The drive to know "more"—what Bill Nichols terms "epistephilic desire"—may underlie all documentary forms (2010, 40), but I argue that it finds one of its sharpest and most overt expressions in the true crime documentary through the genre's emphasis on solving mysteries, uncovering buried truths, and capturing visual "evidence." The desire for images to constitute "visible evidence" has long been central to what Tom Gunning calls the "documentary impulse" (1999, 46). It is noteworthy that the name first given to the new technological device of the hand camera in the 1880s was the "detective camera." Although this name was quite quickly suppressed because of its associations with "devious ways" and prurience (49), it is nonetheless deeply significant, as Gunning notes, that it was called this in the first place. In the early decades of cinema, there "was a virtual explosion of accounts" in which "a movie camera captured either a moment of private indiscretion or evidence of a crime," sharply indicating the fantasies and anxieties regarding the "juridical effect" of the cinematic apparatus (46–47). There is a close historical association, in other words, between the development of the photographic/cinematic apparatus and the activity of "uncovering wrongdoing and gathering evidence" (53). As Gunning writes in a statement that could well be applied to the sharing of photos and videos of crime on social media today: "The detective camera allowed bodily language to be captured for display and comment, and even condemnation" (54). This sense of the unique potential for cameras to capture documentary images of crime continues to exert fascination for audiences; as Gunning notes, it fuels "the recent popular entertainment use of video surveillance" (61), which I will discuss in detail in chapter 2 when I turn my attention to the elevator surveillance videos of violence that now circulate on TMZ, YouTube, and other sites as a source of entertainment.

While true crime has long been popular in its more sensational "pulp" formations, from "lurid true crime magazines" to "ubiquitous documentary cop shows on television" (Browder 2010, 124), many of today's true crime entertainments have an added cachet that comes from their increasing association with the social and political purchase of the documentary form. To fully consider the development of true crime as a form, it is essential to reference Errol Morris's 1988 *The Thin Blue Line*, a true crime documentary that was seen to usher in a new era of more stylized, more dramatically charged—and more "cinematic"—documentaries. *The Thin Blue Line* is famous for its expressive, stylized reenactments that complicate the idea of a single, "stable" truth and that run alongside a series of compelling interviews with subjects that reveal the vagaries of memory and human testimony (Williams 1993; Musser 1996). Nonetheless, at the same time as it exposes the complexities of truth and narrative, Morris's investigative, self-reflexive documentary is driven by the determination to reveal the truth of Randall Dale Adams's innocence, a purpose that is accomplished very dramatically in the film's final moments via the device of the tape recorder. This thrilling moment of revelation is echoed in Andrew Jarecki's recent true crime docuseries *The Jinx*, discussed in chapter 4, which also ends with an explosive "reveal" of criminal guilt through audio recorder in a very direct throwback and homage to Morris's now classic documentary.

Voted number 5 in *Sight and Sound*'s 2017 poll of the greatest documentaries of all time, *The Thin Blue Line* famously resulted in the overturning of Randall Dale Adams's death row conviction for the 1976 murder of police officer Robert Wood. Adams was released from prison a year after the theatrical release of Morris's documentary, leading Harvey Weinstein, then the head of Miramax, to proclaim: "Never has Miramax had a movie where a man's life hangs in the balance" (Perren 2001/2002, 31). Notably, at the time of its release Morris's film was not marketed as a documentary but as a "movie mystery," largely in order to counter the public perception of the documentary form as dry, serious, and educational. Morris's official website includes a scanned copy of a humorous letter in which Weinstein admonishes the director for coming across as "boring" in his promotion of the film:

> It's time you started being a performer and understand the media. Let's rehearse: It's a mystery that traces an injustice. It's scarier than Nightmare on Elm Street. It's like a trip to the Twilight Zone. People have compared it to *In Cold Blood* with humor. Speak in short one sentence answers and don't go on with all the legalese. Talk about the movie as a movie and the effect it will have on the audience from an emotional point of view. ("The Thin Blue Line" n.d.)

Weinstein's concern with pitching *The Thin Blue Line* as a "movie" and not a dowdy documentary indicates the extent to which documentary was often seen as "a subordinate cinematic form" (Aufderheide 2016, 376). *The Thin Blue Line* is a significant turning point, as documentaries begin to be more vigorously marketed as "thrilling" movie experiences in their own right. As I will discuss in the next chapter, from the 1990s into the 2000s, there is a growing emphasis on the visceral, emotional appeal of documentaries as they increasingly deploy devices more typically associated with fiction genres—including cliffhangers and suspenseful plot twists.

What makes the true crime documentary so significant a subgenre for the newfound interest in "entertainment with a purpose" (Aufderheide 2016, 378) is its apparent ability to step in where the law failed, to effect meaningful and measurable social change. While the idea of social change has always been a key component of documentary filmmaking as an art form that "lend(s) us the ability to see timely issues in need of attention" (Nichols 2001, 2), it has been difficult for documentary studies to pin down just precisely *how* documentaries actually do effect social change, if indeed they do at all. Does the so-called change derive from how documentaries can raise social consciousness? Or do socially committed documentaries merely preach to the converted? How do we define and measure the idea of "social change" anyhow? Jane M. Gaines has noted that the "myth of sweeping social change" has remained stubbornly attached to the documentary film, despite a real "vagueness" in documentary studies regarding what actually constitutes "social action" or "social consequences" (1999, 84–85). Gaines further asserts that it can be tricky to make claims of "social influence" when so "few of the classic documentaries have ever had mass audiences" or "been box-office blockbusters" (85). I agree with Gaines that the question of documentaries and social change is an exceptionally thorny and undertheorized one, but it is striking just how much has changed with the rise of digital culture: many documentary films and docuseries *are* now "blockbusters," securing large audiences, yielding high profits, and initiating much cultural chatter and debate.[25] The subsequent rise of "clicktivism," whereby people show their support for a documentary cause by clicking on various links on social media, has led to ensuing debates over the efficacy of such "feel-good online activism" (Morozov 2009)—debates that have arguably only exacerbated the murkiness regarding the links between documentaries and social change.

Gaines refers only briefly to the crime documentary as a genre relevant to her discussion of "political documentaries" and social change, mentioning the "concept of documentary pathos" in relation to "films that document cases of social injustice" (1999, 92). And yet, it is the crime documentary that has yielded some of the most prominent historical examples of how documentaries can intervene in social reality, thus inspiring the kind of wider "fantasy" described by Gaines, which is "based on some powerful documentary mythologies that have become intertwined with actual historical events," of "an audience that is collectively *moved* to get up out of their theater seats and take some kind of group action on behalf of a political cause" (1999, 89).

In addition to the example of *The Thin Blue Line*, there is the *Paradise Lost* trilogy (Joe Berlinger, Bruce Sinofsky 1996, 2000, 2011)—a true crime documentary series that spans from the 1990s to the first two decades of the twenty-first century. The *Paradise Lost* trilogy did indeed inspire people to move off their seats (and sofas) to take group action in an effort to free the "West Memphis Three"—the three men (wrongfully) convicted as teenagers of the murder of three boys. In *Paradise Lost 2: Revelations* (2000) and *Paradise Lost 3: Purgatory* (2011), the social protestors inspired to action by the first film, *Paradise Lost: The Child Murders at Robin Hood Hills* (1996), have become key players in the documentaries, which show images of activists fighting to free the "West Memphis Three" huddled around bulky desktop Web 1.0 computers. The final documentary in the trilogy ends with the successful release of all three men, over eighteen years after they were first imprisoned.[26] The *Paradise Lost* films,[27] along with *The Thin Blue Line*, provide extraordinarily powerful examples, then, of the kind of change that documentaries can affect in righting egregious social wrongs. While not all crime documentaries result in such dramatic action occurring, I would suggest that these historical examples help to fuel a fantasy of the cultural purchase of the documentary form, which is also further energized by the rise of participatory media culture.

Errol Morris has recently reflected on the differences between the public engagement with *The Thin Blue Line* and the overwhelming interest in Netflix's *Making a Murderer*, which attracted millions of viewers and initiated wide-scale public outrage. As he notes:

[I]n 1988 there was no Internet. Miramax was the distributor of *The Thin Blue Line*. It was in . . . not all that many theaters. Probably well under a hundred. But people started spontaneously signing petitions. And it spurred a kind of movement. People started writing about it. But much, much more slowly and on a much smaller scale. . . . Today, with the Internet, it's possible for—I don't how many millions of people have seen *Making a Murderer*, but there's a lot of awareness of that story. (quoted in Butler 2016)

As Morris's comment reminds us, while documentaries about true crime stories have always contained this potential to attract public attention and raise social concern about miscarriages of justice, it is important to explore how the documentary format has "evolve[d] in digital networked contexts" (Gye and Weinstein 2011) and what the speed and spreadability that characterize the digital environment have meant for how we watch—and respond to—documentary films, as well as for how such films address themselves to us.[28] It is also necessary to explore how the construction of the spectator's agency is held in tension with the affordances of technological platforms, which work to define and circumscribe what that agency looks like and consists of. The true crime documentary, and its positing of an idealized vision of the spectator as "poised to intervene in the world" (Gaines 1999, 92), is a significant site for exploring how changes in the ideological "apparatus of capture" (Gye and Weinstein 2011) work to shift understandings of the affective relations between documentary films and spectators. There is a pressing need, in other words, to consider how documentaries "respond to their new exhibition platforms both formatively and narratively" (Benson-Allott 2013, 7).

While individual feature-length true crime documentaries such as *The Thin Blue Line* (1988), *Capturing the Friedmans* (2003), *Standard Operating Procedure* (2008), and *The Act of Killing* (2012) have been subject to serious analysis from film scholars as individual films, less sustained attention has been paid to the workings of this subgenre overall in documentary film theory. One significant exception to this is the work of documentary film scholar Kristen Fuhs, who has argued for the significance of what she terms the "juridical documentary" as a "particularly loaded space for analyzing the ethical and epistemological responsibilities of documentary representation as well as for revealing truths about the legal process and the ordering of a just society" (2014, 781). Crime documentaries, in other words, are especially charged objects for bringing documentary ideals of truth-telling to the fore. In particular, Fuhs writes, crime documentaries articulate the "desire that people have long held for documentary—that its images have the potential to precipitate direct social change" (2017, 6). In the digital era, the desire for documentary to initiate social change is heightened through participatory media technologies, which afford new opportunities for viewers to directly respond to, and engage with, documentary images of crime and violence. As Nichols notes in the second edition to his classic textbook *Introduction to Documentary*, with the rise of internet culture the "participatory mode" of documentary has expanded to "embrace the spectator as participant" through interactive websites, through digital cameras and recording devices, and through internet databases (2010, 80). The success of true crime blockbusters, which I discuss in detail in chapter 4, is directly connected to the ways in which they enable user web-based interaction and provide viewers with a sense of control over the material.

The notion that audiences can participate in true crime has, of course, always been a feature of the genre on both film and television. While traditionally the invitation for audiences to assume a metaphorical seat in the jury box has often only been implied in true crime feature-length theatrical documentaries (Clover 2000a, 248), audience interactivity has been a much more overt feature of televisual true crime. Television scholars such as Jermyn, Gray Cavender, and Mark Fishman have theorized the significance of "real crime" and its participatory elements to the origins of reality television. Real crime shows such as *Crimewatch* in the United Kingdom, and *America's Most Wanted* in the United States, which both came to prominence in the 1980s and 1990s, are credited with originating the forms of reality television that proliferated in the first decade of the 2000s. Jermyn suggests that "in its appeal to a mass audience to take a participatory role" by phoning in tips and therefore "actually shaping the programme as it unfolds," *Crimewatch* "was arguably a notable forerunner of numerous strands of the current Reality TV movement" (2004, 74). Likewise, Cavender and Fishman, writing in an American context, assert that shows such as *America's Most Wanted*, *Unsolved Mysteries*, and *Cops*, all of which sought to present the "realities" of crime in "an entertaining way that [drew] upon traditions of crime fiction and tabloid journalism" (1998, 14), were central to the rise of "infotainment" in American popular culture.

BBC's *Crimewatch*[29] (1984–2017) and Fox's *America's Most Wanted*[30] (1988–2011) were broadcast-era prime-time television shows that invited viewers to help fight crime and capture criminals. Using a combination of dramatized reenactments and interviews, the shows always drew to an end with the host making an appeal to viewers to share information and phone in tips. The results were tangible: one in three cases featured on *Crimewatch* apparently "ended in arrest, and one in five resulted in a conviction" (quoted in Bird 2017). During its twenty-five years on American television, *America's Most Wanted* is said to have helped catch 1,203 fugitives, "including 17 people off the FBI's Most Wanted list" (Cochran 2013).

However, notwithstanding these figures, which were only ever revealed much later—months, sometimes years after the initial airing of the programs themselves—it is significant that *America's Most Wanted* was cancelled in 2012, and *Crimewatch* in 2017, following declining viewership. The rise of new digital media technologies and the shift in viewing patterns to self-scheduled viewing on streaming services or "appointment viewing" of serialized dramas was cited as a primary reason for the decline of interest in the public service format of these shows (Lawson 2015). British newspaper the *Telegraph* refers to former *Crimewatch* host Nick Ross's suggestion that "the format had become dated in an increasingly digital world where police forces issue appeals with CCTV footage of suspects on Twitter and other social media" (quoted in Bird 2017). Indeed, while Twitter was seen to increase audience responses to *Crimewatch*, it also allegedly "reduced the quality" of those responses because "the ease of texting or tweeting means that the show is now more at risk of the pet theories of sofa detectives" (Lawson 2015).

But while interest in these foundational real crime TV franchises may have declined, significant elements of their format have been "replicated" (Lawson 2015) and repurposed elsewhere. Indeed, real crime TV is an important context for this book's consideration of the growth of digital true crime in the contemporary cultural moment. As I will discuss in chapter 4, true crime continues to play a pivotal role in the establishment of new forms of television, including, most prominently, the rise of Netflix and streaming TV. The long-form true crime serial is one of the genres that Netflix has mined and developed in order to construct and promote the notion—central to its business model—of audience participation through "binge-watching." With the rise of the blockbuster true crime serial, the "'sobriety" of the true crime documentary meets the thrill-seeking nature of the reality TV show, coalescing around the increasingly popularized and rejuvenated expectation that "entertainment changes things" (Glassman 2015) and that "television documentaries could offer justice to a cold case" (McNamara 2015b).

Throughout this book I look at the different formats and platforms that distribute and exhibit true crime images in a twenty-first-century media ecology: from podcasts to feature-length documentaries, to short-form trailers and long-form Netflix series. As Richard Grusin has asserted, "At our current historical moment there is almost no sense of a medium that exists in itself, but rather only media that exist in relation to or in collaboration with other media" (2016). This notion of "distributed media" buttresses my approach to the texts I examine, as does Grusin's critical observation that "television or the Internet or film should be understood as networks or systems of technologies, practices, and social formations that . . . in the process of circulation and exchange tend to fluctuate or perhaps overlap at various nodes or crossings" (ibid.). While I interrogate the specificity of different platforms, and the kinds of responses they invite from viewers, I also want to consider how notions of interactivity with the true crime image are distributed across different "media forms and practices" (ibid.).[31]

My particular concern in the book that follows is with the emotional appeal of true crime images and the ways in which they position the listener or viewer, working to construct a notion of a collective "feeling public" (Petersen 2011, 29). In her research on the documentary and emotionality, Belinda Smaill has explored how "individuals are positioned by documentary representation as subjects that are entrenched in the emotions, whether it is pleasure, hope, pain, empathy or disgust" (2010, 3). Noting that "emotions are not only private matters" but also "circulate in the public sphere," Smaill argues for the value of exploring "how emotion is produced in particular documentaries and how the audience is addressed by this emotion" (3). Through my analysis of a range of case studies, I explore how the audience is affectively imagined, addressed, and commodified by true crime, in order to consider the ethical and political significance of the genre for a twenty-first-century media ecology. Central to my reading of the discursive construction of true crime and its audiences is Petersen's assertion that "one of the most important political functions of the media is not the capacity of media texts to convey information but the way these texts and their circulation, project or invite felt proximities, distances, desires, disgust, and disconnections" (2011, 12). The question of how true crime gets remediated across documentary modes and formats, "inviting or disinviting" public response and engagement, is central to my consideration of the genre's significance for a theorization of twenty-first-century forms of participatory media spectatorship.

In her book *Updating to Remain the Same: Habitual New Media*, Wendy Chun argues that to focus on new media as "simply viral or disruptive" is to miss out on the vital fact that "our media matter most when they seem not to matter at all, that is when they have moved from the new to the habitual" (2016, 1). After all, it is "through habits," Chun writes, that "users become their machines: they stream, update, capture, upload, share, grind, link, verify, map, save, trash, and troll" (1). While images of violence and real crime emerge as moments of "crises," the volume and accessibility of real crime images in the digital era has also led to their increased habituation—"networks make crises habitual," as Chun puts it (17). For Chun, "a focus on habit moves us away from dramatic chartings and maps of 'viral spread' towards questions of infrastructure and justice" (15).

Justice on Demand seeks to explore the kinds of habits that are being formed through watching and listening to true crime images in the digital era. Where previous studies of crime films and TV shows have tended to take a representational focus, my approach is to examine the kinds of relations and affects solicited by true crime at this particular historical juncture. If, as Chun contends, "habit is ideology in action" (7) then my contention is that what needs to be urgently examined are the kinds of habitual relations being solicited by contemporary true crime and its remediations of violence. In the chapters that follow, I therefore pay close attention to the connections that get made between the solicitation of audience engagement, user practices, and true crime: in particular, I am concerned with the kind of distracted, "clickable" viewing associated with short-form true crime in contemporary "clip culture," and the more immersive, absorbed viewing associated with longer-form true crime as valorized through the activity of "binge-watching." Rather than seeing these forms of viewing habits or practices as distinct or opposed, my argument is that the short form and the long form, the "distracted" and the "immersive," need to be understood in relation to one another in order to fully comprehend the affective and visceral appeal of true crime in a digital media ecology.

The aim of the book that follows is to interrogate the kinds of affective relations to true crime being established through new media protocols, and the attitudes and ideas about criminality and race, class and gender that are being shaped through digital-era listening and viewing practices. It is not enough to merely observe the rise to popularity of true crime in participatory digital culture; it is imperative to examine the kind of participatory subject being imagined, recognized, and captured in the ever-expanding networks of true crime. What are the "cues" and "rewards" (Chun 2016, 8) through which viewers are incentivized to remain caught up in the true crime loop and to keep listening and watching?

Thinking about the nature of our habitual relations to true crime returns me to *My Favorite Murder,* the popular true entertainment with which I began this introduction. In both its "minisodes" and its longer episodes, *MFM* is constructed in relation to a wider "media flow" that, as Dominic Pettman suggests, "demands a compulsive refresh of our screens" (2016, xiii). Episodes of *MFM* are released on a weekly basis, but they are also available for binge-listening, or for dipping into and out of, as the occasion may dictate. As with other "binge-worthy" audiovisual texts of the early part of the twenty-first century, self-curation and audience autonomy are talking points in online discussion threads on *MFM*: people can decide where, when, to how many, how often, and on which device they want to listen, thus facilitating a further sense of intimate, user-based involvement with the podcast.

In its extremely self-conscious address to a networked community, *MFM* explicitly foregrounds the pleasures—and the perils—of true crime as the perfect click bait entertainment for the internet age. Although taking pleasure in true crime as a form of entertainment is certainly not new, what *is* decidedly different about *MFM* and the other true crime case studies I examine in this book is how their pleasures are bound up so explicitly with what Dean calls "the intense circulation of information in the networks of contemporary technoculture" (2002, 1). As much as they talk of the gory details of true crime cases, the hosts of *MFM* talk of the mundane but addictive activities of googling, searching, and clicking through online sites in search of more and more information about murder. The *MFM* podcast renders visible the affective charge of true crime as a form of networked communication that facilitates various "online connections and disconnections" (Paasonen, Hillis, and Petit 2015, 1).

A key element of the rise of "murderino culture" as epitomized by *MFM*, resides in its modulation of positive and negative affective response. To appreciate *MFM* one needs to be able to accept the dicey terms of its tight-rope walk across the modalities of positive and negative affect and humor and violence. Even as the female cohosts make an effort to discuss gendered murder through a feminist-filtered lens,[32] the grim, systemic violence of the cases they consider is sometimes undercut by their cheerful, positive tone and their cute witticisms, their signature phrases, and their gentle ribbing of their mustachioed sound man, Steven Ray Morris; listeners can count on the fact that every episode, no matter how depressing, ends with Georgia's cat Elvis's meows and their cute and quirky "bye-eeees!" The "feel good" vibe of the podcast was extended on the Facebook page, which operated as a "humming positivity machine"—a memorable phrase Erin Gloria Ryan uses to refer to the "uplifting posts" on the "Pantsuit Nation" Facebook page (2016). The feminist critique that is at times gestured toward on *MFM* often went missing on the social media forum in favor of sharable mottos, funny sayings, and listicles. As I discuss throughout this book, this is a problem that underlies digital-era true crime more generally: too often, the potential for true crime to offer a feminist analysis of violence against women is overlooked in favor of delivering a series of microaffective nuggets or thrills.

Hosts Karen and Georgia openly privilege their affective responses over rigorous research. For example, Karen describes their approach to true crime in the following terms: "We're not trying to be *48 Hours* (the popular CBS investigative TV crime series), we just want to retell you a 48 Hours we saw that we liked" (*MFM* minisode 52). If their lack of informed research can, at least initially, be a point of real annoyance for some listeners (and I include myself here), it is also surely a huge part of the ad hoc appeal of the podcast and the wider culture of amateurism that is extolled and normalized in digitized culture. *MFM* can be considered an especially striking example of how, in neoliberal affective regimes, expertise is sidelined as "affect trumps knowledge" and feelings are channeled into "reliable revenue streams" (Pettman 2016, 18). The issue of the kind of affective work being performed by true crime—as it is rerouted through socially networked culture—forms the basis of this book.

In the final analysis, what I find most interesting about *MFM*, and the reason why it is my primary case study in this introduction, is how sharply it brings into focus the issue of audience address. *MFM* routinely incorporates metacommentary on the reasons for the contemporary cultural obsession with true crime through its frank address to the consumer as a "fan." Listeners are welcomed as part of a like-minded community and told that they no longer have to "hide" their love for stories of gruesome murder. Just as they imagine a group of listeners who "want to jump into the pool of terror" with them and "know all about bad things so it will never happen to us" (*MFM* episode 6, "Stay Sixy"), so, too, they routinely imagine a disgusted, angry audience that is outraged with them for enjoying true crime or for getting their facts wrong. *MFM* thus attempts to normalize the sense that it is okay to be "obsessed" with true crime—that "murderinos" are part of a much wider, more mainstream community—while simultaneously constructing a sense of listeners as special, as part of a marginalized "cult" fandom. It thus caters to the fragmented niche audiences of twenty-first-century media culture, capturing significant shifts in how true crime narratives are constructed, distributed, and responded to in an era of competing listening and viewing platforms. *Justice on Demand: True Crime in the Digital Streaming Era* aims to explore the significance of such shifts for an evaluation of the political potential—and limitations—of networked true crime and its promotion of a participatory "murderino" culture.

Chapters and Structure of *Justice on Demand: True Crime in the Digital Streaming Era*

My main case studies in this book are (North) American, even though the examples I discuss extend far beyond US borders through their digital circulation. Part of what I am interested in exploring is the transmedia, global appeal of audiovisual true crime texts, as they spread through the media stratosphere. The questions I examine regarding the politics and ethics of true crime and the kinds of visibility afforded to crime images on digital platforms are therefore relevant across a range of national contexts. The audiences for true crime blockbusters such as *This American Life* spin-off *Serial* or Netflix's *Making a Murderer* are international, so even as I am attentive to the specificities of cultural context, I am keen to explore the types of interactions with true crime facilitated by global digital platforms such as Facebook, Twitter, and Netflix.

In chapter 1, I begin with a discussion of the 2008 true crime documentary *Dear Zachary*, a film that continues to attract attention for the intense emotional experience it affords viewers. Directed by Kurt Kuenne, this deeply personal, low-budget documentary was released on the cusp of the explosion of cultural interest in true crime and the corresponding rise of social media networks, which occurred post 2010. It was the intensity of the emotional response to *Dear Zachary* that first kindled my interest in the affective resonances of true crime and that signaled what I saw as a definite cultural shift in the reception of true crime and documentary as intersecting media formats. The cultural reception of *Dear Zachary* remains a point of fascination over ten years after its release. On the *MFM* podcast, Karen and Georgia note that *Dear Zachary* is one of the true crime films that their fans most often tweet them about and tell them to watch. There is now a subreddit on *Dear Zachary* under "Documentaries," where viewers share, and relish in, their emotional reactions to the "saddest film they've ever seen." "Top comments" include: "Dear Zachary: Or, How I learned about the sensation of Rage sobbing" and "Warning: only watch this movie with a full box of tissues" ("Dear Zachary: A Letter to a Son About His Father"). Many redditors describe their corporeal experience of watching the film in even more colorful terms: they speak of muscles tensing up, veins bulging, tears streaming, and guts wrenching. Situating *Dear Zachary* in relation to other popular feature-film-length true crime documentaries before and after it, such as *Capturing the Friedmans* (2003) and *The Imposter* (2012), I consider the kinds of affective responses solicited by, and enacted through, its public remediation of "private" home video footage, as well as its afterlife on DVD and on the internet—in discussion threads and review forums. My examination of the strong affective attachments to *Dear Zachary* sets the stage for the questions that will preoccupy me throughout this book regarding the ethical and ideological implications of our emotional encounters with true crime in the digital era.

Though I provide a close textual analysis of the representational content of individual true crime texts in all of the chapters that follow, my overriding concern is with the forms that true crime, and its modes of audience address, take in a digital media environment. In chapter 2, "Caught on Tape": Elevator Assault Videos, Black Celebrity, and the Politics of Surveillance, my case study is the celebrity gossip website *TMZ* and its publication of two surveillance videos of American black celebrities committing acts of violence in elevators. These elevator videos are not true crime texts in the same way as some of the other examples I discuss: where traditional "true crime" typically features murder, these short CCTV clips feature physical assault. They are nonetheless significant as striking case studies of the ways in which closed-circuit television videos now circulate across networked spaces and link to the true crime genre through their solicitation of a participatory spectatorship that invites viewer judgment. CCTV videos, along with the social media systems that track our data, are an intrinsic part of wider digital surveillance culture and regimes (van der Meulen and Heynen 2016, 3). Indeed, these CCTV surveillance videos are part of an economy of real crime images that now circulate through networked spaces, and it is therefore important to consider their racialized and gendered dynamics. The first video, released on May 12, 2014, captures superstar Beyoncé with her husband, Jay-Z, and sister Solange in a hotel elevator, and shows Solange kicking out at Jay-Z. Without any audio to accompany the video, the public fascination with the video—which instantly went viral—focused on what Jay-Z might have said to Solange to provoke such a violent outburst. The second video, released a year later, shows American football star Ray Rice punching his then fiancée Janay Palmer Rice in a hotel elevator and knocking her unconscious. This chapter examines how both of these videos, released without the consent of the subjects involved, went viral and were turned into internet memes that drew on racialized stereotypes of criminality. Referencing work by digital race scholars such as Lisa Nakumara and meme theorists such as Limor Shifman, I examine the process by which these two highly mediated surveillance videos became entangled with one another in online meme culture, as racialized and gendered spectacles of violence. It is glaring, if largely unacknowledged, that *TMZ*'s most "popular" surveillance videos should focus on black subjects and that the memes that emerged out of the videos should actively work to reproduce black bodies as toxic and criminal. Although these elevator videos of violence are culturally framed as "authentic" and unmediated instances of real crime—thus distinguishing them from authored true crime—I argue that it is important to think further about the boundaries of what counts as "true crime" in the digital era, in order to interrogate the whiteness of the genre and its imagined audiences.

In chapter 3, "Tagging" the True Crime Audience: Netflix Trailers for True Crime Documentaries, I turn my attention to short-form true crime in the shape of the one- to three-minute trailers that promote true crime documentaries and docuseries in online spaces. More specifically, my focus is on the Netflix trailers for *Making a Murderer* and *Amanda Knox,* both of which, I argue, demand to be seen as blockbuster texts in their own right. Garnering millions of views on YouTube, these short-form trailers offer short, powerful rushes of affect and play a vital role in establishing a notion of true crime as an interactive digital commodity. While the true crime trailers I examine here work to fashion an idea of the "active," socially engaged viewer with the power to decide questions of guilt and innocence, I investigate the ways in which they also feed into, and crystallize, the logics and operations of what Dean (2010) calls "communicative capitalism." By way of historicization, this chapter considers the role of "tagging" in earlier true crime network–era TV through a brief examination of the short-lived but significant 1950s American true crime TV series *The Court of Last Resort,* based on the real-life organization of the same name led by Erle Stanley Gardner. In a postnetwork era, I argue that Gardner's documentary "tags" have now migrated outside of scheduled television and the confines of the TV shows themselves and have become a crucial part of the curation of true crime streaming television through internet distribution. Looking at the significance of Netflix's "tagging" of its audience through its use of algorithms and targeted trailers, I explore how viewers are interpellated in the terms of an endlessly deferred and extended crime-solving scenario that binds them ever more tightly to the commercial platforms and interfaces seeking to capture their attention. Trailers, I suggest, are a crucial part of a wider attempt to "tag" the true crime audience and are therefore in need of theorization as objects that work to construct and to premediate the very formulation of our affective interaction with true crime in the digital era.

Chapter 4, Over Her Dead Body: Binge-Watching Long-Form True Crime, is the companion piece to the previous chapter, as I argue that the short form and the long form in contemporary media culture are two sides of the same coin, and therefore need to be understood in relation to one another. Although the extended, long-form true crime serial, which has become so popular in the age of streaming TV, might appear to be vastly different from the fast-food affective thrills of the trailer, they have more in common than it might first appear. As Linda Williams has noted in relation to *The Wire,* long-form serial TV does not necessarily encourage longer attention spans; instead, it proceeds in short segments or "beats," which requires "us to see the pieces *as* pieces" (2014, 50–51). Montage, money shots, direct address, cliffhangers, hooks, and the lure of sex and violence: these are all central elements of the condensed one- to three-minute true crime trailer, but they are also features associated with long-form true crime series. Evaluating the claim that true crime is "tailor-made" for the activity of compressed viewing, or "binge-watching" as it is more commonly known, this chapter examines the affective attachments engendered by long-form serialized true crime, through a close analysis of three of its most significant contemporary examples: the twelve-episode-long podcast *Serial* (2014), the six-episode-long HBO television series *The Jinx* (2015), and the ten-episode-long Netflix docuseries *Making a Murderer* (2015). Although claims have been made for the critical potential of long-form true crime, especially in terms of how it initiates a participatory, socially involved form of spectatorship, I argue that these texts generate affective judgment in highly predetermined ways, which are attached to the dynamics of binging. What is of further concern here is the way in which these binge-worthy true crime serials simultaneously deploy—and then elide—the dead female body in the service of stringing out their long-form narratives. I argue that the extended structure of these long-form serials, designed for binge-watching, make visible the problematic raced and gendered mechanics of the true crime format.

My focus throughout this book is on how new digital protocols, platforms, and interfaces are reframing our affective interactions with true crime images and stories. While I seek to problematize accounts that herald new modes of audience engagement and participation in digital-era true crime as inherently progressive, this is not to say that I want to foreclose the possibility of critical resistance entirely. In the Afterword, Feminist True Crime, I therefore reflect on the #metoo, post-Weinstein era and some of the new possibilities that digital media networks open up for a feminist interrogation of rape culture. While the internet has created devastating new forms of violence and image-based sexual abuse, as well as serving as a breeding ground for men's rights activists (MRAs) (Ging 2017) and "toxic technocultures" (Massanari 2017), it has also simultaneously enabled collective feminist organization and resistance against violent crimes and the misogynistic cultures that fuel them. With reference to hashtag feminist activism, as well as to recent attempts to deploy new media formats for a feminist repurposing of rape narratives, I conclude this book with a discussion of the critical, feminist potential of true crime. My case studies in this afterword are the Netflix American true crime series *The Keepers* (2017) and the Canadian Broadcasting Corporation podcast series *Missing and Murdered* (2016–), both of which, I argue, make significant efforts to stay focused on the victims and to open outward to the social contexts of crime. In reflecting on the scope for a feminist repurposing of true crime, I consider how such an approach might eschew the production of knee-jerk emotional reactions to individual "villains" and "heroes," in favor of a more considered, collective approach to social justice, one that exposes and interrogates the social causes and dimensions of crime and violence. If, as is my central assertion in this book, true crime flourishes in the digital era because of how it lends itself to the operations of a Google search culture, then it is essential to interrogate the particular demands it makes upon our attention. By exploring how true crime captures and positions its audiences, *Justice on Demand: True Crime in the Digital Streaming Era* provides insight into the cultural and political significance of true crime for an "on demand" digital entertainment culture.

"A Film that Will Rock You to Your Core"

Emotion and Affect in *Dear Zachary* and the True Crime Documentary

THE FOLLOWING PROMOTIONAL DESCRIPTION of *Dear Zachary: A Letter to a Son About His Father* provides a good summation of its critical reception: "A true crime story so gripping, devastating, and ultimately unforgettable that it easily trumps any thriller Hollywood has to offer this year" (Tsai 2008). Released in 2008, *Dear Zachary* was part of a new breed of feature-length true crime documentaries, including Andrew Jarecki's multi-award-winning *Capturing the Friedmans* (US, 2003) and Bart Layton's *The Imposter* (UK, 2012), which were marketed as "edge of your seat" thrillers "with unbelievable twists and turns" (Sciretta 2012). In review after review, the contention was that these emotionally "gripping" and "gut-wrenching" true crime stories would stimulate cinema audiences better than any Hollywood blockbuster.

This new style of dramatic true crime documentary emerged out of the wider "mainstreaming" and popularization of the documentary form (Arthur 2005, 18) that occurred in the first decade of the twenty-first-century. During that time, there was a growth in the financial success and accessibility of documentary film, with soaring revenue figures for the theatrical releases of documentary, as well as an expanding online and DVD market.[1] As Patricia Aufderheide has noted, the "business of making and selling documentaries has expanded dramatically" with the emergence of digital technology and new viewing formats and, as a result, the "very notion of what a documentary is has been stretched and changed" (2005, 24). There are a number of theories regarding why there has been such an increase in the popularity of documentary formats, including, as noted above, the emergence of new digital technologies; a post-9/11 context in which there is a greater need for emotional "connection" with real life stories; the rise of reality TV; and the rewriting of boundaries between the private and the public in the YouTube age (Arthur 2005, 18–23). At any rate, changing commercial distribution models and viral online marketing processes led to an increased DVD market for documentaries, with viewers expecting them to be "packaged like feature-length fiction films" (Aufderheide 2005, 26).

That documentaries were "edging ever closer to the stylistic prerogatives of fiction film" during this period was the subject of much debate, with critics such as Paul Arthur lamenting the use of unbridled "dramatic tactics" in a range of contemporary documentaries (Arthur 2005, 20). Arthur was particularly critical of the kind of emotional "manipulation" and titillation he saw at work in a crime documentary such as *Capturing the Friedmans*, which "doles out its information in a manner intended to build suspense and provide 'shocking revelations'" (Arthur 2003, 6). Winner of the Grand Jury Prize at the 2003 Sundance Festival and nominated for an Academy Award in 2004, *Capturing the Friedmans* tells the story of a middle-class Jewish family from upstate New York whose lives are thrown into turmoil when the father, Arnold Friedman, and one of the three sons, Jesse Friedman, are accused of child sex abuse. At the heart of the film is dramatic found home video footage of the family during the time of the arrests and trials.

As a documentary that makes the "*technologies* of re-presentation the subject matter throughout" (Bell 2008, 94), *Capturing the Friedmans* marks a decisive moment for the true crime documentary as it moves into the digital era. Not only was it released theatrically, becoming a "breakout hit" and grossing over the three million mark, but it was also accompanied by the release of a noteworthy interactive DVD, which enabled viewers to pore over evidence and further reflect on the explosive home videos at the heart of the film. What Jodi Dean calls the "lure of the secret" in contemporary technoculture (2002, 77), was exemplified in the operations of *Capturing the Friedmans*—a documentary that drew viewers in by asking "who do you believe?", only to leave them with a heavy "burden of sensation" (Bell 2008, 90) by failing to resolve the issue of guilt or innocence.

Since the release of *Capturing the Friedmans* in 2003, there has been a steady increase in true crime documentaries that employ dramatic "tactics" and structures more commonly associated with fiction film in order to heighten the emotional viewing experience. In fact, following the promotion and branding of the 2012 crime documentary *The Imposter* as a "white knuckle thriller" (Bradshaw 2012), some viewers appeared not to realize—at least initially—that it was a documentary at all.[2] The recent trend for long-form true crime documentaries, which I discuss further in chapter 4, further amplifies the emotionality of the format. A post-2010 long-form streaming docuseries such as *Making a Murderer*, for example, is recognized for the strong emotions of outrage it evokes in its social media–savvy audiences, who then spread their reactions across online spaces. Moreover, there is a growing acknowledgment among cultural criminologists that the diverse emotional involvement with true crime documentaries and series on platforms such as Reddit provides an illumination "into how citizens comprehend issues related to crime, criminals, and justice, and should be taken seriously by scholars" (Kennedy 2018, 404).[3]

In this chapter I seek to examine the emotional mechanics of *Dear Zachary*, a film that, I argue, is a precursor for more recent affect-driven true crime blockbusters. Widely received by its viewers as an emotionally devastating and heartbreaking film,[4] *Dear Zachary* is an important, if critically underanalyzed, film in the contemporary true crime documentary canon not only for its strong emotive value but for its graphic revelation of the affective stakes involved in cinematic retrospection and the mediated reenactment of the past through home video footage. As Stella Bruzzi has noted, although "documentary is commonly thought of as a cerebral, intellectual genre (Bill Nichols' notion of a "discourse of sobriety"); quite often it is virtually the opposite: emotion driven, sensual and—in that it sometimes asks its spectator to respond to it spontaneously on a gut, almost physical level—primal in its appeal" (Bruzzi, 2006, 248). What is suggestive in the case of crime documentaries especially, which often circulate in the public sphere as objects of emotion—whipping up social outrage by campaigning against wrongful criminal convictions, or exposing gross injustices (as with *The Thin Blue Line* and the *Paradise Lost* trilogy, as discussed in the introduction)–is how this emotive, primal address relates to the wider social, political, and ideological messages such films are attempting to impart.

With its use of dramatic reenactments and its strong emphasis on affective response, *Dear Zachary* exemplifies the wider "affective turn" in true crime documentaries in the early twenty-first century. While it may lack the sophistication and polish of films like *Capturing the Friedmans*, *The Imposter*, and

The Act of Killing (Oppenheimer, Denmark/UK, 2012), in its low-budget rendering of violence *Dear Zachary* lays bare the emotionality of the true crime documentary and raises important questions regarding the affective stakes of the visual consumption of crime.[5] In what follows, I will consider the strong emotional appeal made to the viewer by Kuenne's documentary, through an analysis of its dramatic and affective redeployment of home video footage in the context of crime scene reenactment. While I am interested in the kind of emotional responses solicited by *Dear Zachary*, I also want to analyze the affectivity of its crime images. In my use of the term "affective" here, I am drawing on the work of criminologist Alison Young, who refers to affect in its "post Deleuzian sense" as distinct from emotion and who considers how we register cinematic images prior to cognition (2010, 9). For Young, an affective approach to analyzing the crime image "broadens the interlocutive possibilities to ask questions . . . of those who name or respond to crime in various ways: What affect arises from an encounter with crime? What affect arises from an encounter with an image of crime?" (10). Following Young's emphasis on the "matrix of intersections between the spectator, the image and the context of reception" (10), this chapter will critically explore how *Dear Zachary* repurposes personal home video images and family photographs, calling upon the affective labor of spectators to reaffirm dominant social values regarding crime, victimhood, and the family. Following my exploration of the affective circulation of *Dear Zachary*, in particular its afterlife in online discussions and its cultural formatting as a DVD, I will argue that the vehemence and intensity of the emotional response to *Dear Zachary* is ultimately not only about the horrible crimes it reveals but about the anxieties it raises regarding what is at stake in the public circulation of "private" family images.

A Documentary Tragedy

Kurt Kuenne is a filmmaker who wears his heart on his sleeve, which is due in no small part to the deeply personal attachment he has to his subject matter—the murder of his best friend. In a statement on the film's website, Kuenne writes that he set out to make *Dear Zachary* as a memorial to his dead friend:

> I wish that I had never had the opportunity to make this film. I wish that
> my friend Dr. Andrew Bagby was alive and well and that I was blissfully

ignorant of the lessons I've learned along this journey. Alas, this is not the case. When bad things happen, good people have to take what they've learned and make the world a better place, and that is precisely what I hope this film will do—make the world a better place. (Kuenne 2006)

While this heartfelt statement indicates the idealism underlying Kuenne's film, it is interesting to note that *Dear Zachary* utilizes a very similar marketing campaign to other crime documentaries of the time period such as *Capturing the Friedmans*, the *Paradise Lost* trilogy, and *The Imposter*, in that it, too, attempts to entice viewers by referring to a "mystery" at the heart of the story. Where *Capturing the Friedmans* asks "who do you believe?", the *Paradise Lost* films invite us to "make up our own mind," and *The Imposter* advertises itself as containing "shocking revelations,"[6] *Dear Zachary* draws its viewers in by getting us wondering about the horrifying "twist" that has all the film's viewers in tears. Here is a brief recount of the story: The filmmaker's best friend, Dr. Andrew Bagby, was allegedly murdered by his ex-girlfriend, Dr. Shirley Turner, who then fled to Canada, shortly after which it was learned she was pregnant with Andrew's baby. The Canadian government let her out on bail, and she evaded prosecution. Andrew's devastated parents, Kate and David Bagby, moved to Canada so that they could be close to their grandson, a circumstance that meant they "were forced to stomach a civil relationship with the woman they knew had murdered their only son."[7] In the trailer for the film, Kuenne's voice-over states that his mission with this film was "to bring a man back to life" by interviewing people and recording those interviews on digital tapes so that one day Zachary, his dead friend's child, would get to know his father. The trailer concludes with this voice-over from the director: "But I never could have guessed what happened next."

This question of "what happened next" is the hook of the film. Reviews of *Dear Zachary* generally characterize it as a very powerful and emotional documentary film, one that contains a major "plot twist," which reviewers are careful not to reveal. As one *Time Out Chicago* reviewer argues, "some twists deserve to be kept secret, because the twist is central to the experience of the film. . . . *Dear Zachary* earns our discretion, for the simple reason that we want you to experience this movie the way we did, as a series of emotional shocks. Just take our advice and bring tissues. You're going to need them" (Sartin 2008). No doubt, it is the "emotional experience" it provides that is the most remarkable thing about this documentary for its viewers, as indicated by the public responses to the film found on internet forums. There is an emphasis on the viscerality of *Dear Zachary* in audience responses, which refer to the bodily experience of viewing the film—the chest tightening, the breath quickening, and the gut "wrenching."[8] This response is echoed in reviews of the film; as one review declares, "Several gut-wrenching twists and turns later, we're left with a film that will rock you to your core. You will cry. You will hurt—and this film will sit with you for days, weeks, months" (Davis as quoted in "Accolades" 2008). Repeating the idea that the film is "best seen with as little foreknowledge as possible," Jenni Miller of *Premiere* wrote that she was "so devastated in the first five minutes" that she "had to watch it over the course of two days. . . . It's impossible to fully explain the pain, sorrow, and love this documentary holds without ruining its effects on future viewers" (2008). The strong emotional responses to *Dear Zachary* are seen as inextricably tied to the temporal unfolding of the film and its withholding of key narrative information. In order to experience the maximum amount of pain and emotion and to be "hit so much harder" by the documentary, as one viewer notes, it is important to let it unfold in a temporal structure of "real time" (IMDb User Reviews 2008).

If I am to critically explore the function of the plot twist in *Dear Zachary* it is necessary to reveal the tragedy that is so carefully withheld by the film's reviewers, which is that during the filming of the documentary, Zachary, the thirteen-month-old son of the murdered Andrew Bagby and his alleged killer Shirley Turner, was murdered by his mother when she regained custody of him after she was let out on bail. She drugged him and walked into the ocean with him strapped to her chest and they both drowned. *Dear Zachary* holds back this information from us until near the end of the documentary, when it is revealed to great dramatic effect. In this way, Kuenne's film changes from being a letter to a son about his father to being a memorial of a murdered father and son and a touching tribute to the grieving grandparents who were left behind and who feel so betrayed by the Canadian government's bail system, which allowed Turner out of jail as a decision was pending on whether she should be extradited to the United States on murder charges. Turner died before she could stand trial for the murder of Andrew Bagby. According to Kuenne, he structured the film in the way he did because he wanted to give us "the cinematic equivalent" of his "emotional experience" (quoted in Rich

2008). As Kuenne declares: "It is my hope that this film puts people right inside that experience and that no one will be able to come away from it unchanged" (Kuenne 2006).

This notion of the film as a traumatic yet transformative experience has been tied to a recognition of its apparently cathartic nature. Some reviews of *Dear Zachary* stress the idea that you need to first make your way through the "black" despair to find the "life-affirming message of hope" at the film's end (Buchanan n.d.). Such a response articulates the Aristotelian "paradox of tragedy," in which, as Stacie Friend suggests, "we appear to enjoy tragedy not despite, but precisely because of, the painful emotions we feel in response" (2007, 184–85). This is one of the "best" films they have ever seen, according to many viewers, precisely because it managed to make them feel so very bad. In the end, though, this bad feeling is arguably converted into positivity because of how the emotional experience of viewing the film is tied to its project for activism and social change. As Kuenne writes in his "filmmaker's statement" on the film's website: "I will be making every effort to get this film seen by lawmakers in Canada and abroad, where applicable. As Andrew's parents, Kate and David Bagby, have said repeatedly, 'The best we can get out of this is change in the future to prevent a reoccurrence. It's too horrible to let it happen again'" (Kuenne 2006). This positioning of the spectator as a worthwhile, empowered citizen is further facilitated by the DVD version of the film, in which supplementary material invites you to sign a petition urging bail reform in Canada. Even if you do not sign the petition, the rhetoric of intimacy and the very personal appeal made to viewers by director Kuenne do give a strong sense of an active, involved spectator.

While true crime documentaries such as *Capturing the Friedmans* and *The Imposter* also work to generate feelings in viewers, there is a purposeful "lack of resolution" to these other films that "leaves the viewer with unresolved emotions" (Bell 2008, 91). By contrast, *Dear Zachary* is unabashed in its courting of raw emotion and is very clear in its direction of our feelings. The judgment on the crimes it discloses has already been made: Dr. Shirley Turner is presented as an evil, psychotic killer and the victim and his family and friends are shown as kind, decent people. The viewer learns almost nothing about Dr. Turner and her experiences of depression, insomnia, and suicidal despair.[9] Viewers are instead asked to join director Kuenne in his very personal grief and outrage over the death of his friend and to harness our emotions to the public cause of law reform. Kuenne's obvious anger against the Canadian legal system, which failed to keep Turner in jail, is articulated through his depiction of the legal system and its agents: legal representatives are mocked and derided through a variety of techniques, including a Monty Python–style facial distortion of their television interviews and a vehement repetition of key phrases from their legal judgments in Kuenne's emotional voice-over. Visits to the film's website consolidate the idea of the social and legal importance of *Dear Zachary*. In a 2010 addendum to his original statement regarding his documentary, two years after its release, Kuenne announces that, thanks to *Dear Zachary*, a new law was finally passed in Canada regarding bail reform, "which likely could have saved Zachary had it been in place in 2003." He thanks the "thousands of you who wrote to Parliament in support of our cause" and notes that he has been "humbled and overwhelmed" by the response to his movie. He concludes with the following: "Please stop by the 'Bail Reform' section and read a letter of thanks to you from Kate & David Bagby. Thank you so much for your passionate support, and for helping make the world a safer, better place" (Kuenne 2010).

But despite the emphasis placed on the social good of *Dear Zachary*, there are serious questions that linger about the nature of our emotional encounter with the images of crime it displays. What, for example, does it mean to use the murder of a boy as a documentary "plot twist"? For some critics, there is something uncomfortable about this narrative strategy, which raises ethical questions. As Karina Longworth writes:

> As a viewer it's hard to not feel as though your sympathies have been taken advantage of. Ironically, in being honest about how, when and why his project changes focus, Kuenne has to initially lie to his audience. He documents an undeniably affecting personal story . . . but there's something about it which feels false enough to undercut some of its potential power. In its title and initial structure, *Dear Zachary* sets up a foundation which it knows it's going to pull out from under us, and that makes it every bit as emotionally manipulative as a studio film. (2008)

In this reading of the film, *Dear Zachary* is seen to capitulate to the fictional machinations of the dream factory and therefore lose some of its documentary integrity and its commitment to the "real." And yet in the majority of broadsheet reviews, as well as in the online forums, the manipulation of the plot twist is seen to be key to the powerful visceral experience of the film, hence the countless recommendations to watch it with no "foreknowledge" so as not to spoil its emotional impact (IMDB user reviews 2008). It is important, therefore, to take the powerful affective responses to *Dear Zachary* seriously (rather than merely dismissing the audience as duped or tricked by the film), in order to open up a set of crucial questions about our embodied relationship to documentary crime images.

One of the most striking things about the reception of *Dear Zachary* and other contemporary crime documentaries is how the emotions they evoke continue to circulate as the films are distributed as DVDs, on the internet, and in marketing publicity and reviews. What becomes paramount, then, is the issue of how emotions are harnessed and transmitted through various affective channels and media platforms; after all, it is not only, or not even primarily, at the "movie theater" that our emotional engagement with the moving image takes place. In the sections that follow, I will trace the affectivity of the crime image as it is routed through the remediated home video footage in *Dear Zachary* and then through the "extras" on the DVD format. Following Sara Ahmed's lead, I am interested not in what our emotional attachment to the documentary "is" but in what such an attachment "does" (2004, 4). As Ahmed argues, the interesting question is how "objects of feeling, circulate and generate effects: how they move, stick and slide. And how we move, stick and slide with them" (14).

The Politics of Reenactment: Remediating Home Video Footage

Dear Zachary is representative of what Jonathan Kahana has described as a "renewed interest in the powers of re-enactment" in contemporary moving-image culture (2009, 46, 47). Although documentary film theorists do not always acknowledge it as strongly as they might, the true crime documentary is one of the most interesting and significant sites in contemporary culture for the performance of reenactment.[10] Among the examples of true crime documentaries deploying reenactment are Errol Morris's *Standard Operating Procedure* (released in the same year as *Dear Zachary*, 2008) and the aforementioned *The Act of Killing* and *The Imposter*, both released in 2012. In all of these crime documentaries, reenactment calls upon the affective involvement of the audience and is a powerful way to interpellate viewers in the scene of the crime.[11]

Out of the above list of films, *Dear Zachary* has the most in common with *The Imposter*, a documentary that was similarly marketed as "edge-of-your-seat stuff" and where there was an emphasis placed on not giving away the central "mystery" (Barnard 2012). But in contrast to *Dear Zachary* and its raw, amateur look, *The Imposter's* reenactments are glossy, high-production affairs that use actors. *Standard Operating Procedure* and the Academy Award–nominated *The Act of Killing* (produced by Errol Morris) are also recognized for their stylized—and in the case of the latter, highly surreal—renderings of violence. As Kahana notes, *Standard Operating Procedure* was criticized for what some felt were its "luridly stylized dramatizations" of the violence against detainees by American military personnel at Abu Ghraib (2009, 49). Morris himself has written eloquently in defense of reenactment in the *New York Times*, asserting that a "story *in the past* has to be re-enacted" and that reenactments allow him "to burrow beneath the surface of reality" (2008). The director of *The Act of Killing*, Joshua Oppenheimer, has similarly argued for the value of reenactment as a way of allowing viewers to get "inside" violence (Whittaker 2013). Oppenheimer's film shows men who participated in the genocidal killings in Indonesia in the 1960s reenacting their murders in the style of Hollywood fiction films. While these reenactments were widely lauded by critics as remarkable, there were some dissenting voices. Tony Rayns, writing in *Sight and Sound*, criticizes *The Act of Killing* for its "near total lack of context" and for its "emotionally manipulative use of some of the material" (2013).

The charge of emotional manipulation has also been leveled against *Dear Zachary* and its distinctive remediation of amateur fiction film scenes and home video footage in the context of crime reconstruction. I now want to turn to a close examination of these reconstructions to explore what they reveal about the emotional and affective potency of reenactment. To give an example found early on in the documentary, Kuenne's voice-over is delineating "a summary of the evidence against Shirley Turner" in a staccato, true crime delivery, with *Psycho* theme–style music playing in the background. "He [Andrew] was shot five times, in the face, the chest, twice in the buttocks and in the back of the head, he also received a blunt trauma to the back of the head." As this information is recounted for us, we do not, à la *CSI* and countless other forensic crime dramas from the early twenty-first century, see graphic crime scene images; instead we are shown a sequence of photos of Andrew as a toddler and a young boy. The voice-over and the images work closely together so that as we hear about how Andrew was shot in the chest, there is a zoom in on Andrew's chest in a photo of him as a toddler; in this image of Andrew as a little boy, his T-shirt has a red stain on it, which is here made to connote the blood from the gunshot wounds that killed him.

To a certain extent, what Kuenne is doing here with photographs of the victim draws on an established tradition of crime reporting. It is common practice, for example, to show photos of victims before and after dramatic reconstructions on popular reality crime television programs. As Deborah Jermyn suggests, the purpose of such photos is to "communicate enough about the victim to make the viewer respond on some kind of emotional level, be that guilt, empathy, sympathy or outrage" (2007, 90). *Dear Zachary* also uses photos of the victims to communicate emotions, but takes it even further, and ratchets up the level of affective involvement considerably, by remediating family photos of the victims into the narrative of the crime itself. In other words, the photos and video footage of the victim do not just bookend the story of violent crime; rather and crucially, it is through these very images that the crime is presented to us, so that, as in the above example, when Kuenne's emotional voice-over describes a bullet going through his friend's chest, we see a close-up image of Andrew's chest not from a crime scene photo but from a photograph of Andrew as a young boy. Indeed, *Dear Zachary* relies heavily upon the emotive use of the figure of the child: it is vital to its ideological project that the photos used during the crime reconstructions are of Andrew as a baby and young boy and not of him as an adult. As with the coverage of other contemporary crime stories, there is a strong emotive force assigned to the image of a lost child, which "represents the face of innocence" and which is "universalized through the imagined loss of *any* child as a loss that could be my loss" (Ahmed 2004, 192).

Dear Zachary's affecting brand of crime reenactment reaches its emotional crescendo in the reconstruction of the murder of young Zachary. As Kuenne's rapid-fire voice-over provides a "summary of the evidence" of the murder of Zachary by his mother, Shirley Turner, actual home video footage and family photos are again employed to affective ends. As we hear Kuenne say, "The night she killed you," the film provides images of Turner in a paddling pool with baby Zachary on a sunny summer's day, playfully throwing a ball at him. When describing how Turner fed her son prescription drugs before she drowned him, the film shows home video footage of baby Zachary refusing some food in his high chair. The film then zooms in on an extreme close-up of baby Zachary dozing off to sleep with his face made up as a cat in yet more home video footage from happier times. Kuenne's voice-over breaks down with emotion as he tells us that "the only good thing we know about this [the fact that the boy was drugged] was that you were not conscious and did not suffer." The happy image of baby Zachary drifting off to sleep is here recast as the scene of his death.

As Kuenne recounts the details of how Turner strapped her son to her chest and walked into the Atlantic Ocean, an image is shown, again from previous home video footage, of Turner in a swimming costume, kissing and carrying along baby Zachary, in a wading pool. This footage, which presents a recontextualization of the past for the viewer, is here re-viewed, retrospectively, as deeply ominous and disturbing. A voice recording of Turner saying "Mummy loves you" then plays over a series of still photographic images of a smiling Turner in the pool with baby Zachary, finishing on an image of her holding her son as he swims under the water (all the while, the sound track plays of her voice from a series of recorded telephone calls made to Zachary's grandparents while she was in jail; in a feedback loop of the recording, Turner is heard saying "Mummy misses you, Mummy loves you").

The repurposed or remediated family photo and home video sequences in *Dear Zachary* highlight the tension between dramatic and documentary modes of viewing, and between the private and public consumption of family photos and home video footage. Marsha and Devin Orgeron have noted that the "extensive use" of home video footage in contemporary documentaries "signals a shift in recent documentary production, one that compels us to consider the implications of using home videos as narrational and illustrative tools" (2007, 47). While there is an undeniable power in taking the images of baby Zachary from a happier time playing in the pool and making them perform the dramatic, illustrative work of crime reconstruction, there is arguably a certain violence involved with this move. As noted by Minette Hillyer, critics such as Roger Odin and Eric Kuyper have argued that "screening home movies out of context can perform a kind of violence that is not only textual but also social"; or to put it even more strongly, the "exposure of intimate home video material out of context is an 'obscenity'" (2010, 768). Whether or not one considers such a recontextualization "obscene," the emotional charge of the home movies of *Dear Zachary* comes from the way in which they are taken out of their (private) context and reworked in the public context of crime and death.

To further think through the affective force of the home video footage on display in *Dear Zachary*, it is helpful to reflect on theorist Richard Grusin's observations about the public reaction to the photographic images of criminal acts committed by American soldiers in Abu Ghraib. Grusin has argued that what was so shocking about the photographs was not only their horrible content but rather, "the stark contrast with the kinds of affective responses we normally associate with viewing digital photos on our computers or on TV and in the newspapers" (2010, 89). That is to say, that what was recognized, "at some level," was that:

> what these soldiers were doing with their Abu Ghraib photos or their photos of maimed and mutilated bodies was not fundamentally different as media practices from what we do with our digital cameras and video cameras when we capture scenes of a wedding or birthday party. . . . And that part of the horror of these images, if the unarticulated or non-symbolic part of that horror, is this bodily feeling both of the affectivity of these digital images and of the affinity between our own practices of distributing affect across and through other media as well. (89)

The point Grusin is making here is a subtle but important one: on an affective level, before there was a chance to process feelings or express emotions about the disturbing photographs from Abu Ghraib, there was a recognition that we also use photos in this way to distribute our affect (happiness, sadness, etc.) and that there was therefore a disturbing affinity between our own media practices and torture and violence. The public response to the Abu Ghraib photographs needs to be understood as "not only a response to what the photographs reveal or mean or to the emotions they evoke, but as an unqualified bodily response independent of, and perhaps phenomenally prior to, our understanding of the emotions they evoke or the meanings they entail" (81).[12] The embodied affective response to the photographs should be understood in relation to their circulation in terms of familiar media habits, so that the shock that was felt over the photos was not just about the content but about the "prior affective relationship with our everyday media practices" (81).

Grusin's analysis of the public outrage over the Abu Ghraib photographs is useful for thinking through the powerful affective responses to the family photos in *Dear Zachary*. The home video footage and the still photographic images on display in the film are a familiar part of everyday media practices, and it is the dramatic reframing of those images in the context of violence that draws attention to the potential proximity of such documentary images to crime and death. By shifting home videos away from their initial context, that is, *Dear Zachary* is making visible what happens more generally when terrible events place home photos and movies into a public record of violence and retrospective reading. It is useful here to refer to José van Dijck's arguments regarding the widespread public awareness of digital cameras and recording devices as tools for "producing future memories" (2008, 71). Even young children today, as van Dijck suggests, are acutely aware of the "pliability of mediated experience" and of how the registering of private lives via new digital technology "may help shape (future) public identity" (71). While the emphasis in constructing this kind of "cinematic hindsight" may be on manufacturing pleasing and desirable images, I would argue, along with van Dijck, that there is also a growing sense of how such "audiovisual retrospectives" (71) play a role in public articulations of grief and death, something that is made dramatically apparent by true crime narratives.

When we watch the family photos and footage of Andrew and Zachary, overlaid by Kuenne's voice-over, which provides us with details of their violent deaths, it is painful not because of how horrible it is (which it *unquestionably* is) but because of our more basic and prior sense of material familiarity with the mundane video images and photographs on display, images that structure our own affective lives. That is why one reviewer who castigates the film for being *too* personal and therefore not relevant to a wider cinema audience beyond the victims' friends and families is missing the point.[13] It does not matter that viewers did not know the victims, as testified to by the emotional outpouring over the documentary in online forums. The reason it does not matter is because the emotional involvement with the documentary is predicated upon the affective familiarity with the images it displays and the graphic ways in which it foregrounds the increasingly blurred boundaries between what we might imagine is "private" and what we are increasingly asked to do with and through those private feelings and images in public life.

In fact, I would like to suggest that the recontextualized home video images and family photographs in *Dear Zachary* underscore the more disquieting elements of the affective relay that occurs between the private and the public in today's media culture, the formulation of which theorist Brian Massumi has referred to as a "quasi-public sphere." Speaking of the "relay and overlap between private and public messaging that blurs the boundaries between them," Massumi uses the example of Facebook: "you friend your friends' friends, and they friend yours, and soon you're sharing 'personal' news with total strangers. The mode of expression is still 'personal,' but the presupposition is of a certain degree of publicness, more restricted than broadcast but not exactly intimate or personal in any way previous generations would have understood that word" (2012). For Massumi, it is not just that the private has become public but that there is a

> whole new relational field where the act of expression is already informed and formatted by its quasi-publicness, so that it is marked from within by the presence of others. It's an example of expression becoming explicitly what Deleuze and Guattari called a 'collective assemblage of enunciation.' To the extent that we produce ourselves through social media—in pretty much the same sense as when we refer to what film producers do—we are fairly explicitly participating in a collective individuation under the flimsy guise of "the personal." (ibid.)

There is a striking example of just such a "collective individuation" in one of the better-known scenes from *Capturing the Friedmans*, in which David Friedman speaks to the camera in home video footage he took of himself from 1988 ("private" footage that he turned over to director Jarecki for inclusion in his documentary). In this intimate footage, David Friedman, wearing his underwear, utters the following: "Well this is private, so if you're not me then you really shouldn't be watching this because this is supposed to be a private situation between me and me. This is between me now and me of the future, so turn it off, don't watch this, this is private . . . If you're the fucking cops go fuck yourselves, go fuck yourselves because you're full of shit." This monologue exemplifies Massumi's idea that so-called private expressions are "marked from within by the presence of others" (2012).[14]

In its remediation of home video footage in relation to crime reconstruction, *Dear Zachary* is also making explicit the kind of collective and public enunciation that already exists within our so-called private expressions. It is noteworthy how this relay between the personal and the public manifests itself at the level of the film's distribution as it shifts across various viewing platforms producing different circuits of affect. In its extensive deployment of still and moving images of the murdered Andrew, *Dear Zachary*, by Kuenne's own admission, was initially intended only for family and friends, as a kind of "cinematic retrospection" or memorial video, which, as van Dijck has noted, is gaining in popularity "as part of a funeral experience" (2008, 85). It was only later, after the various twists and turns the story took, that the film's viewing context shifted to the public domain, to film festivals and television screenings, in which emphasis was placed on withholding information about Zachary's death. While it is common practice to try to retain some secrecy around major plot twists in fictional films, it is slightly more curious in a documentary film, especially one about a violent crime that has already been heavily publicized in the media.[15] That so much effort is put into concealing the open secret of the murder of Zachary for "future viewers," not only by the film's marketing team but by critics and online reviewers, goes to show the extent to which the true crime documentary operates as what Vikki Bell, writing on *Capturing the Friedmans*, refers to as a "compound of affect," a "materiality that . . . promises to hold and deliver sensations at a future encounter" (2008, 93).

Given the emphasis placed on the sensory experience of the film and its emotionality, the question then becomes: what are the "cultural politics" of such emotions, to borrow Sara Ahmed's phrase? To help get a sense of the kind of cultural work performed by the emotional responses to *Dear Zachary*, it is instructive to consider the outrage directed against (the very few) reviewers who criticized the film for its crass aesthetic and blatant emotionalism. Noting how her "analytical response to the documentary seem[ed] to be [so] thoroughly out of tune with the emotional responses of MSNBC viewers," critic Karina Longworth reprinted several viewer comments that took her to task for reviewing the film in the first place. In response to her charge that the film is a "blanket of overlapping sentiment" (2008), legions of outraged viewers wrote in to passionately defend Kuenne's film and to criticize Longworth for her lack of "empathy." In similar fashion, another reviewer, Ron Wilkinson, who argued in even stronger (and arguably more glib terms) that the film was nothing but "maudlin tabloid journalism," faced an onslaught of comments from viewers who were furious at his failure to empathize (2008). Among the arguments put forward by these viewers was the idea that *Dear Zachary* "isn't just a documentary" but a "profound act of love." To quote from one viewer in full: "What an awful review! This film was so moving to me. . . . Are you that heartless to write something that cruel and negative? It was wonderfully done and heartwrenching. Andrew's parents are to be commended for having to accept and overcome what they have. Andrew definitely got his amazing spirit and love of life from them" (quoted in comments on Wilkinson 2008). This kind of comment is echoed in the general viewer response to the film found on IMDb.com, in which viewers express how much the film has affected them emotionally, offer love to the "Bagby friends and family," and emphasize how "inspirational" they find David and Kate Bagby (IMDb User Reviews 2008). In these responses, feeling grief for the other "moves the subject" into what Ahmed calls a "position of charitable compassion," which can be characterized by the following formulation: "In being moved by this pain, I show myself to be full of love in the midst of the violence" (2004, 192). The problem, as Ahmed points out, is that there is a certain conservatism that underlines such compassion and sympathy.

What is indeed noteworthy about the public response to *Dear Zachary*, I want to suggest, is the extent to which strong emotions, underlaid by a prior affective recognition of the dangerous proximity of crime and violence to everyday media practices, appear to reinforce conventional ideals about love, family, and society. Noting the close historical relationship between criminal identification and Western culture's reification of the family, Jermyn has pointed out how closely intertwined the discourses of family and crime remain on contemporary crime programs, which, she argues, "adhere[s] to and promote[s] conventional and conservative ideological structures . . . revering the institution of the family and 'legitimising' victims through their placement within it" (2007, 83). *Dear Zachary* similarly reinforces powerful ideas about the family through its memorialization of the victims of crime; or, to put it the other way around, it is through the institution of the family that it is able to so effectively convey the idea of victimhood and suffering. *Dear Zachary* draws the viewer in through its use of the fictional device of the "plot twist," which,

I argue, serves primarily to heighten the emotional experience of the film, and the audience of *Dear Zachary* ultimately comes together over the scene of violence to affirm certain absolute convictions about the power of love and family, good versus evil, justice and the "norms of acceptable behaviour," ideals that have long been central to crime films more generally (Rafter 2006, 4). It is this kind of emotional interaction with the documentary text and the ideals underpinning it that creates a positive collective affect, one that insulates and protects the viewer from more disquieting revelations.

Bearing in mind how important it is to consider the "extra material that increasingly surrounds and structures our interactions with and reactions to the primary text" (Brown 2008, 96), I now want to consider the DVD format of *Dear Zachary* in order to further reflect upon the kind of affective responses solicited by, and enacted through, the remediation of home video footage in the documentary.

Afterlife

While it had a very limited theatrical release and made some notable appearances at film festivals, *Dear Zachary* first came to most people's attention via its television premiere on MSNBC in 2008; it was later released on DVD in 2009, and has since had an extensive afterlife on the internet—on websites devoted to the film, on internet sites such as Reddit, and in review forums on sites such as Amazon. This is not just incidental detail; though it is often overlooked, the question of distribution and exhibition across different media platforms, and the complex intersection between the private and the public, is absolutely crucial to any understanding of our affective engagement with true crime documentaries. van Dijck observes that the "cultural format of a DVD, which comes replete with 'making of' scenes and evidentiary material," means that the viewer assumes "the position of active co-constructors of hindsight" (2008, 79). This position of the viewer as the co-constructor of hindsight is especially acute in relation to true crime documentaries, which tend to place strong emphasis on the notion of viewers as "armchair detectives," and which, in their search for lost objects and their reconstruction of past events, evoke provocative questions about death and temporality.

The DVD sleeve of *Dear Zachary* includes a review by Erik Childress, the vice president of the Chicago Film Critics Association, which guides our emotional response to Kuenne's documentary. Childress heaps praise on *Dear Zachary*, a documentary that, by his own admission, works him up into a "hyberbolic frenzy." His "shaken" response to the documentary and his colorful description of its viscerality is in keeping with the other vivid emotional responses to the film found in the online reviews discussed earlier. Childress likens the documentary to a "rapidly approaching buzzsaw that opened a pit in my stomach and quickly filled it with sadness, joy, shock, contempt and the helplessness of living in a God-fearing world that would allow this to happen" and describes it as a "furious lightning bolt of *reminiscence* and *outrage* that is going to reach into each viewer's chest and squeeze their heart like a tomato in a vice while it unfolds like a masterful thriller" (Childress n.d.). Such hyperbole is interesting not for what it reveals about individual emotions but for what it suggests about how *Dear Zachary* circulates as an object of emotion, emphasizing Belinda Smaill's point that the "expectations and assumptions that permeate the production, reception and critique of documentary are based in an emotional attachment to the form" (2010, 4).

The "Extras" section of the DVD menu includes six additional scenes that didn't make the final cut, interactive DVD-enabled material regarding bail reform in Canada, and, significantly, three home videos that come together under the heading "Footage of Andrew & Zachary." It is the home video footage that I am particularly interested in discussing for the questions it raises about our affective engagement with the film's staging of documentary facts. DVD reviews of *Dear Zachary* typically frame its three additional home videos as extending the emotional experience of the film and providing "more heartbreak" for the viewer (Humanick 2009). Where *Dear Zachary* is an incredibly fast-paced film, moving from interviewee to interviewee and from sequence to sequence at "breakneck speed" (Sartin 2008), it is significant that the home videos are included in their entirety here, allowing the viewer to linger over them, and calling upon a different, more "pensive" spectatorship than the film (Mulvey 2006, 186). What I find most interesting is how we respond to this footage retrospectively; when we come to the "extras" of the home videos after watching the film, we are already reenacting it—or recontextualizing it—in relation to crime and death. In other words, it is not the content of the home video footage that grips me, and keeps me watching throughout the entirety of a video of Andrew Bagby's "Best Man's Speech," but the mental reframing of that footage in the context of the violent crime and death that we know has already occurred and that we have already engaged with through our experience of the documentary. The documentary footage is retrospectively reframed by the viewer in relation to crime images. The prior affective familiarity of such home video imagery, as well, strongly encourages us to recall our own personal images, and to imagine not only what would happen if those documentary images were viewed in relation to crime and death but, rather, more crucially, to see those images in some way as already *potentially* infused with violence and death.

The final home video extra, "16 mm film of Zachary," is footage of Zachary playing outside with his grandparents. Set to extradiegetic elegiac music, the footage of baby Zachary with his grandparents is poignant and tragic and is meant to elicit tears. It is reminiscent of the emotive footage of other missing and lost children, such as Madeleine McCann, which appears on our television, computer, and phone screens, and which strongly appeals to mass public sentiment. The ethical purchase of *Dear Zachary*, I believe, is located within this footage. How are we meant to watch these images? Should we be watching this footage at all? On one level, the function of the video footage is obvious: it is a memorial to a murdered child. For Kate and David Bagby, the grandparents, it is a cherished visual memory of the time they spent with their grandson; for friends of Andrew Bagby, it is, almost certainly, an unbearably sad and touching video of their murdered friend's son, a "media memory" of a child they never knew. But what is our relationship to this footage? To borrow John Ellis's phrase, "What are we expected to feel" (2009, 67)? It is indeed likely that such an "extra" provides us with more "heartbreak," but to what end? What are we reenacting in our return to, and review of, this footage of a dead child? As the elegiac music tacked on to the image acknowledges, there can be no "innocent" viewing of this footage outside of the terrible knowledge of what happened to this child. Oddly, while so much emphasis is placed on withholding information about the "plot twist" of *Dear Zachary* so that future viewers of the film can watch the film in "real time" and approach it with fresh eyes, unencumbered by any foreknowledge, here things are turned around so that in watching the home video footage we are being invited to shudder "*over a catastrophe which has already occurred*" (Barthes 1993, 96). In both cases, though, the emphasis is on generating—and heightening—our emotions. While we might well "wonder about the wishes at work in the visual archive of the child in pain, in death" (Lebeau 2008, 149), it is the emotional "truth" of the figure of the child that this crime documentary finally wants to leave us with; a figure that, as I have argued, is mobilized for affective ends, to secure our sympathy and indeed our outrage over the flimsy laws that led an alleged murderer to reoffend, but also, finally, to shore up certain idealized convictions about good versus evil and the power of love and family.

In this chapter I have explored the movement and effects of the emotions mobilized by the crime documentary *Dear Zachary*—and, specifically, the home video footage that lies at its heart—as it circulates through different digital media channels, in particular in online comments and reviews and in its format as a DVD. In particular, I have been interested in exploring the ways in which the affective labor of the viewer is used to shore up dominant ideologies and social values regarding the institution of the family, all the while keeping at bay a deeper, more unsettling set of cultural anxieties regarding the proximity between violence, death, and our own everyday documentary practices. As I have argued, the strong emotional response to *Dear Zachary* is not only about the content of the terrible crimes it discloses but also about our affective familiarity with the materiality of the media technologies it deploys.

Dear Zachary and its attempt to bind feelings to a public cause through its highly affective brand of crime reconstruction can be understood in the context of the growth of digital technologies and the emergence of new distribution formats for documentary, as well as a wider turn to empathy in post-9/11 culture. As I have suggested, however, it is vital that we unpack the cultural significance of this desire to feel or to "refeel" violent events (Bruzzi 2012), and consider the work such emotionality is performing. As Daniel O'Gorman has observed in his discussion of the "empathic line" taken by political theorists in a post-9/11 context, it is imperative that we "acknowledge a need for empathy itself to be 'unsettled' and critically interrogated" (2012). True crime documentaries, with their strong affective pull on audiences, open up a set of vital questions about the politics of empathy and about the functions of emotionality in a contemporary digital culture in which the lines between the private and the public, the individual and the collective, are being rapidly and continuously reconfigured.

In the next chapter, I continue to explore questions about the nature of our affective encounters with images of violence and criminality, but I shift my attention to the circulation of real crime images in wider internet clip culture in order to think about how the boundaries and viewing practices associated with "true crime" are extended in a 24/7 entertainment culture. Examining the online spreadability and replay of CCTV surveillance assault videos published by the celebrity gossip website *TMZ*, I consider the mechanisms by which such videos circulate and the kind of racialized and gendered content being repurposed and shared through the problematic memetic reproduction of a notion of the black body as inherently toxic and criminalized.

"Caught on Tape"

Elevator Assault Videos, Black Celebrity, and the Politics of Surveillance

IN 2014, THE CELEBRITY gossip website *TMZ*[1] published two different surveillance videos of American black celebrities from the respective fields of music and sports committing acts of violence in elevators. The first video, published on May 12, 2014, involves celebrity power couple Jay-Z and Beyoncé, and Beyoncé's sister Solange, in an elevator in the Standard Hotel in New York. It shows Solange kicking and thrashing at Jay-Z as a bodyguard tries to restrain her. "Jay-Z physically attacked by Beyoncé's sister Solange" was the headline to *TMZ*'s video of the incident.[2] The second video, published on September 8, 2014, involves National Football League star Ray Rice, of the Baltimore Ravens, and his then fiancée, now wife, Janay Palmer Rice. It shows Rice punching Palmer in the head and onto a guardrail as she falls unconscious to the floor in a casino hotel elevator in Atlantic City. "Ray Rice—Elevator Knock-out—Fiancee Takes Crushing Punch"—ran the typically brash *TMZ* headline to the video, which was featured on its "sports" page.[3]

Dramatically fulfilling *TMZ*'s stated mission both to dispense "celebrity justice"[4] and to publish only stories that include "documentary proof" of transgression (Schmidle 2016), the two closed-circuit television surveillance videos, released three months apart from one another, were watched by millions of people online and constituted a major coup for the gossip website. The surveillance videos are of a poor aesthetic quality; they are silent, black-and-white, grainy, jerky, and difficult to see. And yet, it is not so much what the videos show as it is the issue of how they are framed, and the ways in which viewers are affectively bound to them, that interests me most. The poor aesthetic quality of the videos, which adds greatly to their sense of authenticity, comes from the fact that, in both cases, hotel employees used their cell phones to film the closed-circuit television footage from a TV screen. They then sold the footage to *TMZ* for extraordinary sums of money. This dishing of the digital "dirt"[5] about black celebrities, although presented to viewers as "raw" and authentic, is thus triply mediated: through closed-circuit television, through cell phones, and through the platform of *TMZ*.

In the case of the Jay-Z/Solange/Beyoncé video, the vociferous public discussion over what Jay-Z might have said to Solange to provoke such an outburst is part of the wider internet "sleuthing" culture discussed in the introduction to this book, with viewers rushing to perform online detective work through a tactile, tangible engagement with the video (pausing, tapping, swiping, replaying, and sharing) in an effort to ascertain what might have happened. I should say from the start that readers who come to this chapter hoping for a solution to the "mystery" of what "Jay-Z said to Solange" will be disappointed. My interest is not in what Jay-Z might have said to Solange but in how the video becomes culturally bound to the Ray Rice domestic violence video as it circulates across online spaces and draws on wider viewing practices associated with digital-era true crime.

Surveillance clips have always featured prominently on reality crime television (Wheatley 2001, 46), straddling an uncomfortable border between "entertainment" and criminal identification and apprehension (Jermyn 2007, 109). In her influential 2007 book, *Crime Watching: Investigating Real Crime TV*, Deborah Jermyn includes a chapter on such "unscripted footage" (109) and discusses how, from the 1980s onward, CCTV and police footage featured widely on "crime appeal programming" and "real crime TV 'clipshow' programmes such as *Police Camera Action!* and *World's Wildest Police Videos*" (110). However, as I noted in my introduction, the advent of social media networks has contributed to a decline in the popularity of real crime shows such as *Crimewatch UK* and *America's Most Wanted*, as people can now readily access such clips online through user-generated sites such as YouTube. It is therefore necessary to look at the circulation of such clips outside of the boundaries of more established true crime formats in order to consider the relationship between new media interfaces and the capture of violent images.

The elevator assault videos discussed in this chapter are not constructed "true crime" products and are presented as "authentic" moments of violence. But while surveillance technologies may appear to "'capture reality unawares'" (Plantinga 2013, 44), they are far from neutral. As digital race scholar Lisa

Nakumara writes: "surveillance does more than simply watch or observe bodies. It *remakes* the body as a social actor, classifying some bodies as normative and legal, and some as illegal and out of bounds. There is no form of surveillance that is innocent" (2015, 221). It is no accident, I argue, that the most publicized surveillance videos on *TMZ* to date involve the depiction of racialized, black bodies. As Nakamura has suggested, "women and people of color are still overwhelmingly the objects of the biometric and surveillance gaze, as they have always been" (2015, 223–24). In the chapter that follows, I examine the process by which these two highly mediated surveillance videos became entangled with one another in online meme culture, in order to consider how they circulate as racialized and gendered spectacles of violence. What is of specific concern to me here is how the apparently "passive" lens of surveillance actively works to reproduce a notion of black people as toxic and criminal in ways that have wider implications for how we think about true crime as a racialized formation.

Not surprisingly, perhaps, the "activity" and "passivity" of the bodies involved in the two elevator videos were a central discussion point in their cultural reception. Consider, for example, this description of the Jay-Z/Solange Knowles incident from the British newspaper the *Independent*:

> The video footage, obtained by TMZ from inside an elevator in the Standard Hotel in New York after the Met Ball Gala last week, saw Beyoncé's sister *transform into a furious battery of fists and legs* as she lashed out at the rapper, *who at no point retaliated*, other than to grab her foot to prevent it from colliding with his face.
>
> A security guard *wrestled her backwards* and slammed on the emergency stop at the twelfth floor, *as Beyoncé remained entirely placid and motionless.* (Selby 2014, my emphasis)

The so-called placid passivity of Beyoncé in the elevator—the fact that she remained "entirely" calm and collected in the midst of the fracas between her husband and her sister—was much remarked upon at the time. Her inactivity was viewed as either dubious or praiseworthy—sometimes both at the same time. As I will later discuss in more detail, the apparent passivity of Jay-Z—the fact that "he at no point retaliated" (Selby 2014)—made him the subject of ridicule in memes and was the occasion for a maligning of his masculinity, even as that very passivity also later served as the grounds for praising him as a chivalrous and decent "gentleman," in contrast to the toxic black masculinity of Rice.

With regard to the Ray Rice video, questions about the so-called activity of Janay Palmer Rice—Did she strike Rice first? Was she somehow actively involved in her own victimization? How could she go on to marry her abuser one month after the incident?—were central talking points, both in the racist, hate-filled comments found on YouTube and also in the mainstream reporting of the incident. However, as I will demonstrate, in both incidents what is most salient is not simply the value judgments passed regarding which individual bodies acted or not—why, and in what way—but, rather, how questions of passivity and agency were framed in regard to what Judith Butler has elsewhere referred to, in a discussion of the Rodney King video, as a "racially saturated field of vision" (1993, 15). For regardless of which actions the bodies in these videos were perceived to be performing, and it must be noted in relation to the Ray Rice video that the actions of Rice are to be roundly and unequivocally condemned, it remains the case that black bodies are "always already performing" certain violent, criminal actions within a "white racist imaginary" and that there is therefore a strong need to unpack how the " 'seeing' of blackness takes place" (20) in our contemporary digital moment. As Butler so aptly puts it: "it is necessary to read not only for the 'event' of violence, but for the racist schema that orchestrates and interprets the event" (20).

While the *Washington Post* and other publications reflected on why "we watch awful things like Solange Knowles's attack on Jay Z," and wondered "what we think we will get out of pressing play" (Rosenberg 2014), it is in the memes that flooded the internet following both incidents that questions of audience participation and involvement in the mise-en-scène of racialized violence really come to the fore. I want to argue for the critical significance of these memes as examples of what psychoanalytic film theorist Elizabeth Cowie calls "public fantasies": mise-en-scènes of "desire" (1997, 143) that render visible the racist logic underpinning the widespread surveillance of black people in contemporary America. Looking at how the elevator scenes get visually reworked and restaged in multiple contexts through the internet memes that proliferated online in the wake of their publication on *TMZ*, I explore the kinds of wishful racist scenarios at work, which revolve around what Cowie calls a "structure of positions" (140), in this case, of acting/not acting, of agency/submission, of violence/nonviolence, of (black) female/ (black) male.

There is a risk of conflating the two incidents in a comparison/contrast exercise, and I agree with Anna Nti-Asare (2015) that there are very different power dynamics of control and dependence going on between the pairing of Jay-Z and Solange (as mediated by male security guard), and Ray Rice and Janay Palmer-Rice that need to be acknowledged. In other words, the two incidents are emphatically *not* the same in terms of the kind of violence they enact and the level of harm that is suffered. Ray Rice is committing an act of criminal assault and domestic violence and Solange Knowles is physically lashing out at her brother-in-law (who is protected by his bodyguard). And yet the proximity of the release of the two elevator surveillance videos by *TMZ* meant that they *were* inevitably compared and contrasted—both in mainstream media and in an explosion of internet memes—in ways that indicate the tenacity of certain deeply rooted and pernicious racial and gender stereotypes.[6]

The time line of the videos is significant to understanding their mutual imbrication. On February 19, 2014, *TMZ* first posted a forty-nine-second video clip of football star Rice dragging his unconscious fiancée out of an elevator at a hotel casino in Atlantic City. The video went viral, resulting in a two-game suspension for Rice from the football league. However, six months later, on September 8, *TMZ* released a second, much more graphic surveillance video, this one taken from inside the elevator, showing Rice knocking his fiancée unconscious, which it purchased for a reported ninety thousand dollars. The release of this video resulted in a full-scale national controversy over football and domestic violence, and Rice was cut by his football team, the Ravens, and suspended indefinitely from the NFL.[7]

On May 12, 2014, in between the publication of the two videos of Rice, and notably *before* the release of the second graphic video showing him knocking his fiancée unconscious, *TMZ* published the surveillance footage of Solange Knowles physically lashing out at her brother-in-law in an elevator after the Met Gala Ball. This footage was allegedly sold to *TMZ* for 250,000 dollars (Schmidle 2016). Viewed over six million times on YouTube, as well on the *TMZ* site itself, which is reported to have seventeen million unique visitors a month (ibid.), the video spawned thousands of internet memes and was the source of much internet humor.

In her work on the prevalence of racist memes in postdigital culture, Nakumara argues that "racism is less a virus in the internet's body than it *is* that body" (2014, 269). Nakumara suggests that what is "badly needed in our so-called post-racial moment" is a "critique of the digital" that closely examines the origins and meanings of memes as part of a wider history of viral racism, which has long traded in derogatory images of black people (260). Following Nakumara's call for "a social media image ethics that acknowledges the conditions of production of memes and their operation within an attention economy that includes racial abjection as both a product and a process" (260), I will examine how the memes and jokes that circulate around the two elevator videos, as published by *TMZ*, disclose widespread social participation in a set of fantasies regarding celebrity, blackness, and violence.

Finally, and importantly, these elevator incidents need to be situated in relation to a "Black Lives Matter" cultural moment. A major part of the cultural traction of these surveillance videos of violence featuring black superstars from the arenas of pop music and sport, unconscious or not, is that they were released in a moment of social unrest and anxiety regarding widespread racism and police brutality against black Americans. Citizen videos of wanton police brutality resulting in the deaths of African American boys and men, including, for example, Trayvon Martin (2012), Eric Garner (2014), and Michael Brown (2014),[8] circulated before, during, and after these elevator videos as shocking instances of murderous anti-black racism. Captured on mobile phones, and shared widely across the internet, these politicized citizen videos led to the intervention of the "Black Lives Matter" movement, which seeks to expose, and fight back against, the systemic dehumanization and criminalization of black people.[9] The extent to which these subjective digital videos disturb the white conservative status quo is sharply underscored by the fact that the bystanders who record and distribute them have been subsequently arrested or held by police.[10] By contrast, the apparently "objective" *TMZ* surveillance videos—filmed by "nobody"—depict black-on-black violence involving black American celebrities and work to reinforce dominant white culture and its evidentiary ideals of neutrality and impartiality. As I will further demonstrate in the discussion that follows, the *TMZ* videos, and their remixing and recoding in meme culture, ultimately work to reproduce racist ideas of black people as dangerous and criminally threatening.

Elevator Time

To begin with, it is not incidental that these surveillance videos of violence should take place in elevators. On the contrary, I would argue their appeal has to do with the striking way in which they operate within the bounds of what film theorist Alanna Thain calls "elevator time." Reminding us of the history of the passenger elevator, and the fanfare that attended its unveiling in 1853 before its widespread adoption in early-twentieth-century "modern urban life" (2009, 51), Thain writes of the significance of elevators as "time based mediums of transportation." Elevators are "zones of duration where the potential for difference is made manifest" (53), Thain writes, "even if that difference is usually 'held in check' through the observance of 'unspoken' social norms" (53). As a liminal, "suspended zone" (64), elevators are an "exaggerated micro-ecology" of social rules and regulations (59).

The "micro-ecology" of the elevator and its "condensation" of social encounters (66) is made explicit, I would suggest, in its racial history as a mode of transportation. Elevators, like other social spaces, were segregated in America under "Jim Crow" laws. For example, Hanno van der Bijl notes that in 1903 in Atlanta, Georgia, "African-Americans could not ride a building's passenger elevators—they were relegated to the freight elevators, as if they were cargo. Whites were free to ride the freight elevators if they wanted to. Ironically, some buildings in Atlanta allowed African-Americans to go down but not up" (2015). Moreover, for many years after the end of slavery, it was common practice for a uniformed black elevator attendant to press the buttons for white passengers. The elevator, then, is historically a racially marked space in the United States, and it is therefore important to take that history into account when considering how it operates as a "spectacular attraction" (Thain 2009, 52).

According to Thain, the elevator "holds a natural affinity with cinema. Both are machines for creating non-habitual space and time" (52). Central to the evocative nature of both is a strong sense of temporality; elevators, like films, have a strange "ability to make one *feel* duration" (63). As Thain points out, elevators are banal spaces of duration, at the same time that that very banality is often the means of covering up or concealing the terror of their vertical movement down a shaft (56). The banality of the cage of the elevator, with its range of sounds, lights, buttons (and occasionally "elevator music"), is designed to give the passenger a sense of control and agency, however illusory this may be (62).

The affective sense of duration described by Thain is apparent in the *TMZ* surveillance videos under discussion in this essay. There is a rhythm to the elevator videos and their particular clocking of time: the doors open and close, the elevator rises and falls, a "private" altercation occurs in the public space of the cage and a set of social rules are breached, the elevator ride comes to an end, the doors slide open, and the passengers exit back into the social realm. The sense of a "before" and an "after" is central to the fascination the videos exert; it's no surprise, for example, that the pre- and post-elevator photos of Jay-Z, Beyoncé, and Solange in their Met Ball sartorial finery were objects of intense fascination, circulating as affective artifacts that might hold clues to the mystery behind the elevator quarrel.

Both elevator videos center on the movement of bodies in an enclosed space; the motion of the bodies is arguably emphasized even more in the absence of any audio. In the Jay-Z/Solange Knowles video, it is motion itself that is on display: there is a scuffle of bodies in movement, of legs kicking and of arms hitting out. Because the visibility is so poor, it is hard to discern exactly what is happening (hence *TMZ*'s heavy labeling of the incident with large red arrows identifying the participants and its careful selection of precisely which moments to select for the thirty-seven-second clip it showed on its website).

What becomes more noticeable on repeated viewings of the full three-minute-thirty-second-long video, available on YouTube, is the role of the black security guard. Not only does the security guard act as a proxy for Jay-Z, restraining Solange and physically containing her, but he is also pictured pushing at the buttons of the elevator. Reports that the guard "pushed the emergency stop button in the elevator on the 12th floor" (Proud 2014) may recall the history of black elevator attendants but they also underscore how central the question of agency and the "regulation of movement" (Thain 2009, 62) is to the scene. The security guard's role, in addition to restraining Solange and protecting Jay-Z—both in the sense of making sure Jay-Z is not hit but also, and even more significantly, that Jay-Z does not have to hit and therefore enact a violent masculinity—is to contain the situation and ensure that this private argument does not spill out into public space.

The boundary between private and public space is also brought into dramatic relief in the Ray Rice video, which begins before the couple even enter the elevator, with a surveillance camera showing the two arguing in the corridor. Ray Rice appears to spit on Janay Palmer Rice, and she slaps at his face in retaliation. When they enter the elevator and the doors close, the verbal altercation continues (though, again, the video is without audio). Rice then delivers one brutal punch to his fiancée's face and knocks her unconscious. The *TMZ* video shows the punch, and then it shows it again, in slow motion. The rest of the remaining two-minute video, which feels acutely prolonged, is of Rice picking up and dragging Janay Palmer Rice's limp, unconscious body out of the elevator. He drops her on the ground so that she is lying face down, her bare legs exposed, with her feet still in the elevator and the rest of her body in the public space of the corridor. An African American security guard comes over to talk to Rice, and Janay Palmer Rice slowly regains consciousness. Other (unidentified) people arrive on the scene, including a white woman who appears to comfort Janay Palmer Rice and eventually leads her away. During this two-minute portion of the video, the doors of the elevator remain open (so the view is from the inside of the elevator *and* of the corridor just outside); this heightens the emphasis on the elevator as a liminal space, between the inside and the outside, between "private" transgression and the public realm.

Although *TMZ* was criticized, including by Ray Rice's legal team, for editing the footage,[11] the website was, in fact, careful to include the "raw surveillance footage" just below the edited video, with a caption that declares: "the raw is jerky." Indeed, the jerky, glitchy movement of the bodies as they enter the elevator both anticipates and dramatically demonstrates the extent to which these scenes of elevator violence are especially suited to internet culture and in particular the culture of GIFS—the "compressed image file format" that has experienced "newfound popularity" in the contemporary networked age (Grindstaff and Murray 2015, 120). It is the gifability of these elevator scenes—the way in which they lend themselves to the "small snippets of physical action" favored by GIFS (ibid.)–that is particularly apposite to a contemporary attention economy in which affect is commodified, and where "the most attention-grabbing images become the most valued" (McKay 2009).

TMZ is known for the sensationalized click bait design of its website; the Jay-Z and Solange and Ray Rice videos exemplify its brash, emotive, and "video-heavy style" of gossip journalism (Petersen 2010, 70). As Anne Helen

Petersen notes, *TMZ* "combines the immediacy of the blog, the technology of new media, and the content of a tabloid" (63); its format "exemplifies the demands of our hyperlinked, intensely visual culture" (71). It is worth noting that *TMZ* debuted in 2005, the same year as YouTube; it is part of the same culture of media production and spectatorship that relies on "spreadable" videos (Jenkins, Ford, and Green 2013) that are "shocking" and visceral. As the anti–*Entertainment Tonight* (Petersen 2010, 69, 71), *TMZ* seeks to dethrone celebrities rather than venerate them, and mainly consists of videos with some very basic, crude, accompanying text. As Petersen suggests, "there is little explanation of the videos, other than a title and brief phrase (Disgusting! Racist! Unbelievable!) to guide user reaction" (71).

Thus, the Jay-Z and Solange video is simply and descriptively labeled "The Fight Video." Just beneath the video, *TMZ* includes a short, if flamboyant, description of what happened in the elevator and emphasizes *TMZ*'s role in obtaining the footage: "Jay Z was ferociously assaulted by Beyoncé's sister Solange . . . who was wildly kicking and swinging at him inside an elevator . . . and the attack was captured on surveillance video . . . obtained by *TMZ*." In similar fashion, the Ray Rice video is labeled "The Brutal Attack," with the first line of the accompanying text garishly describing the incident in the same language it uses to describe sporting events and again branding the video as a *TMZ* exclusive: "This is what a two-game suspension looks like . . . Ray Rice delivering a brutal punch to his fiancee's face, knocking her out cold . . . and *TMZ* Sports has the shocking video."

TMZ's original report of the Jay-Z/Solange incident consists of a thirty-six-second-long, truncated clip from a longer three-minute-thirty-second-long version. The video is available in two different guises on *TMZ*: in the first instance, there is a screen labeled "The Fight Video," with red arrows identifying Jay-Z and Solange and their positions in the lift; the user clicks on the play button, the *TMZ* logo appears, and the edited version of the scene begins playing.[12] In the second version, the video is cued to "auto-play" so that when the user opens the website, the elevator video automatically begins playing.[13]

The Ray Rice video is not set to auto-play on the *TMZ* website but is instead presented in the form of a GIF: a silent, looping fuzzy moving image of Ray Rice hitting Janay Palmer Rice. In the GIF, Janay Palmer Rice is hit and falls to the floor, Janay Palmer-Rice is hit and falls to the floor, Janay Palmer Rice is hit and falls to the floor, repeatedly, on a loop. To activate the video, which runs to three minutes and thirty-four seconds, users must press the play button located in the bottom left-hand corner of the GIF.

The technical formats through which users are able to access the Ray Rice video and its images of violence are central to the affective responses it enables. As Jason Eppink notes in "A Brief History of the GIF (so far)" the GIF is a data format certainly, but it is much more than that: "it has an ethos, a utility, an evolving context, a set of aesthetics" (2014, 298). GIFS, as Eppink points out, are "encountered not in theaters or in living rooms, but on networked screens that are physically private but socially public" (298). GIFS are not passively viewed either: they are shared and commented on, "collected, copied, modified and performed" (298). With the GIF of Ray Rice hitting Janay Palmer Rice, the moment of violence is "'looped, extended and repeated" (McKay 2009); the repetition of the image invites viewer's affective involvement in the decontextualized action of Rice punching and punching and punching.

It is interesting to track what happens to the affective trajectory of the video as it is copied and shared and moves to other sites, such as YouTube, which reframe it in a wider context of "fight videos." After I watched the Ray Rice video on YouTube (along with twelve million other people), another video titled "Knockout Compilation of 2014" automatically began playing. This video consists of edited clips of (mainly white) men being hit, kicked, hurt, or "knocked out" in some way. As Carol Vernallis has noted, the algorithms of YouTube clips seek to elicit audience participation by creating "an urge to continue on through YouTube. . . . Like a wind-up toy, a web user needs to keep moving through the web to diffuse energy and affect. . . . YouTube clips are concerned with getting linked up" (2013, 200–201). Other videos in the suggestions bar of what's "Up Next" after the Ray Rice video include: "Best 2014 Fights Punches Knockouts Compilation," "Extreme Idiots Compilation," and "Epic Knockouts." These "fight" and "knockout" videos, which are performed in a "JackAss" generic style where people get hurt and wounded for laughs, are filed under the category of "comedy." Beneath the videos are thousands of comments, in which users share their reactions to the various knockouts and find them either funny or disturbing. That images of domestic violence are included in this loop of "hilarious" knockouts indicates the kind of ethically suspect linking and intermingling so characteristic of new media formats.

Getting "linked up," and culturally sharing the visual experience of violence, are also motivating factors behind the creation of the hashtag

"WhatJayZSaidToSolange." In the next section of this chapter I will track the spread of this hugely popular hashtag—and the public fantasies of gendered and racialized violence that cohere through it.

#WhatJayZSaidToSolange

Immediately after *TMZ*'s release of the Jay-Z/Solange Knowles "fight video," the hashtag #WhatJayZSaidToSolange began trending on social media, producing legions of memes creating jokes about the incident. Spurred on by the video's lack of audio, the memes spun theories about what Jay-Z must have said to Solange to make her so angry.[14] As the *Independent* put it in a tongue-in-cheek headline to a story on the incident: "What Jay Z really said to Solange . . . According to the Internet. As Twitter followers debate which of their kidneys they are happy to sell in exchange for the elevator audio, the memes flow thick and fast" (Selby 2014). While many of the memes consist of tweets that create gendered jokes around Jay-Z's imagined insults to Solange, such as—"Solange: The elevator isn't going anywhere! Jay-Z: Like your career!" and "Solange Knowles attacks Jay Z? The first hit she's had in years"—it is the image memes that I will focus on for what they can tell us about the uniquely visual methods through which racial and gendered stereotypes spread.

As Limor Shifman defines them, internet memes are "units of popular culture that are circulated, imitated, and transformed by internet users, creating a shared cultural experience" (2013, 367). Memes consist of phrases, remixed videos, photo images, and animated GIFS, which are "extensively circulated, transformed, and incorporated into public discussion" (Milner 2013). While memes seem to proliferate with abandon in the digital age—with it taking "only a couple of mouse clicks to see hundreds of versions of any meme imaginable" (Shifman 2014, 341)—it is not, in fact, as much of a free for all as it may first appear. As Shifman argues, memes tend to fall into very specific and rigid generic boxes, thus underscoring the "important social function" they serve, and enabling researchers to "trace the social and cultural logics underpinning the ostensibly chaotic world of meme creation" (342).

The visual memes of the Jay-Z/Solange incident tend to fall into two categories or "meme genres," as identified by Shifman in her discussion of photo-based memes: "reaction Photoshops," which are "collections of edited images created in response to a small set of prominent photographs," and "stock character macros," which "refer to a set of stock characters representing stereotypical behaviours" (343). Not only do these two meme genres often overlap in the memetic explosion around the Jay-Z/Solange incident, but the very success of the memes—what ensured that they traveled far and wide—was their mutual deployment of two stock racist "character macros" or stereotypes: the black male "thug"/domestic abuser and the angry black woman. The perceived relationship and incongruity between the celebrity success of power couple Jay-Z and Beyoncé and the "stock macro" racist stereotypes of black criminality endemic in dominant culture provided the "stable core" (Milner 2013) by which a range of preexisting celebrity photos were remixed and recaptioned.

My aim is to interpret these memes as "technosocial production(s) of race" (Sharma 2013, 47) and gender, in contradistinction to approaches that rely on "identity-based explanations" and focus on questions of "user identity and behavior" (Sharma 2013, 48). As Sanjay Sharma has argued in his research on Black Twitter, it is important to examine "the contagious effects of networked relations in producing *emergent racial aggregations*, rather than simply representing the behavior of an *intentionally acting* group of Black Twitter users" (2013, 48, my emphasis). Against an approach that understands race in "representational terms" bound to notions of the identities of users, I follow Sharma's lead in taking a materialist approach that examines how "race *works* in online networks" (54).[15] To quote Ganaele Langlois, who is cited by Sharma, instead of trying to determine the identity of users constructing these memes, it is more compelling to ask: "What kind of technocultural assemblage is put into motion when we express ourselves online?" (quoted in Sharma 2013, 55). Paramount to an understanding of race as it relates to the materiality of digital networks is the notion of digital contagion and what Helen Wood refers to as the "affective properties of media forms," which have both a transformative social potential *and* the ability to reproduce certain problematic social formations and stereotypes (Wood 2018, 3).

The first prominent set of visual memes around the elevator incident that I want to discuss consist of "reaction Photoshop" photos of Jay-Z and Beyoncé taken from previously published publicity photos of the celebrity pair on tour, on holiday, or at various social and sporting events. On Tumblr, Twitter, and other social media sites, these photos were repurposed to generate humor by attaching "witty" captions to them. Thus, one notable meme recaptions the

Fig. 2.1. "On the Run" from Solange Meme

poster from Beyoncé and Jay-Z's 2014 joint stadium tour, in which the couple wear black ski masks playing the role of criminals on the "lam," with the line: "On the Run—From Solange—Tour."

This visual joke, in which the famous couple is running away from a crazy and out-of-control Solange, is extended and repeated in the recaptioning of other well-known publicity photos. For example, a photo of Jay-Z and Beyoncé jumping into a pool together while on holiday is recaptioned to say: "Fuck! Solange coming!" The image of Jay-Z in his swimming trunks jumping into the pool was in turn playfully relocated onto a stock photograph of an elevator. In this Photoshopped image, Jay-Z appears to be jumping out of the elevator, and the caption reads: "Hop out da elevator like!"

The Jay-Z/Solange memes enact what theorist Ryan Milner calls the "logic of lulz" (a version of LOL, an acronym that stands for "laugh out loud"), which "favours distanced irony and critique" (2013). Although the "logic of lulz" can be used to "make political points," memes tend to "commonly replicate well-entrenched hegemonic stereotypes" (Shifman 2014, 348). In a key strand of memes, for example, the apparent disjunction between Jay-Z's "tough guy" rapper status and his lack of retaliation against Solange is the source of much ridicule. One meme reproduces an awkward still image of Jay-Z from his 2013

Samsung commercial and mocks him as effeminate with the caption: "Ouch! Stop Solange!" In the same vein, but with even more disturbing connotations, are the memes that recaption preexisting photos of Jay-Z with singer Chris Brown, who in 2009 pled guilty to felony assault of his then girlfriend, the pop star Rihanna. In this group of image memes, a photo of a tuxedoed Jay-Z as he laughs with, and greets, Brown is repurposed to imagine a violent, threatening, and misogynist scenario in which Jay-Z seeks "help" from the convicted domestic abuser; the image's various captions have Chris Brown saying: "If she touches you again, call me" and "That's her?? Say no more." Yet another creative caption to the photo has Jay-Z giving Brown the details of Solange's location: "Jay Z: 'Solange is on the 6th floor room 229'—Chris Brown: 'I got this.'"

Using a similar template, other memes repurpose publicity photos of a smiling Jay-Z and Rihanna and attempt to generate humor by comparing them as victims of domestic violence: "I'm Jay Z and I'm Rihanna . . . And Together We Are Against Domestic Violence." While there is potential for such memes and their humor of "incongruity" to make politically resistant statements—for example, a generous reading of the Jay-Z/Rihanna meme I just mentioned could say it is at least drawing attention to the issue of domestic violence, however

L.A.S. ✅
@SartoriallyInc

hop out da elevator like:
♡ 842 4:44 PM · May 12, 2014

Fig 2.2. Jay-Z vacation photo repurposed as mocking meme

problematically—for the most part they tend to employ race and gender discourse in limited ways that "reinforce oppressive ideologies" (Milner 2013). This is evidenced even more clearly in another variant of the Jay-Z/Rihanna meme strain, which repurposes a photo of Jay-Z and Rihanna onstage at an awards ceremony, and imagines Rihanna saying: "Man Chill Out Jay—My Ass Whooping Was Way Worse Than Yours." Such jokes manage to at once emasculate Jay-Z and demean and trivialize the scene of Rihanna's domestic abuse.

While Jay-Z is openly mocked as "feminine" for his passivity, Beyoncé's perceived lack of response is the occasion for a more subtle gendered derision, as she is depicted as cold, unfeeling, and self-involved. One very popular meme consists of two photographs taken the day after the Met Gala and the elevator incident, of Jay-Z and Beyoncé at a New York Knicks basketball game, chatting courtside with white Hollywood actor Jake Gyllenhaal. The photos are recaptioned to poke fun at Beyoncé's passivity in the face of the violent fracas between her husband and sister. In the first photo an animated Beyoncé is smiling and chatting with Gyllenhaal; the caption imagines her telling him: "And then Solange was kicking him and screaming in the elevator." In the second photo, Jay-Z and Gyllenhaal are laughing together, as Jay-Z points at Beyoncé, and the caption reads: "And she stood there!" Despite their grounding in a culture of amusement and "lulz," there is an ambivalent undercurrent to these memes regarding the cultural stakes of Beyoncé's perceived indifference that becomes even more apparent as they further replicate.

In fact, as the memes of the Jay-Z/Solange Knowles incident travel and are remixed, new combinations emerge that make visible the extent to which the stereotype of the "black male abuser" is wedded to the stereotype of the "angry black woman" in strange and often complicated ways. Thus, one meme repurposes an image from Jay-Z and Beyoncé's 2002 music video "Bonnie and Clyde," of the couple in a car together; Jay-Z is captioned as saying to Beyoncé: "Oh, you just gon' watch . . . Yo sister Chris Brown me?" Conflating Solange and the stereotype of the "angry black woman" with Chris Brown and the stereotype of the black man as abuser, this meme also makes explicit the cultural unease over where to locate Beyoncé in the scene of violence.

I would like to suggest that the felt ambivalence over Beyoncé's enigmatic position in the mise-en-scène of elevator violence has to do with her status as a megastar that—in a pre-*Lemonade* world at least—was seen to "transcend" race.[16] Hannah Hamad has suggested that in the postracial era of Obama, the

Fig 2.3. Jake Gyllenhaal meme, poking fun at Beyoncé's apparent passivity

issue of embodiment is especially charged for black celebrities. In her work on the "(Post-) Racial Familial Politics of Hollywood Celebrity Couples," Hamad notes how "the cultural politics of coupledom and family have always been particularly charged spheres of debate where African Americans have been the subjects" (2015, 117), and that that remains the case even in an era of so-called racial transcendence.

Discourse on the politics of coupledom and the African American family is certainly prevalent in the memes generated around the elevator incident. In this regard, it is significant that one dominant strand of memes feature two other famous "post-racial" celebrity families—the Kardashians and the Obamas. The Kardashian women, while not black, are often framed in the media as women of color. As Rachel Dubrofsky and Megan Wood argue, Kim Kardashian's "dark complexion and curvy body are used to racialize her in the popular press, as are her relationships with black men," most notably, of course, with Kanye West (2015, 102). What the memes involving the Kardashians and the Obamas make visible is the racialization of the memes, which encourage humorous participation through unchallenged racist stereotyping (Milner 2013). It is telling that none of the memes about the elevator incident involve white celebrity families such as, for instance, Gwyneth Paltrow and Chris Martin, who, consciously uncoupled now or not, were known to be good friends with Jay-Z and Beyoncé. Memes featuring a white family simply would not work in the same way because the memes referencing the elevator incident are about fantasies and anxieties concerning blackness itself.

Consider, as an example, one very popular meme following the elevator incident that features Kanye West eating an ice cream cone; the tagline attached to the photo is: "Khloe know better"—a reference to one of his Kardashian sister-in-laws. The misogynistic and racialized humor here derives from the celebrity one-upmanship over Jay-Z; the joke of the meme is Kanye's imagined smug surety that Khloe would never dare to attack *him*. In another derivation on the same theme, another meme captions a previously published photograph of a scowling, angry-looking Kanye with the heading: "I Wish Khloe Would." Such memes invoke long-standing gendered and racialized stereotypes of the violent and thuggish black man, and plainly draw on "persistent discourses of African-American masculinity that characterize black men as promiscuous, misogynist, materialistic irresponsible partners and fathers" (Hamad 2015, 120).

The memes featuring the Obamas are also of interest for their racial marking of the elevator scandal. Both the Obamas and the Carter Knowles, who are widely known to be good friends, embody a vision of "postracial" coupledom that is seen to transcend race. Bearing this in mind, it is interesting to see how the Obamas as an idealized postracial couple are used to generate humor over the elevator violence. In one Photoshopped image, the famous photo of Michelle Obama holding the "Bring Back Our Girls" placard, to publicize the plight of the kidnapped Nigerian schoolgirls, is altered so that the First Lady is instead holding a screen shot of the *TMZ* surveillance video. The humor comes from how the meme reattaches or repurposes the look of dismay and concern on the First Lady's face to the scene of black-on-black familial violence in her hands.

The "Bring Back Our Girls" meme had considerable traction, as it spawned several derivatives, including a Photoshopped meme of Jay-Z as the First Lady, holding a placard saying "Bring Back my Dignity," which vividly emphasizes the undermining of his black masculinity. Yet another meme remixes the image so that it is Solange dressed as the First Lady, holding a placard that states: "#Bring JayZ Back in the Elevator."

Fig 2.4. President Obama and "Queen Bey"

If Jay-Z is denigrated via his Photoshopped insertion into a picture of the First Lady, Beyoncé is elevated to a position of postracial transcendence in the meme that features her with President Obama. The meme in question repurposes a highly publicized photo of President Obama with Beyoncé from the presidential inauguration. In this photo, the President is whispering into Beyoncé's ear and the caption reads: "Let's call this problem number 100," in reference to Jay-Z's well-known rap song, "99 problems," the chorus hook of which is "I got 99 problems but a bitch ain't one". In this fantasy pairing of "Queen Beyoncé" with President Obama, Beyoncé's imperturbability puts her on the "outside" of the elevator scene of black-on-black violence, and arguably locates her in a position of postracial distance and superiority.

The "constitutive omission" (Snead 1994, 8) within all the memes that riff on Beyoncé's passivity is the "stock macro" of the angry, out-of-control black woman. Indeed, I would argue that Beyoncé's so-called passivity only garnered the attention it did because it was held in such dramatic contrast to the racially coded and stereotyped "activity" of her sister. As Huda Hussan notes, the "angry black woman," also known as the "Sapphire," is "one of entertainment's most reliable tropes": the "short-tempered, emasculating black woman who is angry without reason" (2015). This "controlling image," as Patricia Hill

Fig 2.5. "Slay Jay" meme

Collins (2000) would call it, serves the interests of white patriarchy in erasing the interlocking nature of racism and sexism and the way in which it impacts on black women.

By far the most prevalent strand of memes featuring Solange Knowles are those that feature her as a fighting ninja; these visual images accompany the racially inflected written descriptions of her as "ferociously," "savagely," and "wildly" attacking her brother-in-law. So, for example, Knowles is inserted into the roles of white film characters for comedic effect—*The Matrix* and *Kill Bill*, respectively. The *Matrix* meme shows an image of Neo (Keanu Reeves) floating in the air in a ninja pose as he fights against the "agents," with the caption: "Solange—in the elevator with Jay Z." The *Kill Bill* meme superimposes Knowles' face onto the body of the Bride (Uma Thurman), with the caption: "Slay Jay."

The animated GIFS of Solange Knowles as a fighting ninja are most interesting to consider for how they relocate the elevator "action" to a video game cultural aesthetic in order to further mine the stereotype of the "angry black woman." One GIF superimposes the heads of Jay-Z and Knowles onto computer game characters and depicts Knowles repeatedly kicking Jay-Z; the words "Finish Him!!" are in red in the background as a scoreboard keeps a tally of her wins. Another popular GIF, this one entirely cartoon animated (without the superimposition of any photos), shows a heavily built black man with no shirt on and a muscled black woman fighting in an elevator. The movement of the GIF is of the black woman's leg kicking the black man, as he tries to block the kick. Again, the graphics frame the GIF as a video game and label the animated characters as "Jay-Z" and "Solange." Such GIFS make explicit the spectacularization of the elevator scene of racialized violence and indicate the process by which the racially abjected body becomes the site of what Shifman calls a "hypersignification." As Shifman explains, in the genre of memes she calls "stock character macros," "hypersignification is located in the overt construction of stereotypes," which take "stereotypes to their extreme" (2014, 348). The GIFS mark the overdetermined bodies they show in perpetual motion as black, making the "blackness" of the violent black body itself a central "part of the joke" (349).

Laura Grindstaff and Susan Murray suggest that GIFS, which they describe as "encapsulated moments of motion and emotion," are "ideal carriers of branded affect" (2015, 121). Looking at Reality TV GIFS in particular,

Fig 2.6. Video-game GIF of Solange as fighting ninja

they explore how GIFS circulate as "categories of reaction," such as "crying," "shocked," and so on, where "viewers and fans use these GIFS in social media to comment on or react to news, information, or opinion" (121). The GIFS featuring the "stock macro" of the "angry black woman" are part of this wider culture where "branded affect is distilled to its most minute and precise level and then disseminated throughout the Internet"; GIFS, as Grindstaff and Murray explain, "capture memorable moments of affect and package them as digital caricature" (121).[17] The question of how memes and GIFS circulate and travel across the internet as "digital caricature" and packaged affect is central to any understanding of how they figure in the wider media ecology and attention economy as a process.

The operation of memes as constructive processes of racial and gender stereotyping was made manifest when the second Ray Rice video was released four months later. The Jay-Z/Solange video—and the responses to that video already in public circulation in the form of memes and GIFS—helped to manage feedback and to shape public response to the Ray Rice video, in which the coordinates of the mise-en-scène of elevator violence changed from "an angry black woman is beating a black man" to "a violent black man is beating a black woman."

Milner suggests it is important to consider "how memes stand in relation to each other and broader discourses" and to examine, among other features, their "participation structures (which voices are included and silenced)" (2013). As I now turn my attention to a consideration of the Ray Rice video, the issue of which voices are silenced becomes paramount. Looking at how the Jay-Z/Solange memes travel and replicate as they become entwined with the Ray Rice incident, I will demonstrate that there is one notable figure missing from the memes: the victimized black woman. That the memes cannot countenance this figure, I will suggest, is ultimately revealing of their visual trade in racial and gendered abjection.

The Ray Rice Video

The Ray Rice surveillance video shows what did not happen in the Jay-Z/Solange surveillance video: it shows a black man hitting a black woman. It is deeply significant that this video emerged in the wake of the widespread circulation of the memes belittling Jay-Z and his black manhood. As I have shown, these memes generated humor around Jay-Z's lack of "retaliation," and created wishful misogynistic fantasies in which a violent black male—incarnated as Chris Brown—seeks vengeance against Solange on Jay-Z's behalf. The Ray Rice video therefore provided the internet with the image of black male violence it had already been memetically dreaming of through its deployment of the stock macro of the black male thug/domestic abuser.

In the wake of the disturbing video showing Rice knocking his fiancée unconscious, which was watched by nearly sixteen million people on You-Tube, the White House issued a statement:

> President Obama is the father of two daughters. And like any American, he believes that domestic violence is contemptible and unacceptable in a civilized society. Hitting a woman is not something a real man does, and that's true whether or not an act of violence happens in the public eye, or, all too often, behind closed doors. Stopping domestic violence is something that's bigger than football—and all of us have a responsibility to put a stop to it. (quoted in Korte 2014)

While race is not mentioned here, it is nonetheless present in this curiously paternalistic utterance by America's first black president (note that it is not that he is a husband but that he is a *father* of two daughters). As already noted, the "semiotic power" of the Obamas as a famous black family offers an image "at odds with entrenched and pernicious rhetoric that paints and pathologizes the black family as perennially in crisis" (Hamad 2015, 119). When President Obama speaks of a "real man," then, it cannot help but be postracially inflected as a "real *black* man." Jay-Z and Beyoncé offer another such vision of postracial superstardom, as the content of their elevator video is recycled and reworked in the context of the Ray Rice video to differentiate between nontoxic and toxic forms of blackness.

Following the White House statement, Jonathan Capehart, of the *Washington Post*, wrote a piece called "What Jay Z Could Teach Ray Rice." Pondering Obama's White House statement, Capehart asks: "What I found myself wondering was what does this "real man" look like? Yes, I know plenty of men who would never hit a woman. But in our visual society, what does a 'real man' do when he's involved in a heated situation with a woman? You need look no further than to Jay Z" (2014). The article then provides a link to the elevator video of Jay-Z and Solange, as if to supply visual "proof" of what "good" black masculinity looks like. Capehart writes that:

> Back in May, everyone was talking about Solange Knowles' elevator set-to with her brother-in-law Jay Z. The music mogul, his wife, Beyonce, and Knowles were leaving a party at a New York hotel when Knowles attacked Jay Z on the small elevator. She pushed him. She kicked him. She slapped him. She hit him with her purse several times. Other than raising his hands to block her blows or keep her away from him, Jay Z did nothing violent to Knowles. (ibid.)

At this point in Capehart's article, a link is inserted to the Ray Rice video to offer a visual contrast of "bad" black masculinity in the form of Rice, before Capehart concludes: "Contrast that gentlemanly behavior to the viciousness of Rice" (ibid.). In this article, then, the elevator videos function as spectacularized shorthand for ideas of "good" and "bad" black masculinity. Where previously Jay-Z was mocked for his failure to stand up to the black woman's anger, here his passivity has been recouped as chivalry.

A set of similar discursive moves happens in the memetic culture that sprung up around the Ray Rice video. Similar to the memes involving Chris Brown, Ray Rice is depicted as the black male abuser who can "teach" Jay-Z how to discipline black womanhood. The most popular strand of memes is in this vein; striking examples include a photo of Jay-Z that is captioned "Where was Ray Rice when I was on the elevator?"; a Photoshopped image in which Rice is teaching Jay-Z "Elevator Defense 101," which is captioned: "I am Ray, Your Instructor . . ."; and finally, a publicity photo of Ray Rice from his football glory days, which is captioned: "Solange wouldn't do that/Shit to me in an elevator."

A racist vision of Ray Rice and Chris Brown as the celebrity embodiment of endemic stereotypes of the violent black man is made explicit in a meme that inserts the two men into the roles played by white actors Will Ferrell and John C. Reilly in the buddy slapstick 2008 comedy *Stepbrothers* (McKay, US). The tagline for this mocked-up, Photoshopped publicity poster for the film, "starring Chris Brown and Ray Rice," reads: "The hardest hitting comedy in decades. . . . From the guys who brought you NFL memes." As with

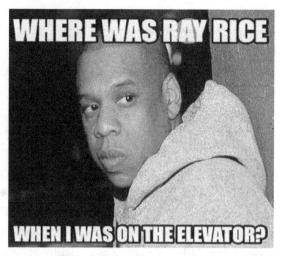

Fig 2.7. "Where Was Ray Rice?" meme

Fig 2.8. Chris Brown/Ray Rice *Stepbrothers* meme

the commutational memes that inserted Solange Knowles into iconic white film roles, the racially inflected humor here comes from the visual staging of "blackness" as savage and violent in juxtaposition to a normative whiteness.

This template of the black male abuser, and its comic juxtaposition with whiteness, emerges in another set of memes that feature the white tank top, commonly known in North America in slang terminology, as a "wife beater." One meme shows the torso of a white male body wearing a white tank top; the caption reads: "Just got my new Ray Rice jersey." In yet another example, a photo of a white tank top is captioned in bold white letters: "Ray Rice's New Endorsement Deal." Such memes imagine the black man as the violent racial other, with the internet user assumed to be white. Associations between blackness and savagery emerge in the multimodal construction of race that takes places through what Milner describes as a mixture of "image and text," whereby "familiarity with racist tropes is necessary to get the joke" (2013).

In my discussion of the Jay-Z/Solange memes, I noted that there was a suggestive mutual deployment of the stereotypes of the "angry black woman" and the violent black male "thug." Following this, it is fascinating to observe how Ray Rice and Solange Knowles become conflated as black aggressors in the memetic culture that welds the two elevator incidents together. The same animated GIF used in the Jay-Z/Solange incident, for example, of a cartoon muscle-bound black man and black woman fighting in an elevator, is here recycled. Retitled "Final Battle," with a subtitle of "KO" (Knockout), the fight is now labeled as: "Ray Rice vs Solange". One of the most popular of all the memes, there are many derivations of this "Ray Rice vs Solange" theme, which depicts the football player and the pop singer in "Mortal Kombat," or a final "Showdown."

In these prevalent memes, Ray Rice and Solange Knowles become conflated as gendered images of toxic blackness: they are depicted as the inverse to Jay-Z and Beyoncé, who are now conversely recuperated as examples of a healthy postracial, nontoxic blackness. The "good" postracial personas of Jay-Z and Beyoncé as a power celebrity couple, in other words, are used to siphon off a separate realm of "bad" blackness represented by long-standing and insidious stereotypes of African American men as brutish, "ghetto" thugs and of African American women as wild and angry. The work of the memes across the two elevator incidents, therefore, is to reshuffle and restructure the oppositional set of positions and pairings of man as victim/woman as

Fig 2.9. "Final Battle" between Ray Rice and Solange meme

aggressor, man as aggressor/woman as victim, Jay-Z vs. Solange, Ray Rice vs. Solange, and so on. In the sliding of positions that occurs across the two incidents, Jay-Z is transformed into the very image of a good husband and father, in order that he and Beyoncé can be held up as postracial icons against the newfound memetic pairing of a criminalized Ray Rice and Solange Knowles.

There is, of course, one figure conspicuously missing from the memetic culture surrounding the elevator incidents: Janay Palmer Rice. While many memes feature photos of Jay-Z and Beyoncé, together, or on their own, with captions imagining them apprehensively hiding or running away from Ray Rice and Solange, it is notable that there are no such memes imagining Janay Palmer Rice "on the run." While it is true that Janay Palmer Rice is the only one who is not a celebrity in her own right, and that that could partially explain why she does not figure in the memetic response, I also think that her absence from the memes is significant for other reasons, especially in light of how poorly she was treated as a victim of domestic abuse. Police initially arrested Janay Palmer Rice for assault, alongside Ray Rice, following the brutal elevator incident. Although these charges against Palmer Rice were later dropped, the fact that she was charged at all is indicative of her widespread criminalization as a victim. In the months after the publication of the video depicting her abuse, Palmer Rice was subjected to extraordinary victim blaming, with speculation and cultural chatter along the lines of "why did she marry him after he beat her?" After *TMZ*'s release of the first video, which showed Rice dragging his fiancée's unconscious body out of the elevator with a disturbing lack of concern, the Baltimore Ravens released this tweet (which was later deleted): "Janay Rice deeply regrets the role she played in the incident." There was also a press conference initiated by the Baltimore Ravens, designed to try to turn around Ray Rice's image, where the couple, now married, appeared united and where Janay Palmer Rice expressed public contrition for her "part" in the incident.

As noted in my introduction, it was only after the release of the second videotape, which showed Rice knocking his then fiancée unconscious, that the NFL took action and indefinitely suspended Rice. Chief NFL commissioner Roger Goodell claimed not to have seen the second video until *TMZ* released it, and said that the video, which was "extremely clear," "extremely graphic," and "sickening," led to the decision to take "action" ("Goodell" 2014). It is only when the scene of abuse was revealed as a public spectacle, that is, that the organization of the NFL had *to be seen* to deal with the issue of domestic violence.

But even after the release of that second video, there was a persistent inability to "see" Palmer Rice as a victim of violence; her voice was ignored and her agency effaced in ways that make clear the extent to which black women are silenced (Hussan 2015) in white male supremacist culture. The video of Janay Palmer Rice's assault was released by *TMZ* against her will; she did not give her consent and she expressed her deep unhappiness at its public circulation: "To make us relieve a moment in our lives that we regret every day is a horrible thing," she is quoted as saying (quoted in Macatee 2014).

While the memes are curiously silent when it comes to Janay Palmer Rice, in the comments section on YouTube incredible levels of toxicity are directed against her. She is blamed for the elevator incident because, some users claim, she "deserved" it by lashing out at Rice initially. As one user argued: "If a woman hits a man then the man has every right to hit her back. Feminism is about equality . . . Women cannot turn around after fighting for equality and play the victim when they are punched in the face by a man after punching him in the face." The stereotype of the "finger snapping, antagonistic, and assertive . . . Angry Black Woman" (Hussan 2015) is at the root of these comments, even when race is not mentioned. There are over sixteen thousand comments beneath the Ray Rice video on YouTube, and many of the comments are in this vein, with users declaring that "She had it coming." Some of the user comments on YouTube reference the Jay-Z/Solange video, but it is intriguing to find that it is an animating scenario even in those comments that do not directly cite it: "If you switch genders, everything would be fine, in fact everyone would think its badass and funny"; and: "Yes . . . if the gender roles were reversed, so that she knocked him out, people would think it's fucking funny and call her a boss." Putting the misogyny of these comments to one side for the moment, they are right in one respect: the scenario of a black woman hitting a black man—of Solange Knowles lashing out at Jay-Z (if not "knocking him out")—*was* treated as hilarious. As I have shown, what made the scenario of Knowles lashing out at Jay-Z in an elevator so funny was the ease with which it enabled the internet to playfully engage with certain deeply entrenched stereotypes of gender and blackness.

I believe that the same racial optics or field of vision that allowed the internet to laugh at the Jay-Z/Beyoncé/Solange video is responsible for the astonishing lack of empathy for Janay Palmer Rice as a victim of gendered violence and domestic abuse. The label of the "strong black woman," who is "perpetually tough" and "uniquely indestructible" (Harris 2014), leads to an inability to imagine black women as vulnerable or in need of help. As Hannah Giorgis writes: "Black women are often systematically excluded from both the category of 'woman' and that of 'victim'" (2014).

By the same token, part of the reason Janay Palmer Rice was so vilified, I argue, is that she was depicted as *not being resilient enough*, as someone who does not overcome patriarchal damage in the way she is supposed to. In *Resilience & Melancholy: Pop Music, Feminism, Neoliberalism*, Robin James argues that discourses of resilience are central to "Multi-Racial White Supremacist Patriarchy," or what she calls "MRWaSP." According to James, "resilience discourse . . . follows a very specific logic" so that "resilient populations who can overcome their race/class/gender/sexual/immigrant/religious damage in *socially profitable ways* move closer to the centre of white supremacist privilege whereas less resilient, precarious populations move further and further from this center" (2015, 8, 15). Being resilient, and "overcoming" damage, is a kind of "affective labour" that women in particular are expected to perform in contemporary neoliberal visual culture; significantly, it is not just that women are expected to be resilient but that their "resilience must be performed as a spectacle for others" (88). In deciding to stay with Rice, and to marry him, Janay Palmer Rice failed to perform a spectacle of "overcoming" her damage and demonstrating "her resilient subjectivity" in ways acceptable to postfeminist, postracial culture (110).

As James further argues, "MRWaSP visualization racializes 'non-resilient' women as black. Whereas traditional virgin/whore dichotomies separate out 'pure,' virginal white women from everyone else, MRWaSP resilience separates out 'toxic' black women from everyone else" (103). In our supposed postracial cultural moment, James writes, "the overcoming of blackness and its supposed toxicity is what composes the multi-racial 'we' as such" and that "overcoming is . . . facilitated by . . . digital social media," which "actively produce insufficiently resilient populations as both toxic and black" (103). Or to put this argument another way, because "visible sexism and racism is inconsistent with the neoliberal myth of postracialism and postfeminism . . . MRWaSP visualization resolves that paradox by making visible sexism and racism *look black*" (113).

The same scapegoating process by which black male rappers have long been made to shoulder the blame for a more widespread cultural misogyny, as discussed by James, is also at play in the singling out of Janay Palmer Rice in internet trolling and online commentary as a retrograde black woman who "stands by her man" despite the fact that he beats her (114). That white patriarchal culture itself constructs and supports the structures by which abused women of all colors might be unable to leave their partners is not taken into consideration here; instead, Palmer Rice is conveniently singled out as pathological. That is to say, the process by which Janay Palmer Rice was culturally assigned as "backwards" in her "acceptance" of her own abuse is a clear example of the gendered and raced "MRWaSP visualization" described by James. The cultural disdain for Janay Palmer Rice as a "non-elite" or noncelebrity black woman is part of a wider "toxicity narrative" that "treats black women as themselves problems, not people with problems: they can cause toxicity, but they cannot experience it" (105).

In the wake of the castigation of Janay Palmer Rice and the widespread victim blaming that went on, feminist commentators such as Hannah Giorgis urged against watching the Ray Rice video and took issue with the argument that we need to see the video as "evidence" of abuse (2014). As Giorgis states:

That we feel entitled (and excited) to access gut-wrenching images of a woman being abused—to be entranced by the looks of domestic violence—speaks volumes not only about the man who battered her, but also about we who gaze in parasitic rapture. We click and consume, comment and carry on. What are we saying about ourselves when we place (black) women's pain under a microscope only to better consume the full kaleidoscope of their suffering? (2014)

I share the outrage felt by Giorgis regarding the repetitive play of the Ray Rice video, and yet it is important to acknowledge that the fallout over the video opened up a critical space for campaigns against domestic violence on social media networks. Following the release of the Ray Rice video, and the media response to it, a hashtag, #WhyIStayed, was created by domestic violence survivor, writer, and activist Beverly Gooden. Gooden says she was inspired to start the hashtag after seeing how people kept asking why Janay Palmer did not leave Rice after the incident and "how she felt shame when she saw people ask that question" (quoted in Warren 2014). "It was the same shame that I felt back when I was in a violent marriage," Gooden said (quoted in Warren 2014).

Gooden's #WhyIStayed tweets began trending on Twitter almost immediately, with over ninety thousand tweets recorded through the hashtag in the first day of its existence (Clark 2016, 788). These tweets recorded the myriad of reasons why it might be difficult for a woman to leave a physically abusive relationship and acknowledged a range of sociocultural factors. #WhyIStayed is a striking example of feminist hashtag activism and joins other campaigns, including #EverydaySexism, #RapeCultureisWhen and #StopStreetHarassment,[18] that fight back against the rape culture that normalizes violence against women. According to Melissa Jeltsen, writing in the *Huffington Post*, "the Ray Rice video changed the way we talk about domestic violence" (2014).[19] Indeed, on the back of this hashtag campaign and others like it, Rosemary Clark suggests that significant change occurred, as #WhyIStayed "became a central referent for the public's understanding of not only the Ray Rice case but domestic violence more generally" (800). The hope, Clark suggests, is that: "More media outlets adopt feminist frameworks for interpreting domestic violence, more resources are made available to victims, more productive legislation is passed, and more survivors gain the confidence to seek support" (Clark 2016, 800). Just as online abuse emerges from the affordances of social

Bev ✓
@bevtgooden

I had to plan my escape for months before I even had a place
to go and money for the bus to get there. #WhyIStayed
♡ 89 3:52 PM - Sep 8, 2014   ℹ

♡ 115 people are talking about this   >

Bev ✓
@bevtgooden

I stayed because I thought love was enough to conquer all.
#WhyIStayed
♡ 75 3:53 PM - Sep 8, 2014   ℹ

♡ 138 people are talking about this   >

Fig 2.10. Beverly Gooden's tweets

media platforms and technologies, so does the possibility for critical resistance. One of the central challenges for any technosocial account of crime,
violence, and criminality is how to negotiate the complex ways in which social
media sites "are havens for hatred at the same time they are progressive tools"
(Malkowski 2017, 197).

Conclusion

This chapter has discussed the subgenre of CCTV elevator assault videos on
the internet and their memetic repurposing across networked spaces. While
the elevator assault videos featuring Jay-Z/Beyoncé/Solange and Ray Rice/
Janay Palmer Rice cannot be considered traditional "true crime," I have suggested the importance of looking at how such CCTV clips featuring moments
of violence now circulate across a mediascape that continues to push at
established borders of genre. In the end, it does not matter "What Jay Z Said
to Solange"—there could never be an answer that would satisfy. Rather, it is
the process by which contemporary participatory media culture engages in
a highly visible mixing—and remixing—of raced and gendered stereotypes
in relation to scenarios of violence that is of interest here. As Shifman has

observed, "photo-based meme genres . . . are more about the *process* of mean-ing-making than about meaning-making itself" (2014, 344). Through explor-ing the distribution and circulation of memes in the broader media ecology of the digital era, it is possible to trace the process by which certain bodies are made to matter, while others continue to be excluded and treated as cultural detritus. In my reading of online true crime texts in the chapters that follow, this question of the framing of bodies will be central. As Judith Butler argues, "the frames through which we apprehend, or indeed, fail to apprehend the lives of others as lost or injured (lose-able or injurable) are politically satu-rated" (2009, 1). This insight informs my analysis of the affective properties of the true crime "frame" and the ways in which it works to ascertain "whose lives can be marked as lives, and whose deaths will count as deaths" (Butler 2004, xx–xxi).

3

"Tagging" the True Crime Audience

Netflix Trailers for True Crime Documentaries

THIS CHAPTER EXTENDS THE discussion of the cultural relevance of short-form videos for a consideration of contemporary true crime by focusing on the online circulation of the promotional trailer. While existing trailer scholarship focuses almost exclusively on fiction films,[1] this chapter centers attention on trailers for true crime documentaries. My argument is that trailers hold special significance for an understanding of the affective purchase of digital-era true crime because of how explicitly and intensely they generate affect through judgment. As trailer scholar Keith Johnston has noted, "new screen technologies and dissemination media have changed the structure, aesthetics and availability of trailers" (2008, 146). Significantly, the "new mobility" of trailers across a range of "multiple screen technologies"—including "cinema, television, home video, the Internet, games consoles, mobile phones and iPods"—has led to a heightened level of involvement from consumers, who are encouraged to share, download, and archive them (158). It is within the context of this multimedia, digitally networked environment that true crime trailers, with their "promise of interactivity" (Andrejevic 2007, 51) and their emphasis on a notion of the spectator as a digital detective, have flourished. In exhorting viewers to help "decide" questions of criminal guilt and innocence, true crime trailers are well suited to the dynamics of a networked society that privileges participatory media spectatorship.

In his work on paratexts, Jonathan Gray writes that "while promotional materials are constitutive in terms of hailing an audience for a text, they also create meanings for those who will not be in the audience. For every person who has watched any given film or television program, there are likely more who have watched a trailer, poster, or preview of it, and not the thing itself"

(2010, 52). Certainly, the new accessibility of trailers, which appear on Facebook or Twitter feeds, or which pop up in the context of a film review or in a listicle of "top ten crime documentaries to watch," means that they reach those who are not necessarily able—or willing—to spend the time it takes to watch (for instance) the ten-episode-long Netflix series *Making a Murderer*. In this chapter, I want to extend Gray's point and suggest that in the digital era, trailers are increasingly "the thing itself," and that, as a media format, the trailer exemplifies a postdigital attention economy in which attention itself is commodified, as Jonathan Crary has asserted (2013). Before turning to a consideration of the forms and functions of longer form contemporary true crime texts, as I do in the next chapter, I want to first explore the "growing significance of short-form content" through platforms such as YouTube (Grainge 2011, 7). Rather than seeing the "short" and the "long," the fast and the slow, as "binary opposites," it is important, as Tina Kendall writes, to "acknowledge the simultaneity and co presence of a wide range of speeds, velocities, and rhythms that confront us with our daily interactions with media culture" (2016b, 118). The two-minute-or-so-long true crime trailer and its rush of affect is connected in interesting and important ways to the longer-form serial narrative and its microtemporal measuring out of affective jolts and revelations, which I will discuss further in chapter 4.

In the post-YouTube attention economy, the short, sharp burst of affect derived from the two-minute trailer, watched, for example, in a number of different contexts and in a range of public or private spaces, is designed to provide individual viewers or users with a quick fix of feeling. Building on this observation, I will examine more closely how trailers for true crime documentaries operate as *"machines for generating affect,"* a phrase Steven Shaviro uses to describe film and music videos, which, he argues, work to actively construct "the social relations, flows, and feelings that they are ostensibly about" (2010, 3, 6).

More specifically, I want to ask: What can a closer examination of trailers tell us about the kind of spectator that is being hailed and inculcated by true crime texts? And what does this "profile" of viewer engagement have to tell us about the "social identity" of true crime in the digital era? If, as Barbara Klinger has suggested, "it is a matter of industry policy to design a consumable identity for a film" (1989, 5), I am interested in exploring how digital-era trailers work to construct a notion of the true crime text as an interactive commodity. Performing more important cultural work than their commonly perceived status as mere adverts might suggest, I argue that the promotional values of the trailer work to construct and to premediate the very formulation of our affective interaction with true crime in the digital era.

It is not *just* that trailers for true crime documentaries prime us to watch the longer texts they are promoting; it is that they also construct and sustain a powerful notion of the viewing public as participating in questions of social justice. But while trailers work to fashion an idea of the "active," socially engaged viewer, I will investigate the ways in which they also feed into, and crystallize, the logics and operations of what media theorist Jodi Dean calls "communicative capitalism" (2002; 2010a; 2010b). According to Dean, the digital circulation of media content through incessant acts of clicking, sharing, and spreading creates a powerful *fantasy* of participation—one that actually forecloses more meaningful social change and political commitment. Drawing on Dean's work on communicative capitalism, this chapter considers how true crime trailers construct a notion of the viewer's agency as revolving around the "key technocultural fantasy" that "the truth is out there'" and that all can be revealed through the affective labor of watching—and then clicking, spreading, and searching (Dean 2002, 8). In the networked digital era, trailers for true crime documentaries extend and revitalize tabloid crime journalism's long-standing attempt to give readers and viewers a sense of interactivity in crime solving, even as they show up the limitations of such involvement.

In looking at true crime trailers as something more than "gateways into the text" (Gray 2010, 18), my aim is to think about how they operate in terms of wider "clip culture," to borrow Paul Grainge's phrase (2011, 7). While it has become commonplace to bemoan the ways in which the internet leads to a distracted and inattentive viewer, I am interested in how the two- to three-minute trailer concentrates attention, generates affective intensities, and drives the participation of users forward through networks (Dean 2010b, 37). To evaluate the new significance of true crime trailers in a digital ecosystem where "short and readily streaming" is what "maintains attention in an environment designed to distract" (Torchin 2012, 197), I focus on recent examples of true crime trailers produced by global streaming giant Netflix.

Founded in 1997, Netflix has since greatly expanded its online film and television offerings and, at the time of writing this chapter, has amassed 125 million subscribers worldwide (Boland 2018). Since 2013, Netflix has produced its own original content, with true crime featuring as one of its most highly marketable products. There are now numerous separate search tags for the genre on Netflix, including, for example, "True Crime TV Shows," "Critically acclaimed True Crime Films," "Dark True Crime Films," and "Gritty True Crime Dramas." As *Time* magazine has declared, Netflix is now recognized as "the frontier for American true crime television" (Jenkins 2016).[2]

Although there is a growing body of research on Netflix's curation of its offerings, and the dynamics of its interface, there is an absence of critical scholarship on its deployment of trailers. In this chapter I seek to redress this lack of scholarship through an analysis of the trailers for two of Netflix's original true crime "blockbusters": specifically, the megahit docuseries *Making a Murderer* (2015)[3] and the feature-length documentary *Amanda Knox* (2016). The trailers for these Netflix "Originals" are produced post-2010, in an intensified social media environment where trailers are addressed not to a theatrical audience but to individual viewers watching in online networked spaces. These Netflix trailers have viewing figures of a million plus on YouTube and are therefore striking examples of what can be dubbed "high concept" true crime, designed for a global streaming audience. Situated in a wider context of reaction video culture on YouTube, where Netflix has its own channel with over seven million subscribers, these short-form true crime texts generate what Susanna Paasonen calls "publicly shared displays of affect" (2017, 464). Paasonen writes that: "the visual economy of social media is elaborate, finely tuned, operates at expansive scales and speeds, and revolves around the imperative of capturing and optimizing user attention" (465). Although, at first glance, true crime trailers might appear to be worlds apart from the memetic sea of cute cat videos and humorous reaction gifs that dominate the visual mediascape described by Paasonen, they are similar in so far as they meet the internet demand of grabbing attention in as "sticky" a way as possible: they lend themselves to the sharing and proliferation of response in the wider circuits of a social media attention economy where if "it doesn't spread it's dead" (Jenkins, Ford, and Green 2013, 1). To explore the kinds of affects generated by these trailers, I perform a textual analysis of their rhetorical modes of "jury box" audience address, in which viewers are invited to weigh in on questions of guilt and innocence. To further consider the ideological traction of true crime trailers and their harnessing of affect, I also examine the comments that get attached to them through their exhibition on YouTube. These comments demonstrate the significant role that trailers play in how many viewers now experience true crime texts. By considering how Netflix crafts a specific "house style" for its trailers, one that digitally updates a true crime tradition of positioning the audience as "viewers with a job to do" (Clover 2000a, 246), I am interested in the extent to which these ubiquitous, if often critically ignored, short-form texts commodify viewer attention and judgment and construct miscarriage-of-justice narratives as consumer "experiences." My trailer analysis reveals how a notion of the "viewer-detective" is strategically deployed by the Netflix "culture machine" (Finn 2017, 92), as part of its algorithmic shaping of consumer desire and viewer responses.

Coming Attractions

Before considering the significance of Netflix's deployment of its recent true crime trailers, I want to reflect more broadly on the historical forms and functions of trailers and their modes of audience address. In her influential book, *Coming Attractions*, published in 2004, Lisa Kernan suggests that trailers, from the classical era onward, are fascinating for the ways in which they "offer information about the implied audiences to whom trailers are addressed" (2004, 212). For Kernan, trailers are most interesting for how they "vividly illuminate" the way the "motion picture audience [is] imagined by the film industry" (3).

Although trailers continue to be significant as barometers of how the industry perceives its audience, social media culture (or "Web 2.0") has opened up new forms of user engagement, which, in turn, has led to new ways of gauging audience reaction. For one thing, we now have ready access to much more than the merely "imagined" construction of the audience and their interactions. Where Kernan discusses how the members of the audience for *theatrical* trailers manifest "interactivity among themselves" through the "hisses, cheers and other editorial comments" that accompany the exhibition of trailers at the cinema (2004, 6), the picture of interactivity in the digital age is rather different. With trailers now exhibited on YouTube and other online sites, audience interactivity displays itself in online discussion threads with their hundreds of comments, debates, and "likes" and "dislikes." Subjective judgments are "forever archived in verdicts on screens" (Panse and Rothermel 2014, 1) in highly visible displays of audience response. Indeed, what I find most interesting about the Netflix trailers I examine in this chapter is how they serve as affective objects onto which viewers can pin their opinions of true crime. Trailers invite emotional reactions from viewers, and the online media platforms on which they are now embedded provide viewers with the opportunity—and the tools—to publicly share those reactions (Benson-Allott 2017).

As with other scholarly studies of trailers, the documentary trailer is not covered by Kernan, perhaps because her book is acknowledged as an examination of trailers at the end of the twentieth century and of the "trailer form prior to the Internet" (2004, 167). While trailers for documentaries did indeed exist prior to the internet—on television and on VHS format—it is only with the widespread emergence and dominance of the Internet and social media as a part of everyday life—along with corresponding changes in industrial practices—that there has been a proliferation of documentary trailers. The documentary "boom" that occurred in the early 2000s, as discussed by documentary film theorists such as Thomas Austin (2007), coincides with the rise of internet culture and new viewing contexts for documentaries, which I will discuss further below in relation to Netflix and its streaming of documentaries.

My contention is that true crime documentaries, with their strong pull on viewers' epistephilic urges, are a perfect fit with the trailer format. Indeed, true crime trailers, which have proliferated dramatically since 2000, are worthy of critical attention for how they embody the central tension of the trailer as a media format: that "it has to *communicate* its film and at the same time it has to *hold it back*" (Jensen 2014, 106). This finely tuned play between disclosing and withholding key information may be true of all trailers, but it is also very specific to the appeal of recent true crime texts, which turn on the ambiguities surrounding real-life stories of crime, and which are designed around dramatic, revelatory plot "twists." If, as Kernan asserts, fiction film trailers are organized around an "appeal to audience interest in stars, genres, and story" (2004, 27) then true crime trailers are firmly organized around public interest in (real) life stories. Drawing on a long-standing "you-are-the-jury-you-decide-format" (Clover 2000a, 247), true crime trailers thrive in an internet opinion culture.

Trailers produced in a post-2005 YouTube digital media environment utilize established trailer devices including montage, intertitles, and direct address, but they repurpose them for an interactive internet audience. While, as Kernan suggests, the "montage structure of trailers" has *always* been "key to their production of meaning" (2004, 13), I would suggest that montage takes on a new significance in a digital media environment. In her work on communicative capitalism, Jodi Dean has noted the centrality of montage to digital culture, which has an inherent tendency "to decompose and recombine" different images (2010b, 28). While some cultural theorists see the possibility of critical resistance in montage, and its work of mash-ups and remixes, Dean argues that "decomposition and recombination appear more as aspects of our *capture* in affective networks than as tactics of resistance" (29). In a digital media environment of repetition and digital flow, viewers are incited to continuously "search for information," which is rendered "perpetually out of reach" (29). As Dean describes it: "Outraged, engaged, desperate to do *something*, we look for evidence, ask questions, and make demands, again contributing to the circuits of drive" (41). While Dean's arguments regarding the "affective dimensions" of communicative capitalism and its networks may seem unduly pessimistic, they hold relevance for an understanding of the operations of true crime trailers, which, as I will demonstrate, "promote opinion over analysis" (Benson-Allott 2017) and reaction over (considered) response. The Netflix trailers I examine reference democratic ideals of civic engagement, but I argue that they deploy montage chiefly in order to circulate affect and interpellate viewers in the terms of an endlessly deferred and extended crime-solving scenario that binds them ever more tightly to the commercial platforms and interfaces seeking to capture their engagement.

Tagging the True Crime Audience

Documentary film theorist Leshu Torchin has noted that "a traditional documentary format" does not lend itself to the platform of YouTube; "the length of the videos seems to pose a deterrent to viewing," and "the numbers of views, favorites, and links" are "considerably less than those of shorter fare" (2012, 201). By contrast, trailers are imminently spreadable texts that perform very well on YouTube; their short format facilitates the common internet activities of sharing, linking, and "tagging." Tagging is the practice of organizing videos around key words, labels, and links. It facilitates the creation of affective networks in which individuals are brought together through similar interests and "emotional investments." On YouTube, tagging videos with relevant metadata

Fig 3.1. *Making a Murderer* trailer on YouTube with "Up next" sidebar of auto-play videos

is a way of labeling them and organizing them; it "is the first step to ranking your video in YouTube search results," according to instructional videos ("Proper Use of Tags" 2015). Tags also generate "a feed of related videos," which appear in a sidebar on the YouTube screen (Torchin 2012, 198). In the case of true crime trailers, viewers who "like" the trailer for *Making a Murder*, for example, are algorithmically directed to watch other related videos and similar trailers including the ones for *Amanda Knox*, which I will shortly discuss.

While "tagging" means something specific in the context of YouTube and contemporary digital culture, it is important to note that there is a longer history of "tagging" the true crime audience. As many television scholars have noted, from *America's Most Wanted* and *Unsolved Mysteries* to Britain's *CrimeWatch UK*, true crime TV almost always includes some form of direct audience address that seeks to draw viewers into the crime-solving process (Cavender and Fishman 1998; Wheatley 2001; Jermyn 2007; Jenner 2016a). Such forms of direct audience address sometimes involve what is known in television industry parlance as a "tag." The website "TV tropes" defines a "tag" as: "A one to five minute mini-act at the end of a show, after the dramatic climax of the episode but before (or even during) the end credits, used to show the effects or aftermath of the episode" ("The Tag" n.d.).

This particular kind of "tagging" features in traditional true crime TV. For example, it was used quite prominently in the short-lived but important 1950s docudramatic American TV series *The Court of Last Resort*. A weekly crime series based on real-life miscarriages of justice, *The Court of Last Resort* ran on NBC for twenty-six episodes in 1957–58,[4] and was based on a real-life organization of the same name, established by the lawyer turned author and the creator of *Perry Mason*—Erle Stanley Gardner. The real-life Court of Last Resort (CLR) consisted of Gardner and various white male associates of his, including doctors, private detectives, lawyers, and lie-detector experts, and was dedicated to investigating miscarriages of justice. Described as "the Innocence Project of its day,"[5] the Court of Last Resort was at work from the late 1940s to the late 1950s, during which time Gardner and his team of investigators were deluged with letters from poor and underprivileged men, often from racial and class minority groups, who felt they had been wrongfully accused of a crime and for whom the CLR was their "final hope"—to borrow a phrase used in the opening to every episode of the TV series. The TV version of *The Court of Last Resort* was conceptualized as an attempt to represent the important work of the CLR and find a new way of engaging the public in real-life matters of justice. A structuring notion of the viewer as a juror, so central to the "American imaginary," as Carol Clover has discussed (2000b, 102), is evident in the rhetorical framing of *The Court of Last Resort*, which invites viewers to consider the following question: is the accused "guilty or not?"[6]

The Court of Last Resort bears particular importance for my consideration of true crime trailers as part of a "burgeoning clip culture" (Grainge 2011, 7) because of the emphasis it placed on the role of closing documentary "tags." The "tags" came after the scripted, fictionalized episode had finished and directly addressed the audience through a break in the fourth wall. In these concluding documentary tags, actual members of the Court of Last Resort sit around a semicircular table, which explicitly renders the image of social justice in the form of noble white men.

Gardner had some reservations about the inclusion of this image, and in his lengthy correspondence on *The Court of Last Resort*, he worried that it ran the risk of portraying the CLR as "sermonizing" to the public (Gardner 1957c). Nonetheless, the tags always concluded with one of the CLR members facing the camera and issuing the following second-person address to the audience: "Administration of justice is *your* responsibility. You, the people, are the Court of Last Resort."

The closing tags for *The Court of Last Resort* are an important early example of network television's attempt to hail white, middle-class viewers

Fig 3.2. Noble white men in *The Court of Last Resort*

and inculcate them as participatory citizens involved in the rendering of justice and the righting of social wrongs. Some of the tags include didactic speeches from CLR members about topics including the "social tragedy" of wrongful imprisonment ("The Clarence Redding Case," December 6, 1957), while others, referred to as "clue tags" (Gardner 1957e), tried to solicit a more direct involvement from viewers. In such "clue tags," a description of a criminal case under reinvestigation by the CLR would be followed by an invitation to viewers to write in with relevant information to help rectify a social wrong. Other tags took an even more inventive turn and sought to "test" the viewer's detective skills. In a striking example from the very first episode ("The Gordon Wallace Case," October 4, 1957), CLR member Dr. Lemoyne Snyder speaks directly to the audience: "Earlier in tonight's case, you saw a guard lead Gordon Wallace to his cell. Here is a line-up of 6 men. Is the prison guard in this group? If so, which one?" In a dramatic reveal, one of the men steps forward from the line-up, and Dr. Snyder turns to the camera to instruct viewers: "Many innocent men have been convicted because of mistaken eyewitnesses." Lesson thus delivered, the CLR's resident lie-detector expert, Alex Gregory, concludes the tag by booming out the CLR motto: "Administration of justice is *your* responsibility. You the people are the court of last resort."

Eventually, much to Gardner's chagrin, Hollywood insisted on dropping the closing tags from *The Court of Last Resort* because they viewed them as a clunky inconvenience, one that did not fit in with the rest of the fictionalized and commercialized TV format. Although *The Court of Last Resort* was not, ultimately, a commercial success, documentary film scholar Kristen Fuhs has recently argued for its historical importance as an early attempt to mobilize "a mass audience through reality-based television for the purpose of social and legal reform" (2017, 2). As Fuhs writes, the creators of the Court of Last Resort "wanted to use the television platform and the documentary medium to elevate the subject of wrongful conviction to a national consciousness and encourage wider public involvement in issues of legal policy" (2017, 3). It was therefore "envisioned as a program that would elevate the average television viewer from armchair detective to active crusader for justice" (Fuhs 2017, 3).[7]

The Court of Last Resort, then, is a noteworthy early example of the miscarriage of justice subgenre, which has been reenergized and repurposed by new media formats and the rise of participatory internet culture. Certainly, the tags, as well as Gardner's commentary on them, remain one of the most pertinent features of *The Court of Last Resort* as a precursor for contemporary true crime. Especially apposite was Gardner's conceptualization of the tags as "brief 30–40 second" clips designed to "hammer home" key messages, and activate public participation in justice (Gardner 1957d). Gardner was particularly insistent about the duration of the tags, which, he believed, should be delivered in a short, "slam-bang style" (Gardner 1957b). What both the opening and closing address to the audience of *The Court of Last Resort* needed to do, above all, was to capture audience attention: "In these days when a person only needs to twist a dial when he is the least bit bored, we can't afford to take any chances," wrote Gardner (Gardner 1957a).

Such concern with capturing viewer attention and staving off boredom is, of course, also evident in today's audiovisual culture, characterized by what Grainge describes as the "proliferation of short-form media geared towards mobile audiences whose attentions are more fleeting and dispersed" (2011, 3) and where, instead of twisting a dial, people flit from site to site through the activity of "clicking." The short documentary "tags" so important to Gardner's vision of true crime in the golden age of scheduled network television can be seen as a precursor to the proliferating array of short-form true crime video clips and promos that now circulate in an age of "rapid delivery" and "ubiquitous availability" (Tomlinson as quoted in Grainge 2011, 3), and in which TV is increasingly connected to the internet. While, in the 1950s, Gardner had to fight his Hollywood producer to include the twenty- to thirty-second documentary "tags" at the end of *The Court of Last Resort*, such short clips are now a central part of the online marketing of true crime TV shows through social media networks such as Twitter.

Indeed, in a postnetwork era, Gardner's documentary "tags" have now migrated outside of scheduled television and the confines of the TV shows themselves, and have become a crucial part of the curation of true crime through "internet-distributed television" (Lotz 2017). Thus, for example, *Making a Murderer* has a Twitter page, which is organized around the hashtag #makingamurderer and consists mainly of ten- to twenty-second promos or mini-trailers designed to pique—and maintain—audience interest in the alleged miscarriage of justice examined over the course of ten episodes. The Twitter tagline reads: "One man. Two crimes. Wrongfully accused? You decide. Only on Netflix.#MakingAMurderer." Such Twitter taglines are a digital updating of *The Court of Last Resort's* "It is you, the people, who are The Court of Last Resort."

The short video clips and promos on Twitter serve as digital breadcrumbs or "affective nugget (s)" (Dean 2010b, 21), which encourage users to piece together clues and follow the evidence trail that coalesces around the "Making A Murderer" tag. While the snappy, stylized format of these short-form audio-visual clips differs quite markedly from the more plodding and stilted delivery style of the old-style documentary tags found at the end of *The Court of Last Resort,* they derive from the same basic impetus to amass viewers and involve them in an emergent platform.

Of course, the popularized meaning of a "tag" has now changed: whereas in Gardner's era it referred to the closing segment of a TV show and in particular a final speech addressed to the audience, in internet culture a "tag" is more commonly a kind of metadata used on social media networks that allows people to easily find specific messages or themes. As the *Oxford Dictionary* defines it, an internet tag is: "A word, phrase, or name used to identify digital content such as blog and social media posts as belonging to a particular category or concerning a particular person or topic." In internet culture, the "tag" and the "hashtag" are crucial in reaching and "optimizing" global audiences. As noted on an advice page regarding the "Proper Use of Tags: 4 Tips

Fig 3.3. Cover image for *Making a Murderer* Twitter account, screenshot taken July 15, 2018

to Grow Your YouTube Audience": "A tag is a keyword that you are adding to your video . . . tags are extremely beneficial for getting additional views of your video. . . . The more relevant your keywords the more views you will receive" ("Proper Use of Tags" 2015). Despite the shift in meanings, then, the concept of the "tag," both in Gardner's era and in contemporary digital culture, is about capturing audience attention and attracting "eyeballs."

In certain regards, the kind of public engagement with miscarriage of justice stories facilitated and sustained by digitized documentary tags appears to realize Gardner's long-standing dream of a public awake to the need for legal reform. In today's media culture, one need not look very far to find examples of "public participation" in issues of social justice: with the rise of new media technologies, people are able to follow, share, and comment on real crime images and stories through an array of screens, including their hand-held mobile devices. Not only that but people are also able to produce images and videos highlighting instances of social injustice themselves, as evidenced by the rise of citizen journalist videos. As Jennifer Malkowski suggests, in this newly configured social and technological environment, the "notion of participation is especially charged" (2017, 158).

But the digitized updating of tagging, while paying lip service to the idea of initiating and maintaining audience participation in social justice in the so-called democratic space of the internet, is arguably limited by how tightly it binds users to the affectivity of internet platforms and their profit-making impetus. As Alexandra Juhasz has noted, the worry is that the short-form videos of YouTube, with their " 'pithy, precise, rousing calls to action or consumption, or action as consumption'—may function to produce quick and even strong affective responses, but may be counter-productive to the larger ethical and political needs of movements for social justice" (2016). It is important, therefore, to interrogate the ways in which an idea of social action is being packaged by Netflix, a corporation whose very "brand is algorithmic" and is driven by the goal of binding viewers as tightly as possible to "Netflix itself: the application, the service, the platform" (Finn 2017, 94, 104).

"Are You Kidding Me?": Netflix's *Making a Murderer*

In "Netflix and the Documentary Boom," a chapter written before the release of *Making a Murderer,* Sudeep Sharma writes that documentaries are "widely seen as part of the Netflix brand of providing on-demand content viewers want to watch" (2016, 144). In Sharma's account, Netflix's acquisition and exhibition of feature-length documentary films is not about altruism or a desire to ensure viewer access to an otherwise inaccessible documentary catalogue but about satisfying "commercial needs" (144) and "maintaining viewership" (145). Though Sharma suggests that the educational value of Netflix's documentary provision strategically counteracts the more negative connotations associated with the practice of "bingeing" its fictional streaming outputs, the release of *Making a Murderer* in 2015 altered this approach. With *Making a Murderer*, its first foray into long-form true crime original programming, Netflix found a way to bring together the cultural cachet and "real-world relevance" (146) of documentary with its preferred mode of addictive, binge-worthy, serialized viewing.

Although Netflix's trailer for *Making a Murderer* has received little or no critical discussion, it warrants analysis as a blockbuster text in its own right, one that helps to predetermine Netflix's viewership and that is important to understanding the kind of affective labor being solicited by the audiovisual texts at the heart of the recent true crime boom. Indeed, trailers are a central, if unexamined, part of Netflix's branding of itself and its proactive shaping of the consumer demand it professes to merely cater to. Published on YouTube a week before the series' release in its entirety on Netflix on December 18, 2015, the *Making a Murderer* trailer has accrued high viewing figures for a documentary trailer: at the time of writing this chapter in July 2018, it has been viewed 3,490,566 times on YouTube, with 13.5 thousand "thumbs up," 355 "thumbs down," and 2,078 viewer comments.[8] The *Making a Murderer* trailer also appears on the Netflix platform, in a section labeled "Trailers & More". This section displays the trailer and a set of further algorithmic recommendations for other true crime texts (including, for example, *Amanda Knox* and *The Keepers*).

My main focus here, however, is the exhibition of the trailer on YouTube—"the Internet's highest-traffic and culturally dominant video streaming site" (Malkowski 2017, 160). If it can be difficult to determine whether or not a Netflix series is a bona fide "hit" (given that Netflix does not release viewing figures and we do not know how many people watch it), there is not the same uncertainty regarding the popularity of Netflix trailers exhibited on YouTube, which plainly reveal the number of views.

Founded in 2005, YouTube (which was purchased by Google in 2006) is a natural home for Netflix's branding exercises. As the "world's largest archive of moving images," "YouTube has been and remains the default website for a 'clip culture' that is increasingly defining both Web entertainment and online information," as noted by Pelle Snickars, coauthor (with Patrick Vonderau) of *The YouTube Reader* (Snickars 2009, 293). Operating as "both a node and a network," YouTube videos are distributed everywhere, with the "embedding of clips into various sites, blogs and social-networking platforms . . . crucial

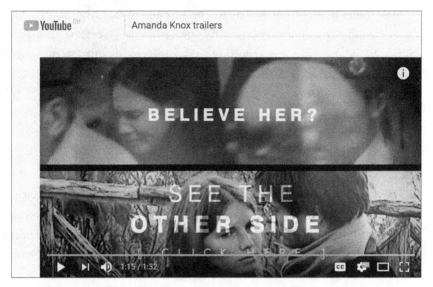

Amanda Knox trailers

BELIEVE HER?

SEE THE
OTHER SIDE
[CLICK HERE]

1:15 / 1:32

Fig 3.4. *Making a Murderer* trailer on UK Netflix site, accessed June 8, 2018

for understanding the success of YouTube" (Snickars and Vonderau 2009, 12). As Grainge suggests, YouTube is "increasingly used as a vehicle for marketing entertainment culture" and is seen as a venue for what *Wired* terms "entertainment snacking" (Grainge 2011, 7). The trailer format is ideally suited to YouTube and its privileging of short, dramatic, and accessible videos. Indeed, the attention-grabbing qualities of the trailer "hook" are fundamental to the very architecture of YouTube and its "'attention economy'—where audience engagement is the sought-after commodity" (Malkowski 2017, 167).

The *Making a Murderer* trailer grabs viewer attention through its solicitation of outrage over a miscarriage of justice by Wisconsin Manitowac County officials against Steven Avery, an uneducated white man from the underclass. The trailer is accompanied by the following tagline from Netflix: "He served 18 years for a crime he didn't commit. Now he's on the line again, and some want to see him put away for good." Running at two minutes and fifty-five seconds, the trailer begins with two printed intertitles (identified as the words of Steven Avery's defense attorney), which immediately interpellate the spectator into its miscarriage of justice narrative: "We can all say that we are never going to commit a crime . . . But that doesn't mean you won't be accused."

The trailer details Avery's wrongful imprisonment for eighteen years for a rape he did not commit (as irrefutably proven by DNA evidence), before shifting to the story of Avery's arrest in 2005 for the murder of a twenty-five-year-old woman, Teresa Halbach, two years after his release from prison. The goal of the trailer is to evoke viewer astonishment over how such a thing could possibly happen, as represented through the emotive reaction shots of the white (primarily male) talking heads who serve as our on-screen spectatorial surrogates. Through a rapid montage of archival footage, talking-head sound bites, and on-screen intertitles—all set to a rousing soundtrack—the trailer strongly implies the incompetence of the police and county officials, while also supplying images of just, morally principled white men who call out that incompetence and summon us to join in their indignation. While the round-table image of noble white men from *The Court of Last Resort* may have disappeared, it is notable the extent to which this twenty-first-century-style true crime trailer nonetheless still revolves around white men as the figures upholding the (broken) justice system and exhorting viewer involvement.

The dramatic climax of the trailer comes at the one-minute-fifty-second mark, when one of the talking heads, a white male lawyer, exclaims in outraged response to the news of Avery's arrest for murder: "Are you *kidding* me?" It is here that dramatic music swells as the show is branded "a Netflix documentary series." This "are you kidding me?" moment is the pivotal, dramatic turning point in the trailer. Documentary film theorist Jason Middleton (2014) has argued that shock (along with pleasure and disgust) is one of the primary emotional responses privileged by reaction video culture, a point confirmed by Facebook's introduction of the "wow" emoji in 2016, which enables users to express if they are "shocked" or "impressed" by someone or something (Betters 2016). The short-form trailer, I assert, is a perfect vehicle for displaying—and producing—an intense "shock" or "wow" reaction. In fact, the "Are you *kidding* me?" moment provokes a kind of mimicry in spectators of the trailer, as demonstrated in a trailer reaction video for *Making a Murderer*, which shows two spectators responding to that moment with their own expressions of shocked disbelief: "What the hell? . . . So he got accused of something *else*?" one of them marvels.

After its interpellation of the imagined viewer into a position of social and moral outrage, the trailer shifts to direct address via a series of printed intertitles: "His Story Will Shock You" . . . "The Truth Will Haunt You" . . . "Where

Will you Stand" . . . "When the Unraveling Begins?" More emotive reaction shots build the affective intensity, as Steven's defense attorney, Jerome Buting, exclaims: "What's *going* on here?" The trailer concludes with two sharply opposing responses: that of defense lawyer Buting, who bemoans the state of the criminal justice system in America, and that of Judge Patrick L. Willis, who proclaims that Steven Avery "is probably the most dangerous person ever to set foot in this courtroom." The final image is a shot of Avery's salvage yard, with a voice-over from Steven (with the printed text on the screen): "the truth always comes out."

Outrage, astonishment, and a desire to find out the "truth": the trailer encapsulates these elements into one neat three-minute-long nugget of affect. It is part of a much longer tradition of trailers as "concise, direct-address cinematic texts that serve as both attractions and forms of persuasion" (Kernan 2004, 2). But while trailers may have long "spoken to us directly, frequently telling us to SEE! COME! JOIN IN! THRILL TO!" (2), Netflix repurposes the trailer's direct mode of audience address for a digital era dominated by the drive to accumulate both positive and negative affect. The *Making a Murderer* trailer epitomizes the turn toward what Silke Panse and Dennis Rothermel refer to as the incessant solicitation of judgment in contemporary television, film, and social media (Panse and Rothermel 2014, 1). This culture of judgment is the strategic focus of Netflix's true crime trailers, which are designed to "heat up" (Paasonen 2015, 33) and feed forward oppositional responses of "liking" and "disliking." As with other transmedia reality-based texts, the extension of further "viewing opportunities" across the internet "enhances the sense of a concurrent, live and open narrative" (Corner 2009, 46) to which everyone can contribute.

My qualitative examination of the two-thousand-plus archived user comments on YouTube for the *Making a Murderer* trailer suggest the diverse ways in which the trailer functions as an interactive, affectively charged object for digital consumers.[9] Not surprisingly, many individuals go to YouTube to watch the trailer as a promo and to learn about the "coming attraction" of Netflix's *Making a Murderer*. As one viewer writes: "I love documentaries and this looks amazing. To me, from just a glance, this guy is being set up by the city law enforcement for being sued for wrongfully jailing him the first time." Other viewers go to the trailer as they would a critical review, in order to seek the opinions of other users on whether the long-form series is worth watching: "is this show really good? i know its critically acclaimed but idk if i wanna watch a 10 hour documentary about some hillbillies?"

However, many more individuals go to the trailer *while* they are streaming the ten-hour Netflix docuseries *Making a Murderer*, as a means of complementing and enhancing their viewing experience. Some viewers' comments even suggest that the trailer is visited in order to provide a form of relief from the intensity of the long-form: "This is so intense. I'm on episode 5, and my brain is fried"; "im [*sic*] sitting just started watching episode 6 i have allmost [*sic*] ripped all the stuffing off my couch and will probably rip the tv off the wall by the end!" A higher proportion of viewers, still, come to the trailer on YouTube only *after* they have completed streaming the long-form series in its entirety: "Just binged all of these in a day. Just shocking, amazing, infuriating, and jawdropping so often it's unreal—seriously, watch this series"; "I watched the entire show in less than 24 hours. Absolutely blown away. How blind some people are. This is the world we live in, full of corruption."; "Just watched all 10 episodes . . . and damn . . . just damn. When the cop called in the license plate . . . like, huh?!"

The majority of the comments are posted near the time of the trailer's and the full series' release in 2015, though there are more recent comments as well, with new comments being added to YouTube every day. Over the course of writing this book, there has been a steady increase in viewing figures for the *Making a Murderer* trailer—from 2,502,073 (in April 2016) to the current tally of 3,691,918 views (as of November 13, 2018). Ongoing developments in the real-life case prompt some viewers to return to rewatch the trailer: "Brendan dasseys [*sic*] conviction got overturned!!!!" wrote one viewer in 2017, for example. But other comments suggest that users also return to the trailer to re-experience certain affects associated with watching the longer-form series: "I finished this 2 years ago and I'm back here getting chills from the trailer" wrote a viewer in December 2017. Such comments indicate how the trailer functions as a way to "top up" and revisit the affective experience of consuming the longer-form series.

Others, however, make it clear they are watching the trailer *in place of* the long-form series: "I'm NOT watching this whole series . . . so can anyone tell me if he's guilty or not?"; "having trouble getting through the first episode After knowing he killed a cat"; "Iv [*sic*] watched episode one i have to admit the beginning was interesting but than [*sic*] it got boring through the second episode does it get better?" For this set of viewers, who will likely never watch the ten-hour-long series of *Making a Murderer*—whether it is because they cannot get past the horror of cat killing, or because they do not have the time, or because they simply find it incredibly boring—the trailer *is* the primary text.

One of the main reasons for visiting the *Making a Murderer* trailer on YouTube is to spin theories about, and share affective responses to, the real-life criminal case and the investigation as it portrayed on the Netflix docuseries. "Just came here to see if im [*sic*] the only one who feels like those two detectives Mark something and Fassbender are EVIL, manipulating a fragile kid like this." Many users discuss how the trailer drives them to seek out further information online: "Now I'm off to go google this so I can find out what happened." As several comments indicate, YouTube is just one of many sites to visit on the journey to finding out more information about the case, with some users referencing the "further research" they have conducted on sites such as Wikipedia: "i just read his wikipedia article. check his "background". i dont [*sic*] even feel a slightly bit sorry for this guy. with that background he seems like a real asshole and even if he didn't commit that rape crime. i think he was an asshole before." Such comments recall Jodi Dean's remarks about the figure of the outraged internet user who is continually compelled to "look for evidence, ask questions, and make demands" (2010b, 41). Often, the YouTube comments seem to illustrate Dean's argument that sharing reactions online is more of a recreational activity than a serious interrogation of the limits of social justice: "React and forward, but don't by any means think" (2010a, 3).

And yet it is notable that the comments section on YouTube does yield *some* significant social insights, particularly regarding the question of race. Although the comments on YouTube are notoriously toxic and often serve as a repository for the most egregious expressions of racism and sexism, it is interesting that there also seems to be space, however small, for critical reflection on the politics of race.[10] A sample of comments attached to the *Making a Murderer* trailer take a critical stance on the whiteness of the Netflix blockbuster by noting the corresponding lack of hit true crime shows featuring black people: "hundreds of black people get wrongly accused and sent to jail daily but no . . . one white guy was sent to jail and they decide to make a whole TV series"; "Black guy spends 40 years no one bats an eye, white guy less than half an eye, the world goes crazy, there is a shows [*sic*], books are written, and laws are changed. See the difference"; "lol, this shit is regular life for black americans but a white man is framed 'omg let's do a show about it!'" These sarcastic, politically charged comments are significant because they reference a cultural context in which miscarriages of justice involving African Americans are ubiquitous and yet too often ignored. If the question of race was largely missing from the critical reception of *Making a Murderer*, it is significantly acknowledged on the YouTube trailer site as an important contextual factor.

Such comments, however, tend to get swallowed up in a wider tsunami of judgment over "universal" questions of criminal guilt and innocence. The trailer site is most prominently used as a space where viewers can indefinitely debate the guilt and innocence of the accused. "I have watched the serie. [*sic*] HE.IS.INNOCENT"; "Setup or no, this guy is guilty as sin. I hope he rots in jail." While much of the critical discussion on the long-form version of *Making a Murderer* focuses on the alleged bias of the docuseries, and the way in which it strongly asserts the innocence of Steven Avery (the argument being that it withholds key evidence that would suggest his guilt), a perusal of the trailer site shows the extent to which viewers remain strongly polarized around the question of guilt and innocence. This is in part related to the true crime genre and its explicit rendering of what Carol Clover calls the "jury challenge," in which spectators are put in the position of the "citizen asked to decide" (2000a, 258). But the extreme polarization of views found in the comments section for the trailer is also connected to the "expressive affordances" (Papacharissi 2015, 67) of YouTube as a platform. The YouTube format, in which comments are organized either by the "newest first" or by the "top comments" (those which have accrued the most "likes"), encourages user interaction with the most recent or the most contentious comments. What Paasonen notes of Facebook also holds true for YouTube: "the platform itself help[s] the sparks fly" (2015, 32). As Paasonen writes, "online exchanges, once heated up, are animated by a search for affective intensity rather than rational argumentation, and by provocation rather than a desire for negotiation" (33). The longest threads—the ones that gain the most traction—are those that vehemently debate, back and forth, over and over—the question of whether Steven Avery is guilty or not.

Related to this, it is compelling to find that disavowal plays a significant role in these threads, as some users imagine a Netflix viewer who, unlike them, is duped by the docuseries. For example, one user states, "The fact that MAM viewers began a petition to ask Obama to spring Avery without researching whether the President even has the power to make it happen (He

Doesn't) tells us how clueless Netflix' audience really is." Other users made similar remarks: "the majority of the public is being ridiculous about this whole situation. 'OMG i just watched a 10 hr documentary! He's innocent! Send letters to Mr. Obama! free Steve Avery!' First of all, you watch a 10 hr documentary and think you know all the details presented in a 6 week trial?" In these trolling statements, viewers are seen as "being played by the media" and putting too much faith in the Netflix docuseries. Paasonen suggests that the "affordances and limitations" of online platforms "facilitates the creation of straw men—projections concerning what the other participants may value, feel, or intend to communicate" (2015, 32). The "straw man" of the naive Netflix viewer is one of the ways certain groups of viewers demonstrate that they are not duped, thus building a "feeling" of affective community (Dean 2010b, 22) around their conviction that Avery is guilty.

Netflix's deployment of the *Making a Murderer* trailer is calculated to play upon the new cultural purchase of the viewer or user as internet detective. As a model for "sticky" user engagement, the user-as-detective is inclined to "stay and revisit" online platforms to offer forth their opinions through mediated online interactions. In inviting users to take a "stand" one way or the other, Netflix is seeking to capture attention and bind people ever more closely to its brand, which is defined not only by its "quality content" but by the unique kind of viewing experience that it affords (Jenner 2017). As Ted Sarandos, chief content officer at Netflix, has declared: "Our brand is really about personalization" (quoted in Finn 2017, 104).

The Netflix viewing "experience" has been described by Lisa Glebatis Perks as one of "insulated flow," in which viewers get caught up in the autoplay features of the interface, undisturbed by branding exercises or adverts (2015, 7). However, in 2017, Netflix introduced its controversial auto-play trailer feature on smart TVs and streaming media players. As users browse through the selection of Netflix originals, for example, trailers automatically begin to play after hovering over a given title for a few seconds. If my Samsung smart TV is left on, trailers for different shows will begin to play on a loop.

Netflix's deployment of trailers both inside—and outside—the "insulated flow" of its interface is central to its wider attempt to colonize viewer attention. If, as Catherine Johnson describes it, a brand is an "interface/frame [that] manages the interactions between consumers, products and producers" (2012, 17–18), then the short, dramatic trailer clip is one of the most expedient ways for Netflix to communicate with, construct, and secure its viewership. In today's digital mediascape, audience address is no longer "relegated" to trailers as mere "promotional" objects but is articulated—and premediated—through them. As Sarah Atkinson suggests, in the age of digital spectatorship, "both pre-cinema and post-cinema engagements . . . extend and intensify narrative affect, heighten spectatorial absorption and enable vicarious audience engagement" (2014, 50). In relation to my analysis of trailers, I would make this point even more strongly to assert that trailer clips are not only important for pre- and post-cinema/TV engagements, but also serve as primary objects for user reaction and absorption. Netflix's attempts to "tag" its true crime audience through trailers are closely connected to its development of a user aesthetic of algorithmic personalization and customization, as I will now discuss further in regard to the trailers for *Amanda Knox*, which some YouTube users dubbed "Making a Murderer 2" (this was before the release of the actual *Making a Murderer Part 2* by Netflix in October 2018).

"See the Other Side": *Amanda Knox* and a Tale of Two Trailers

On September 8, 2016, one year after the success of *Making a Murderer,* Netflix released not one but *two* trailers to publicize *Amanda Knox*, its feature-length documentary by Brian McGinn and Rod Blackhurst. The documentary, which was released by Netflix on September 30, tells the story of Amanda Knox, the twenty-year-old American university exchange student who was twice convicted—and acquitted—for the murder of her roommate, twenty-one-year-old British student Meredith Kercher, in Perugia, Italy, in 2007. It suggests that Knox is innocent and that it was the misogyny and incompetence of the Italian justice system, along with the crass reporting of a tabloid media culture captivated by sudden access to Facebook accounts of the criminally accused, that led to her wrongful conviction(s).

The Netflix trailers, however, frame the matter of Knox's guilt or innocence as a matter of opinion.[11] One trailer, titled "Believe Her," pictures a sobbing Amanda Knox, dressed in a plain pink shirt, speaking directly to camera, as she recounts how scared she was during the ordeal of her arrest and conviction. It presents Knox as innocent and wrongfully accused. The other trailer, titled "Suspect Her," pictures a stony-faced Amanda Knox, dressed in the same

Fig 3.5. Amanda Knox in screen grab from Netflix trailer "Believe Her"

pink shirt, staring blankly ahead as tabloid accusations of her apparent sex-ual depravity flash up on the screen. It is framed as an interrogation of Knox ("Did you kill Meredith Kercher?"). The "Suspect Her" trailer concludes with Knox directly addressing the audience in a much-quoted sound bite: "Either I'm a psychopath in sheep's clothing or I am *you*." The tagline for the trail-ers, which run at 1.32 and 1.20 seconds respectively, is: "Believe Her. Suspect Her. See the Other Side." At the time of writing this chapter, the "Believe Her" trailer on YouTube has 787,556 views, 1,400 thumbs up, 729 thumbs down, and 1,112 comments. The "Suspect Her" trailer has 538,395 thousand views, 1,000 thumbs up, 180 thumbs down, and 761 comments. The two trailers are designed to play on a loop so that whichever one you choose to watch first, the other trailer is cued up to follow: users are invited to "click here" to "see the other side." Such a user-directed interface fits well with Netflix and its cham-pioning of a "user-aesthetic based on instant access and total customization" (Finn 2017, 100).

The trailers were released to great fanfare across the internet and were trending in the days immediately following their release; a Google search in 2018 for "Amanda Knox trailers" yields over 553,000 results (while a search for the documentary yields 335,000). While there are not any official view-ing figures for the *Amanda Knox* documentary, some reports suggest that the documentary "hasn't captivated viewers the way the Amanda Knox case did"

(Otterson 2016).[12] Whether or not this is true, the cultural currency of the trailers is evident. Their block release on the websites for all major UK and US news outlets, and their embedded appearance in a vast range of online publications from *Time* magazine to *Vanity Fair*, strongly indicate that they are no "second-order phenomenon" (Grusin 2016) to the documentary.

The trailers appear to present viewers with a stark binary choice: "Believe her or suspect her." Or, to think about it another way: Netflix creates one trailer for those who think she is innocent and one for those who think she is guilty. As a *Vanity Fair* article on the trailers puts it: "If you believe Amanda Knox is innocent, then Netflix's new documentary about her life and trial is for you. But if you believe she's guilty, then this documentary is *also* for you" (Desta 2016). What is especially notable is how the "Believe Her/Suspect Her" trailers feed into, and are purposefully *designed* for, hashtag social media culture. If, as director McGinn notes, the Amanda Knox case broke in 2007 just before "Facebook and social media were starting to become huge, and the line was starting to blur between hard and soft news" (quoted in Driscoll 2016), then the *Amanda Knox* trailers were released in 2016 into a fully fledged networked media culture, where audiences instantaneously access information and expect to immediately share their thoughts and opinions on criminal cases in online spaces. "Believe her/ suspect her": the titles of the trailers also serve as directives to viewers, who are invited to savor both or either of these positions of judgment as affective, entertainment *experiences* that are infinitely extendable. "Like this? You might also be interested in . . ." is a standard digital-era phrase, as users are continually being directed toward "new options" (Finn 2017, 100) and further algorithmic recommendations.

More than just a promotional stunt, the two trailers for *Amanda Knox* epitomize Netflix's business strategy to "distribute as many different types of content to as many micro-targeted audiences as possible" (Barker and Wiatrowski, 2017, 1). As Cory Barker and Myc Wiatrowski note, "Netflix projects are not only meticulously targeted with audiences' taste profiles in mind, they are also immaculately marketed and 'eventized' to cut through modern popular culture's dense clutter" (2). Netflix researchers are reported to be continually working on inventive ways to employ AI to "craft personalized trailers for movies" (Charjan 2018). Using the vast personal data amassed on subscribers, the idea is that trailers will be automatically generated through software based on "objects, scenery, types of shots, types of music, people, and so on." Film and TV show previews will thus be specifically designed "to correlate to the preferences and dislikes" of individual viewers (Charjan 2018). The Amanda Knox "choose your own trailer" stunt also presages Netflix's recently reported decision to begin producing "'choose your own ending' programmes, incorporating technology that will allow viewers to pick from multiple conflicting story threads" (Hawkes 2017).

This emphasis on user preference, agency, and viewer customization is central to Netflix's business model. In his book, *What Algorithms Want: Imagination in the Age of Computing* (2017), Ed Finn discusses how Netflix uses "microtags" to position various TV shows and films according to various permutations of generic labels and preferences, in a "sophisticated algorithmic model" that puts a premium on viewer personalization. He quotes a Netflix representative who claims that there "are 33 million different versions of Netflix," or, as Finn puts it, "a uniquely tailored system for each individual customer" (95). While they are only briefly mentioned, it is telling that trailers feature in Finn's discussion as crucial to Netflix's self-fashioning as a customized, algorithmic form of entertainment. Finn notes how *House of Cards*, Netflix's first full drop "original," released in 2013, was promoted directly to the company's "millions of users" through "ten highly targeted trailers: Kevin Spacey for the Spacey fans, artful shots for the David Fincher fans, and scenes featuring female characters for viewers who had just seen something with strong female leads, like *Thelma and Louise*." These bespoke trailers embody the Netflix emblem of "instant access to a menu of algorithmically filtered entertainment specially curated for you" (Finn 2017, 104).

As a series that introduced the "Netflix brand" to viewers, Finn points to the significance of the "rhetoric of personalization" at work within the dramatic narrative of *House of Cards*, through Frank Underwood's (Kevin Spacey's) personal asides to viewers (104). As Finn writes:

> Like Netflix itself, Underwood's core audience is you, the individual viewer with whom he makes regular eye contact. The mythos of individualization is complete: Netflix customises its offerings for every single user but drives millions of them to its high-budget creative experiment with tailored advertising. I choose the show, confident in its algorithmically calculated fitness for my tastes, and then Underwood addresses me personally, an illusion of intimacy that is performed with each new viewer.

It's an old trick but it powerfully evokes something novel: the steady gaze of the algorithm looking back through our glowing screens. (106–7)

Television scholar Casey McCormick has also noted how Underwood's direct audience address "take(s) on new meaning in the Netflix context" (2016, 106). McCormick writes that "recent statistics reveal that a growing number of SVOD users watch content on their computers," thus:

> We can assume a certain degree of screen intimacy when analysing the Netflix audience. The screen is likely to be closer to the viewer, perhaps even in her lap or bed, and this screen is the same one used for various forms of personal communication . . . we might even think of Frank's asides in terms of a *Skype ontology*, that we are video conferencing with the narrative, or particularly with Frank himself. This structural choice plays on the dream of narrative interactivity—without, of course, actually allowing the viewer to speak back to Frank. (106)

Both Finn's and McCormick's reading of the intimacy of Underwood's direct audience address hold tremendous resonance for my analysis of the *Amanda Knox* trailers. In the "Believe Her/Suspect Her" trailers, Amanda Knox speaks directly to the viewer, her body framed in midshot in a way that is designed for the pinchable, expandable, and above all, tactile, touch screen. The printed text of her script scrolls across the screen in a way that could be seen as reminiscent of a tradition of screaming intertitles in theatrical trailers, but which much more emphatically resembles the kind of text overlay now found on the auto-play videos that regularly appear on our screens on social media platforms.

Some reviewers have noted that there is something odd and stilted about the *Amanda Knox* trailers: they are an artificial performance of reaction more than reaction itself. The trailers alternate between the display of a weeping, distraught Amanda Knox responding (retroactively) to the charges against her and the trauma of what she went through, and the presentation of a steely-eyed Amanda Knox standing up to her detractors, defiant and recalcitrant in the onslaught against her character. But as Finn argues in relation to Frank Underwood's audience asides, the presentation of Knox as a "knowing performer" is key to Netflix's attempt to "customize the viewing experience" and "assemble its online audience" (2017, 107). As with *House of Cards*, the *Amanda Knox* trailers embody "one of the most seductive myths of the algorithmic age: the ideal of personalization, of bespoke content assembled especially for each one of us" (107).

What makes the artificialized performance of Amanda Knox both strange and compelling is that she is not an actress (or is she? cry the viewers who suspect her of being guilty on YouTube). The fact that Amanda Knox is an actual person heightens the affective charge of the trailer and greatly increases the stakes of audience interactivity. The trailers certainly play on the kind of "Skype ontology" discussed by McCormick in her analysis of *House of Cards*, but the real-life celebrity of Amanda Knox means that audiences feel they *can* talk back to her in a way that is not possible with the fictional Frank Underwood. With the rise of social media platforms such as Twitter, "a range of celebrity figures and behaviours are now accessible to all publics" (Thomas 2014, 243). While the notion that we can access a celebrity's "authentic" self through Twitter may be illusory, such sites "encourage[s] interactive and direct conversation between the formally hierarchical groups of stars and fans" (243).

In his book on Twitter and public shaming, *So You've Been Publicly Shamed*, Jon Ronson argues that with social media "we've created a stage for constant artificial high dramas. Every day a new person emerges as a magnificent hero or a sickening villain" (2015, 74). The recent elevation of true crime documentaries to Hollywood blockbuster status cannot be understood outside of social media networks, in which the drive to issue public judgment functions as a mechanism of the platforms themselves. As with the comments attached to the *Making a Murderer* trailer, but with an added misogynistic twist, the vast majority of the 1,114 comments on YouTube express strong opinions on the matter of Knox's guilt or innocence. My quantitative analysis of these comments shows that, out of those that directly reference questions of guilt and innocence, the majority consider Amanda Knox guilty. As of June 5, 2018, "She is a murderer and yes, i don't believe her" is the "top comment" on the "Believe Her" trailer, which has garnered ninety-three "likes"; while the "top comment" on the "Suspect Her" trailer, which has accrued eighty-four "likes," is "everyone in Italy knows she's guilty."

What bears further analysis is the evident gendering of the trailer's strategic brokering of the guilty/innocent binary opposition. Is Amanda Knox really the sexually depraved, morally bankrupt, murderous femme fatale of the tabloid reports *or* is she a misunderstood innocent who has been unfairly treated by a misogynistic media baying for blood? The traditional "virgin/ whore" dichotomy is here rebooted for contemporary techno-cultures: It's #teamguilty vs. #teaminnocent. The comments attached to the trailer on YouTube indicate how the trailers reinforce long-standing gendered stereotypes and feed into misogynistic discourse. Many of the comments remark on Knox's physical appearance and express misogynistic sentiments, referring to her as a "bitch" and a "whore."

These comments exemplify one of the arguments of the *Amanda Knox* documentary: that there was a rush to judgment, in which the world media and the Italian police made troubling gendered assumptions about Amanda Knox based on her behavior and appearance. As noted in the *Guardian,* the Amanda Knox case "was one of the first examples of the media using social media profiles as 'evidence' (the nickname 'Foxy Knoxy' originated from Knox's MySpace page) and was a disgraceful example of widespread 'slut-shaming' before that phrase was invented" (Lee 2016). Amanda Knox discusses her public vilification in the documentary by McGinn and Blackhurst, remarking that, despite the lack of any physical evidence to implicate her in the crime, people still assumed her guilt. In a direct address to the camera she utters a line that gestures to the appeal of true crime as a genre: "You're trying to find the answer in my eyes . . . You're looking at me, Why? These are my eyes, they're not objective evidence." Although the documentary reveals the damage done by such assumptions, it can't help but play into that culture of judgment by presenting Amanda Knox—and to a lesser degree her former boyfriend Raffaele Solecito—as visual specimens for analysis. In one sequence, for example, Italian prosecutor Giuliano Mignini discusses his (very problematic) views of their behavior after the murder of Meredith Kercher. As we listen to him speak, we are invited to scrutinize the faces of Amanda and Raffaele as though through a glass interrogation screen on a police detective show.

An invitation to scrutinize Knox's face for signs of guilt and innocence is at the heart of Netflix's marketing campaign. The main poster image for the documentary consists of an extreme close-up of Amanda Knox's eyes, with the film's tagline just beneath: "Either I'm a psychopath in sheep's clothing, or I am you."

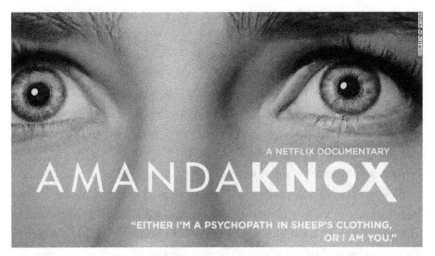

Fig 3.6. Netflix promotional poster image for *Amanda Knox*

This emphasis on a woman's eyes fits into a long tradition of objectifying, fragmenting, and fetishizing female body parts, as, for example, in the opening credits to Hitchcock's *Vertigo*, which emerge in spirals out of a close-up of Kim Novak's startled, wide-open eyes. The focus on Knox's physiognomy can also be seen as part of a wider tendency to fetishize and sexualize female killers, or alleged female killers, as the case may be. Above all, though, the Netflix marketing campaign for *Amanda Knox* epitomizes true crime's newly inflected focus on the "face-to-face" (Steimatsky 2017, 22) in an era of digital delivery technologies and FaceTime communication. While true crime may have always played on the appeal to scrutinize the face for signs of guilt, the ubiquity of mobile screens in the digital era has arguably "changed our experiences of faces," to borrow a phrase from Noa Steimatsky (2017, 1). In part, the change in our "experience of faces" has to do with the strong sense that our digital-age viewing experiences are individualized and uniquely tailored just for us; streaming-video-on-demand viewing and especially clip watching tends to happen on mobile devices—on our laptops and our phones—and is user-directed. As Carol Vernallis writes of her experience of viewing clips on YouTube: "How can it be that 1,257,000 have seen this clip, but now, while I'm with it, I feel I'm engaged in my own private peepshow?" (2013, 105). Vernallis's point is that there is not the same "communual simultaneity" as there was with linear television in the age of networks. I would add, as well, that the public judgments we share on these clips also *feel* individual. Writing on the rise of reality "judgment shows" in twenty-first-century digital culture, Panse discusses how closely emotions are bound up with judgments, whereby it is "the feeling evoked that is judged" (2014, 37). Thus, the judges on a reality music TV show like *The X Factor* will make a judgment not on the worth of the talent they see before them but on the quality of emotion they produce within the judge. In this economy of affective judgment, what matters most is how something makes one feel.

The significance of emotion to the "judging spectator" is visible in the comments on the Knox trailers, which capitalize on a cultural desire to read faces for signs of guilt or innocence and serve as a digitized flip-book version of a mug shot: innocent/guilty, guilty/innocent, innocent/guilty. Viewers of the trailers are invited to be "active," by making a decision about how they *feel* about Amanda Knox. Remarks about Knox's eyes abound in the comments attached to the trailers on YouTube, and are revealing of underlying misogynistic attitudes about the relationship between women, sexuality, and violence: "I don't believe this girl for a second, her eyes are soulless and selfish"; "The eyes are the reflection of the soul and your eyes betray you Amanda"; "her eyes are cold, she killed her"; "she's guilty, she's a psycho you can see it in her eyes."

The comments make plain the intimate relationship between emotion and judgment: "I hate this girl . . . even just looking at her, prior to even knowing about the roommate murder, she just has a look I hate . . . like Casey Anthony meets Drew & Scott Peterson, on top of OJs bronco kinda look." This formulation of Casey Anthony meets Drew and Scott Peterson meets O. J. Simpson may be unusual, but it is notable that some sort of variation on it runs throughout many of the comments on YouTube. Knox is compared to Casey Anthony as an example of "another pretty white woman who can get away with anything," but she is also compared to black athlete O. J. Simpson for her "acting" skills and for getting away with murder.

While the trailers bank on the pleasure audiences take in making a "choice" and taking a stand, it is important to question the nature of the action being performed here. As Panse bluntly concludes of reality TV judgment shows, "We are encouraged to make up our own mind, which might be commendable, but to be active per se—as viewers or anything else—does not necessarily make us better people" (2014, 52). As with the reality TV talent shows discussed by Panse, "the option to be active" in relation to the Amanda Knox trailers "is limited to a binary vote" (53)—for *or* against. Any so-called choice here is strongly predetermined and delimited in advance. Questions of "guilt," "innocence," and social justice fade into the background as reactions to the figure of the criminalized woman play out in the arena of "loving" and "hating."

Conclusion

On April 19, 2018, Netflix launched a new feature on its mobile app: thirty-second previews of TV series and movies. As reported by *Variety*: "The 30-second mobile previews are presented in a slideshow format . . . very much like the presentation of Snapchat and Instagram Stories. As with the popular 'stories' video format, users can tap the screen to play the preview or swipe to advance to the next preview" (Spangler 2018). This development further advances the close links between Netflix and social media networks through its promotion of the kind of tactile, haptic engagement—tapping and swiping—that we have become so habituated to from our engagement with personal mobile devices. Following on from Netflix's 2017 launch of "video previews," described as "a new television user interface that uses video more extensively to bring content alive in real time and helps members decide whether to click play" (Garcia and Jaffe 2016), this latest innovation enhances Netflix's significant use of the short form as what Dean elsewhere refers to as an affective "binding technique" (2010b, 21).

In this chapter I have discussed how Netflix's true crime trailers are not only promotional tools or "afterthoughts"; they are central to the viewing dynamics of contemporary true crime and its digitized, targeted "tagging" of the true crime audience. As part of a wider social media culture of judgment and opinion, trailers work to produce a strong sense of user agency in deciding questions of guilt and innocence, even as the terms of viewer involvement are largely determined in advance. They sustain the fantasy of a spectator's agency in a diffuse network culture where questions of social autonomy, power, and what it might mean to matter or make a difference are often very vague. It is perhaps not entirely surprising that in communicative capitalism such a powerful vision of justice "on demand" should find privileged expression in the one- to three-minute-long promotional trailer. What should invite further reflection from film and media scholars, however, are the cultural stakes of such an intensive marketization of attention and social awareness in contemporary digital screen culture, and the troubling extent to which, as Jonathan Crary asserts, "we choose to do what we are told to do" (2013, 60).

Over Her Dead Body

Binge-Watching Long-Form True Crime

[W]hen people talk of listening to *Serial* and watching *The Jinx*, it's in almost gluttonous terms. They are something to be gulped down, gorged on, binged on, devoured.

—Sarah Hughes, *The Guardian*

At just the point in the 2015 festive calendar when most of us subsided into a coma, something bizarre happened. Thousands upon thousands of viewers on the streaming service Netflix tried out a new programme called *Making a Murderer*—a 10-part documentary series about justice gone awry, made available in its entirety on December 18—and wound up binge-watching it from start to finish. Some paced themselves over a day or three. Some stayed up all night, hanging breathlessly on forensic details till dawn broke.

—Tim Robey, *The Telegraph*

I was addicted from the start and watched it all in one day. So heart-wrenching, it made me sob. Hope they do indeed continue to film Steven's fight for justice because I was gutted when I ran out of episodes—I'm already planning to re-watch it all over again.

—Netflix viewer of *Making a Murderer*

Justice doesn't come on-demand. Systemic change can't be binge-watched.

—Sam Adams, *Rolling Stone*

THE ABOVE QUOTATIONS REFERENCE a viewing practice that has come to be widely known as binge-watching. Awarded 2015's "word of the year" by *Collins Dictionary*, the verb "to binge-watch" is defined therein as: "to watch a large number of television programmes (especially all the shows from one series) in succession." Though there is some quibbling over what exactly constitutes binge-watching (is it two episodes or ten?), a 2014 Netflix survey determined that the majority of people consider it to be watching two to six episodes of a TV show in one sitting (West 2014). It is generally agreed that binge-watching is a mode of consumption that involves watching multiple episodes, one after the other, and it is typically associated with digital streaming, especially Netflix. In this chapter, I want to evaluate the claim that true crime—and in particular the true crime docuseries—is "tailor-made for binge-watching" (Adams 2016). If, in the last chapter, I focused on short-form true crime through my examination of the trailer, here my attention turns to the affective attachments engendered by long-form serialized true crime, through a close analysis of three of its most significant contemporary examples: the twelve-episode long podcast *Serial* (2014), the six-episode long HBO television series *The Jinx* (2015), and the ten-episode long Netflix docuseries *Making a Murderer* (2015).

Together, these true crime shows clock up roughly forty hours of listening or viewing and have inspired remarkably high volumes of cultural chatter and debate. The fastest podcast ever to reach five million downloads on iTunes, *Serial* has been described as "the world's most popular podcast" (Richman 2014); at the time of writing this chapter, it has tallied up over eighty million downloads. *The Jinx*, released episodically on HBO two months after *Serial* concluded, boasted a shocking finale on March 15, 2015, which produced over thirty-five thousand tweets with over eleven million Twitter views, according to Neilson Twitter TV ratings (Kissell 2015). *Making a Murderer* accrued tremendous media buzz[1] with Netflix's share prices "soaring" as subscriptions for the streaming service dramatically spiked in the wake of the docuseries success over the Christmas holiday period (Jameson 2016).

It is important to note that these true crime successes come from notably different formats: the podcast (*Serial*), quality cable TV (*The Jinx*), and subscription video on demand (*Making a Murderer*), respectively. They also have considerably different production and media distribution contexts: *Serial* derives from National Public Radio and the production team of *This American Life*; *The Jinx* is a product of premium cable TV and HBO; and *Making a Murder* is a "Netflix original" that belongs to the domain of digital video-on-demand subscription services. Nonetheless, their shared subject matter of "blood-boiling" true crime cases and their close proximity in terms of release date—*Serial* first aired in October 2014, *The Jinx* in March 2015, and *Making a Murderer* in December 2015—meant that all three true crime blockbusters were continually spoken of in the same breath as part of a "true crime craze."

Of the three true crime docuseries referred to above, only one of them—*Making a Murderer*—was released or "dropped" in its entirety, to be binge-watched at the viewer's discretion. But although *Serial* and *The Jinx* were initially released episodically, on a weekly basis, it is notable that they are still discussed in terms of their binge-ability after the fact. In other words, even though *Serial* and *The Jinx* were released on a weekly basis over the course of their run, they are still indicative of the kinds of viewing habits associated with the "Netflix effect," in so far as they are both discrete series organized around a single case or story and are designed to be consumed in a certain delimited time span.

Though binge-watching might evoke notions of longevity, duration, and endurance, it also points to the reduced attention spans that allegedly char-acterize the age of the internet (Atkinson, quoted in Matrix, 2014, 130). Tra-ditionally, network television's long-running series tend to consist of at least twenty-two episodes per season and therefore require a longer, ongoing com-mitment (130–31). By contrast, long-form binge-able series—following the model of "quality TV" in the TV III era—are shorter, and it is only the act of watching hour after consecutive hour in short blocks of time that makes them *feel* longer and more intense. While it has been claimed that the long form allows for "more storytelling, more richness," (Sarandos, quoted in McCor-mick 2016, 102) it is important to question whether the immersive long form necessarily leads to more in-depth storytelling or greater critical reflection on the part of viewers.

As I have argued in this book, true crime's positioning of the viewer as a "detective" is an important model for the digital era's privileging of a "click-able" interactivity. A notion of the viewer as a detective—deciphering clues and deciding on questions of guilt and innocence—fits in well with the kind of viewer autonomy and activity that is held to be central to the "Netflix effect" and its guiding idea that "binge viewers are actively engaged in con-tent discovery and curation" (Matrix 2014, 133). The dominant perception of digital streaming services is that they offer a high degree of choice and viewer sovereignty in watching television outside of the flow of scheduled network

TV. However, as discussed in the previous chapter, critics of Netflix have argued that this notion of choice is largely illusory and decisions about what to watch are carefully shaped and delimited in advance by capitalist marketing imperatives that submit viewers to new forms of control and surveillance. Netflix, Amazon, and other streaming services operate according to what Sarah Arnold (2016) calls "algorithmic determinism" (56), which shapes the behavior it purports to spontaneously encourage. As Safiya Umoja Noble has argued in her important book, *Algorithms of Oppression: How Search Engines Reinforce Racism,* algorithms are far from "benign, neutral or objective" (2018, 1). In fact, they operate according to existing white patriarchal structures of oppression. Whether tech companies such as Google and Netflix *intend* to reinforce sexism and racism is, as Noble argues, inconsequential: what matters are "outcomes and results" and the ways in which structural oppression imbues "discourses of technology" (91) and digital media platforms.

Such arguments bear relevance for a consideration of the new kind of viewing dynamics created by streaming TV platforms such as Netflix, Amazon Prime, and their various equivalents such as HBO Go and Sky Go. In a *New York Times* article, TV critic James Poniewozik has suggested that the immersive viewing experience of binge-watching creates a dynamic, which he terms "The Suck": "that narcotic tidal feeling of getting drawn into a show and letting it wash over you for hours. 'Play next episode' is the default, and it's so easy" (2015). In what follows I will reflect upon how true crime lends itself to the "user-directed" pull of the binge-able series, where "each episode becomes a new level to be unlocked" (Poniewozik 2015). In the long-form true crime texts I examine here, the calculated capture of audience attention through the use of cliffhangers and plot twists is designed to encourage viewers to hit "play next episode." If true crime is "tailor-made" for binge-watching, it is in large part because of its "enigma-driven" nature (Klinger 2018a, 6), which tantalizes viewers to keep watching over hours of episodes in order to find "answers" and resolutions to mysteries. What's interesting, then, is how such binge-able true crime—in which well-worn themes are extended across several episodes—allows scholars to freshly observe some of the problematic gendered and racialized mechanics of true crime as a genre.

As with the trailers examined in the previous chapter, long-form true crime docuseries operate as prime examples of what Panse refers to as "judgment shows," in which "affect, emotion, and suspense are generated solely through the spectacle of judgment" (2014, 33). Feeding into the incessant solicitation of judgment in digital culture, long-form true crime indulges in the wider "proclivity to judge—to endorse, to favor, to condemn, to denigrate, to remonstrate, to like, to love, and to hate" (Panse and Rothermel 2014, 2). Did Adnan Syed *really* kill Hae Min Lee? Is Robert Durst guilty of killing his wife, Kathie Durst, *and* his friend Susan Berman? Can *we be sure* beyond reasonable doubt that Steven Avery murdered Teresa Halbach? More to the point: *how can we tell?*

To a large extent, these long-form true crime shows facilitate what TV scholar Jason Mittell, quoting David Foster Wallace, refers to as our "lengthy interactions with Hideous Men" (2015, 142). While Mittell is discussing fictionalized serial dramas such as *The Sopranos, Dexter,* and *Breaking Bad,* serial true crime is similarly "distinguished by the long time frames it creates" and the kind of involved "interaction" with "complex" male characters that it allows for (142). But in contrast to the fictional serial dramas Mittell examines, there is a heightened emotional charge to long-form true crime because of its real-world implications. The driving pleasure of these recent long-form true crime shows comes from the activity of passing judgment on guilt and innocence, of distinguishing the "good" guys from the "bad" guys; there is a strong sense that watching (or listening to) and "interpreting" these accused men and sharing our affective responses to them through networked digital media actually counts for something. As journalist Christopher Hooton suggests, the "main reason" for the "sudden success" of these long-form true crime shows

> is the way they can effect change, where perhaps others couldn't preinternet. People love justice and they love to see the truth out, and with it now being easier than ever for the masses to funnel their outrage at prosecutors and police departments online, listeners/viewers feel part of the story, as though they're a million strong group of pro-bono lawyers standing behind the defendant in the courthouse (or angry mob, depending on how you look at it). (2016)

In what follows, I will argue that, although these long-form true crime shows are often presented as extraordinary examples of participatory media culture, they generate affective judgment in highly predetermined ways, which are attached to the dynamics of binging. As Laura Miller notes of the kind of viewership solicited by *The Jinx*, "Every viewer seems to believe that only his or her preternaturally shrewd powers of observation have noticed that Durst is a veritable grab bag of tics, twitches, winks, shrugs and mouth-wipings. Or that his eyes look really weird" (2015). As I will demonstrate, the emphasis these shows place on active individual listening or viewing runs alongside their affective deployment of very familiar narrative devices—including the cold open and the melodramatic cliffhanger—which are designed to evoke collective emotional reactions and which are repurposed in the service of producing a binge-able text that habituates viewers to press the "next episode" button on their screens.[2]

Finally, and crucially: if these true crime digital-era docuseries are seen to solicit new forms of user-directed viewer engagement, then it is important to acknowledge that they do so over dead women's bodies. All three of the long-form true crime texts to be discussed in this chapter center on stories of "lost" and murdered women: Hae Min Lee, Kathie Durst, Susan Berman, and Teresa Halbach. These dead women serve as the inciting means for these true crime long-form narratives, even as they are largely effaced and obscured in the series themselves through the focus on male criminal subjects. In her study, *Women and Death in Film, Television, and News*, Joanne Clarke Dillman calls this the "dead but not gone convention" in which "the woman is put under erasure as a condition of her visibility in the text" (2014, 25). While reviews of *Serial*, *The Jinx*, and *Making a Murderer* have expressed unease over the curious effacement of the female victim(s), I argue that this erasure is in some ways fundamental to the narrative construction of these long-form shows as "binge-able." That these series cannot seem to find a way of adequately acknowledging the female victims whose murders provide the occasion for their "binge-ability" raises questions about the politics of these long-form true crime docuseries and the often-deterministic affective positions they carve out for viewers.

Going Long

A dominant cultural reading of *Serial*, *The Jinx*, and *Making a Murderer* heralds them as examples of a new kind of documentary production that "renew[s]" the "hope for justice" by appearing to fulfill the dream of documentarians everywhere: to effect measurable social change. As John Patterson writes in the *Guardian*:

> First *Serial*, then *The Jinx*, and now *Making a Murderer*: we officially have a new genre on our hands, the long-form, deep-immersion, true-crime documentary that works itself into the courts—perhaps liberating an innocent from jail, or putting the accused there at long last. The ambition here is not to earn Emmys, but to achieve justice. (2016)

As proof of this assertion, Patterson cites the US Federal Court's 2016 decision to overturn *Making a Murderer's* Brendan Dassey's 2007 conviction (when he was sixteen years old)—on charges of first-degree murder, sexual assault, and mutilation of a corpse.[3] Patterson suggests that that decision "marks the third time in 18 months that a TV series or a podcast has played a decisive role in a major murder case" (2016). The other two examples he cites are the high-profile arrest of Robert Durst on the eve of the finale of *The Jinx* on March 14, 2015,[4] and the dramatic announcement on July 6, 2016, that Judge Martin Welch granted Adnan Syed, the subject of *Serial*, a retrial.[5] Syed had been serving a life sentence for the murder of his high school girlfriend, Hae Min Lee, in 1999.

These are undoubtedly remarkable outcomes. Although I do not agree that the drive for "justice" can be so easily separated from the ambition to "earn Emmys," or that the link between the documentaries and the striking legal turnarounds is as "decisive" or direct as Patterson suggests, it is nonetheless evident that a strong sense of contemporary true crime as interventionist runs throughout the opinion pieces on *Serial*, *The Jinx*, and *Making a Murderer*. They are described, variously, as a "sort of medial appeals court, with a subsidiary jury of armchair detectives (us)" (Godwin 2015); an "impromptu branch of the judiciary" (Lawson 2015); a "kind of secondary appeals system" (Nussbaum 2015); and "high-brow vigilante justice" (Schulz 2016). Contemporary true crime shows are seen as notably more critical and suspicious of the criminal justice system than previous iterations of the genre. As David Schmid argues, "these shows are tapping into our culture's widespread sense that our justice system, if not broken, is definitely in trouble . . . viewers get to feel that maybe, in a small way, they can contribute to making the justice system a little more responsive, a little more just. . . . That's something which is relatively new in the history of the genre" (quoted in Serjeant 2016). Where true crime texts from a predigital age, such as *The Court of Last Resort,* which I discussed in the previous chapter, typically worked to confirm belief in the workings of the police and the legal-judiciary system, recent long-form true crime series work to provoke distrust of authorities and encourage viewers to take ownership over the cases themselves, investigating evidential materials and spinning new theories as they feed their reactions into social media networks.

Patterson attributes the critical impact of recent long-form true crime to the viewing "outlets" of "premium cable" and "Netflix" and their ability, as he puts it, "to go long" (2016). As Patterson explains, "free of the confines of TV ads and primetime schedules," filmmakers now have the "freedom to understand old cases anew" (2016). Sarah Koenig, Andrew Jarecki, Moira Demos, and Laura Ricciardi have all respectively noted the importance of the long duration of their documentaries in allowing them to explore their subject matter more deeply and thoroughly. Koenig has noted how the long form enabled her to go "deep inside" the story, so that "the people who are listening will feel like they're learning the particulars of the case in the same manner that I am learning them" (Yurcaba 2014). Using very similar language, Jarecki asserts that the long-style format of *The Jinx* allows the viewer "to dive more deeply into a story" and to go on the same emotional "journey" as he did while making the film (quoted in Bauder 2015). Following suit, Demos and Ricciardi have lauded the critical importance of long duration and said that, although they initially imagined *Making a Murderer* as a documentary feature film, they soon realized that the ten years' worth of material they had "could sustain a much longer form" (quoted in Jones 2015). In a promotional blurb for Netflix, Demos declares that "If we had not been there to witness these events we would have trouble believing they actually occurred. Our goal has always been to share that experience with viewers. Our partnership with Netflix has allowed us to tell this story in a way that wouldn't have been possible anywhere else" (quoted in "Netflix Announces" 2015).

And yet, despite the emphasis placed on the critical, evaluative potential of the "deep immersion" long form, I posit that the appeal of these shows is more thoroughly affective; in other words, what makes them perform so well in the contemporary digital attention economy is not their encouragement of mass critical reflection and complex rational evaluation from viewers, but, rather, their solicitation of emotional responses based on their continuous microtemporal affective modulations from within the long form. Divided into distinct yet interconnected episodes, or "chapters" in the case of *The Jinx*, these true crime shows are designed, above all, to persuade viewers to continue listening, viewing, and interacting their way through the series and through the wider systems of digital media engagement in which they are embedded.

To fully account for the kind of viewer involvement solicited by long-form true crime, it is necessary to explore the affective power of digital interfaces and their calculated capture of audience attention. For instance, when Robert Durst was arrested for the 2000 murder of Susan Berman shortly before the season finale of *The Jinx,* many viewers experienced this as a "spoiler." In other words, the news of Durst's arrest was seen to ruin "the 'ending' of a TV show they'd spent several hours of their lives watching" (Minor 2015). This uneasy line between investigation and obsession, between social concern and televisual entertainment, speaks to the wider issues at stake in a twenty-first-century digital attention economy that, as Jonathan Crary argues, "dissolves the separation between the personal and the professional, entertainment and information, all overridden by a compulsory functionality of communication that is inherently and inescapably 24/7" (2013, 75–76).

Moreover, while it may be seductive and empowering to think of these true crime shows as effecting dramatic legal changes—as evidenced by the individual examples cited above—it is not at all apparent whether they are effecting any serious, substantive, and long-term structural legal transformations. As Sam Adams cautions, in the final epigraph included at the start of this chapter, "Justice doesn't come on-demand. Systemic change can't be binge watched" (2016). What is therefore pressing to explore is how these true crime shows are reframing public interactions with crime and justice through wider social media practices and "networking norms" (Kuntsman and Stein 2015, 7). That is to say, in order to fully understand the ideological work of these shows and their longer-term implications, it is essential to consider how they are mediating and mobilizing the viewer's affective relationship to criminality through digital consumption practices and protocols. That these shows generate strong emotions and moral outrage seems indisputable: what is less clear is the work these emotions are performing in terms of shifting public understandings of agency, crime, and justice. Against a view of these shows as opening up a space for advocacy, I will argue that they are more conservative than they might first appear. Rather than generating new ways of interactively responding to crime—and performing a serious interrogation of male violence as an endemic social problem—this set of long-form true crime texts operate according to presumptive, predetermined binaries that often elide the female victim and actively work to dissuade more profound and contextualized understandings of male criminality and violence against women.

Seriality and Video Game Logics: *Serial*

In an article for *Feminist Media Studies* on "Sexual Violence in Serial Form: *Breaking Bad* habits on TV," Stuart Joy has argued that popular US TV drama, including such shows as *The Sopranos, Breaking Bad,* and *Game of Thrones,* "all operate within, and contribute to, a problematic cultural setting that frequently marginalizes narratives of abuse at the expense of an overwhelming emphasis on the problems of hegemonic masculinity" (2017, 1). Despite the "capacity of long-form television programmes to deal with complex social issues," as importantly discussed by scholars such as Susan Berridge (2013) and Lesley Henderson (2007), Joy argues that serials such as *Breaking Bad* work to marginalize issues of sexual violence and abuse through a focus on the character arc of their male protagonists. Thus, for instance, the strong affective attachment to Walter White (Bryan Cranston), carefully cultivated and developed across all five seasons of *Breaking Bad,* meant that the abuse and violence he inflicted on his long-suffering on-screen wife, Skyler (Anna Gunn), was often overlooked by fans. Even worse, the investment in Walter resulted in overt displays of online gendered hatred toward the character of Skyler and the actress, Anna Gunn, who played her.

Joy's arguments bear relevance to the long-form true crime texts under consideration here because they, too, demonstrate a tendency to sideline the female victims of male violence. What I want to focus attention on more closely is how this marginalization of the female victim is a consequence of the affective operations of these long-form true crime texts and their attempt to capture viewer attention through a deployment of an interactive video-game logic associated with binge-watching as a preferred mode of viewing. The narrative organization of these long-form true crime stories, and their use of seriality as a way of "stringing things out" (Dyer 2015, 27) and suturing viewers into a binge-able flow, rely on a series of binary oppositions that reduce the

Fig 4.1. *Serial* Season 1 website

opportunities for nuanced reflection in favor of a constant sensational staging of affective display and response.

Described as the "first podcast blockbuster" (Zelenko 2014), *Serial's* twelve-episodes-long first season, hosted by American journalist Sarah Koenig, became a "viral internet sensation" (O'Meara 2015) chiefly because of the way it actively involved its listeners as "amateur sleuths" across multiple media platforms. The enticing narrative hook of the podcast—is Adnan Syed guilty or innocent? You decide!—is structured around the unfolding relationship between host Koenig and Adnan Syed, the Pakistani-American who was convicted of the murder of his ex-girlfriend, Korean-American Hae Min Lee, in 1999, when he was a teenager (Syed was thirty-two years old at the time of the podcast). Indeed, the central question asked by *Serial*, as mediated through the voice of white, middle-class journalist Koenig, is: *did* Adnan Syed actually commit the murder? And it is this question that gets reformulated by digitally engaged listeners to: "so do *you* think he did it? Discuss." This call to judgment then reverberates across a multitude of internet sites, including a thriving subreddit, described as a "place to find information about the podcast and to discuss your theories, predictions and other aspects of the show and case" (Serial Reddit n.d.). The *Serial* subreddit received over eighty thousand page views an hour and "a million page views on the day of the finale" (Zelenko 2014). As Michael Zelenko explains, "Some Redditors took it upon themselves to crack the case, going to incredible lengths to uncover some piece of evidence that Koenig hadn't, searching for proof of Adnan's innocence or else a clue that would condemn him beyond a reasonable doubt" (2014).

That *Serial* was a work in progress, and that it could actively change shape according to feedback from viewers, marks it as significantly different from both *The Jinx* and *Making a Murderer*, which were finished products at the time they were released to the public. While Koenig and the *Serial* producers have been candid in interviews about the fact that they "plotted out" all the episodes and had overarching narrative structures worked out in advance, the format, they suggest, nevertheless "allowed them to be responsive and flexible" to new information and developments (Kiernan 2014). This sense of the contemporaneity of *Serial* was key to its appeal as an "unfolding" story and highlights the important temporal dimension of digital culture, in which participation is seen to anchor the interactive subject in the present moment. The temporal currency of the binge-worthy show creates an affective public that converges around these series as shared, participatory objects. As director Andrew Jarecki has noted of his decision to package *The Jinx* in serialized form rather than as a feature-length documentary: "We're living in a binge-watching universe where people are watching 10 episodes at a time of things," in which "millions and millions of people have access to [a TV show] instantly" (quoted in Zeitchick 2015).

As the series that is credited with igniting the current cultural fascination with long-form true crime, *Serial*'s success derived from its hailing of an active, involved listener with the potential to shape events. This kind of intensified sense of viewer agency is part of a wider shift in witnessing practices in the era of digitally networked media. As Paul Frosh and Amit Pinchevski define it, "media witnessing is the witnessing performed *in, by,* and *through* the media" and is a "productive concept" for thinking about "changes in our experience of time" in the digital era (2014, 596). According to Frosh and Pinchevski, ubiquitous media technologies have created a new sense of the "ripeness of any moment as the harbinger of new events" (606). The now routine and "extensive mediation of everyday life" through mobile technologies creates a "condition of conspicuous impendingness . . . in particular through the retrospective examination and discovery of those events by virtue of their routine and incidental recording by media technologies" (595). In a world where we are now accustomed to seeing images of groups of people holding up their cell phones to record events, it has become a truism that "our media witnessing of the event is inherently part of the event" (607). Particularly significant for an analysis of the cultural purchase of true crime is Frosh and Pinchevski's contention that digital networked culture has "engendered a decidedly forensic experience of time," underpinned and enhanced by audience interaction through sociotechnical interfaces in which "images have become operative" (600, 601).

It is the "interactive and operative potential" (Frosh and Pinchevski 2014, 601) of recent true crime texts that is sold as one of their most significant features. In a post-truth era of fake news, long-form true crime is seen to have striking democratic and investigative capabilities; it is celebrated for its potential to show up the failures of the legal system and right social wrongs. However, while *Serial* has been praised as a feminist text for its explicit foregrounding of multiple "voices and perspectives" (Doane, McCormick, and Sorce 2017, 120), I argue that its multivocality works more according to the logic of the video or computer game as it has been described by Richard Grusin. Indeed, Grusin's argument that users "can only work within those potentialities that the Internet allows or has been made to allow, within what has already been networked or premediated—technically, algorithmically, socially and culturally" (2010, 47) is useful for understanding the limited affective operations of *Serial.* Although it has been asserted that Koenig's "core strategy" of raising questions rather than authoring conclusions fits in with "feminist methods . . . to destabilize power hierarchies by representing many different viewpoints" (Doane, McCormick, and Sorce 2017, 120), I contend that the "rhetorical style" of the series and its suturing of listeners into the text through sharply polarized affective responses tends to confirm an "oppositional logics" (Fuhs 2014, 793).

In episode 1, Koenig sets the stage for *Serial* as a competition between opposing sides: "Maybe Adnan is innocent but what if he isn't? What if he did do it? And he's got all these good people thinking he didn't. So either it's Jay or it's Adnan but someone is lying and I really wanted to figure out who." Jay is "the guy" (as Koenig first introduces him) whose testimony ultimately secured Adnan's conviction and who is cast as a central, mysterious character in the narrative of the podcast; he is described in episode 7, for example, as "the thing that confuses" Koenig the most about the case. Jay is African American, a detail that emerges in episode 1, through police audio of a taped interview from fifteen years ago that identifies him as a "black male, nineteen years of age."

The adversarial narrative of the podcast—and the contest it stages between competing narratives—is continuously mediated through the affective experiences of Sarah Koenig.[6] In episode 1, Koenig recalls what it was like to meet Syed in person for the first time. She describes his "giant brown eyes like a dairy cow" and asks: "Could someone who looks like that really strangle his girlfriend?" Koenig admits, in her typically self-deprecating fashion, that this is an "idiotic" line of "inquiry." And yet this initial hunch that "he just doesn't seem like a murderer" is the assumption that animates the whole series; for, after various twists and turns, and copious amounts of information—accompanied by paratextual interviews, charts, and diagrams on the website—this is what the show ultimately leaves listeners with: Koenig's strong attachment to, and "liking" for, Adnan Syed—her gut feeling that someone so "nice" simply could not have committed a murder. With its strong emphasis on the worth of Koenig's intense personal feelings, *Serial* champions the notion of "direct 'gut' access to an unmediated truth," a fantasy that, as Mark Andrejevic has argued, has become central to twenty-first-century reality television and socially networked media culture (2016, 654).

This American Life producer and presenter Ira Glass (whose voice-over, "Previously, on *Serial*," cues the listener into every episode) has noted that Koenig and the other producers "have all flipped back and forth, over and over, in their thinking about whether Adnan committed the murder. And when you listen to the series, you experience those flips with them" (quoted in Larson 2014). Although this statement from Glass makes it sound as if this oscillation is an entirely spontaneous response on the part of Koenig and the producers, it is important to note that, in fact, this "flip-flopping" is the primary structuring device of *Serial* as reinforced through the sociotechnical interfaces through which viewers engage with the series. Consider, for example, the descriptive blurbs for the episodes, found on both the *Serial* website and iTunes. The blurb for episode 2, "The Break-Up," is indicative of how the notion of the case as a series of "choices" between differing views and interpretations is programmed into the very structure of its format: "Friends say Adnan was sad when Hae dumped him but not crazy sad—normal sad. The prosecutors say he was rage-filled and vengeful. Which is it?" Such a blurb is designed to entice viewers to download the episode, but it also demonstrates the extent to which the "back and forth" on questions of guilt and innocence is part of *Serial*'s format and its careful management of audience affective response and judgment. "Which is it?" This is a question that sounds more like a demand, as viewers must choose at regular intervals between a series of competing theories and narratives; some of these "choices" are big, as in, is Adnan Syed guilty or innocent? And some are small, as in, was Adnan "crazy sad or normal sad" when Hae dumped him? You decide.

The sense of how the show operates as a series of "levels to be unlocked" is reinforced through its digital interface and its interactive mode of address. *Serial's* format positions listeners as amateur detectives, and provides us with a set of different options or competing narratives to choose between each episode, as we navigate our way through to the ending. Indeed, critic Justine Elias has argued that *Serial* is a "true crime entertainment" that disturbingly operates as a:

> Choose Your Own Adventure game for the folks playing along at home. "Serial"'s a hit online, with discussion boards, parody video and audio clips; hate-listeners, crime-solvers, and some earnestly, thrillingly living the whole experience as if it were happening to them. Gaming it. You can be Jay! How would it feel to testify against a friend? Or Asia: Why don't you want to get involved? Or Hae Min Lee! Sorry, you can't play. You have been murdered. "Serial" forgot about her. (2014)

As this passage makes plain, Hae Min Lee—the female murder victim—is largely effaced by *Serial*. The show itself accounts for the sense of Hae's absence from the show—despite it being about her murder—by noting that her family declined to participate. In other words, the show's implicit justification for why it comes up short when it comes to rendering the details of Hae's life is that it does not have access to her family's views of the case or to their memories of Hae. Koenig states that she respects that the family did not want to be involved and that all she can therefore tell us about Hae is what she has learned "from non-family members. That she was cheerful and light and funny."[7]

While the fact that the female victim's family is not involved does raise serious issues about consent, my argument is that the disturbing elision of Hae Min Lee from *Serial's* narrative stems more crucially from the show's "choose your own adventure" format and its deep-rooted reliance on binary oppositions. Listeners are invited to adjust their feelings on the crime from episode to episode, as new options and new ways of interpreting "old" evidence are presented to us through a slickly edited montage of competing voices, which are carefully curated by the producers. *Serial's* structuring of the case as a continual series of competing narratives and binary oppositions—Adnan vs. Jay, good boy Adnan vs. bad boy Adnan, bad boy Jay versus good boy Jay, and so on—limits its ability to perform a wider contextualized analysis of the murder of Hae Min Lee.

Serial certainly makes good on its promise in episode 1 to let listeners hear "different versions told by different people of what happened the day Hae Min Lee was murdered," but these versions are constrained by a rigid binary frame that does not allow for nuanced, intersectional thinking. *Serial's* inability to explore the "intersecting oppressions of race, class, and gender" (Collins 2000, 45) is what leads to its failure to contextualize Hae's murder and to render a full and compassionate picture of her as a human being. This failure is all the more striking given the championing of the "in-depth reporting" allegedly afforded by long-form true crime. Why, despite all the claims that get made for the long form and its potential for highlighting social injustice, is the female victim so often obscured?

One of the striking patterns that emerges across the long-form texts of *Serial, The Jinx,* and *Making a Murderer* is the inclusion of extracts from the diary of the murdered woman. In each case, the female victim's diary extracts are included in the second episode of the series, which is significant, given the importance that subscription video on-demand (SVOD) services place on "hooking" viewer attention at strategic moments across long-form series. These moments in which the dead woman is resurrected—through a reading aloud of diary extracts (*Serial*), through voice-over and dramatic reconstructions with actors (*The Jinx*), and through video diary (*Making a Murderer*)—are important for thinking about the problematic ways in which many long-form true crime shows sensationally resurrect the dead woman in the service of seriality and suspense even as they elide the contexts that would assist in producing a deeper understanding of male violence against women.

In episode 2 of *Serial,* "The Break-Up," Koenig quotes from Hae's diary in an attempt to give the listener access to Hae's "own words" on her relationship with Adnan. Strangely, even though this is the episode in which we are meant to gain access to Hae's inner life, it is also the episode of *Serial* in which Hae's voice feels the most ignored and misappropriated. In "The Break-Up," Koenig sets out to interrogate the prosecution's "story that Adnan was 'enraged' after the break up" and that "this was a crime about pride" rooted in a Pakistani culture of honor and revenge. Throughout *Serial* Koenig seeks to put pressure on the notion that Adnan's Muslim religion, race, and culture had anything to do with the murder. While this critical maneuver is not a problem in and of itself, what *is* concerning is how Koenig performs her critique of the possible racial prejudices at work in the case, through a dismissal of gender-based violence.

For example, Koenig introduces Hae's diary, which was entered as evidence at trial, via this curious—and rather disdainful—aside to the listener: "Her diary by the way, well I'm not exactly sure what I expected her diary to be like, but it's such a *teenage* girl diary." This editorializing regarding Hae's diary is important because it highlights the way in which *Serial*, whether it means to or not, works to undermine the victim's voice. "They were *such* teenagers"; "it was just such a *teenage* thing to do"; "Adnan was a teenager in America doing American teenager things." In *Serial*, "teenager" becomes synonymous with a kind of universal experience that the show somehow holds to be outside of the categories of raced, gendered, and classed experience.

Rather than attempting to put domestic violence into a wider context—for example, by interviewing experts who might explain the nature of a controlling relationship—Koenig relies on the he said/she said, competing narrative structure through which *Serial* is curated to create dramatic and affective intrigue around opposing points of view. Thus, Koenig includes testimony from one of Hae's friends who says that Adnan was a very controlling boyfriend. But instead of seriously exploring this claim or giving it any credence as a potential warning sign of a possessive relationship, Koenig uses her own preferred interpretation of Hae's diary to counter that view. As Koenig states: "by far the majority of her diary entries are about how she likes and loves him [Adnan]." Koenig glosses over Hae's expressed concerns about Syed's religious zeal and instead provides Syed with the opportunity to refute accounts of his controlling behavior and remarks as a "joke." *Serial* thus raises the possibility of domestic violence but only to then undermine it and discount it.

Money Shots and Click Bait: *The Jinx*

While in *Serial* the dead female victim is largely ignored, in *The Jinx* she has a far more visible role to play in securing the show's binge-watching mechanics—the revivification of the dead white woman is central to the capture and management of audience attention over the course of its six chapters. But if *The Jinx* places far greater emphasis on the female victim than the other two docuseries I discuss in this chapter, its seemingly more sympathetic foregrounding of the dead woman is ultimately as problematic as the elision that occurs in the other two shows, as I will shortly discuss.

Upon the airing of *The Jinx* in March 2015, director Andrew Jarecki pronounced that his six-part television docuseries "may be the first documentary created for the binge-watcher" (quoted in Bauder 2015). This is a shrewd if debatable claim, and indeed the producers of *Serial, The Jinx,* and *Making a Murderer* all cite the 2004 television true crime documentary miniseries *The Staircase,* directed by Oscar-winning French director Jean Lestrade, as a key influence.[8] Nonetheless, it is important to consider the ways in which *The Jinx* is a series that was specifically designed with "on demand," "water cooler in the cloud" viewing (Seitz 2015) in mind.

Indeed, it was the calculated nature of the show that most disturbed some critics. Documentary filmmaker Robert Greene, for example, in an excoriating review of *The Jinx* for British film magazine *Sight and Sound,* roundly denounced it for being "manipulative," "pointlessly morbid," and "self-congratulatory" (2016). Greene took issue with the "market driven" nature of the series and how it was "so obviously geared to deliver one, single news-making/ratings-grabbing moment" (2016). Greene is referring here to the sensational finale when Durst—off camera in the bathroom via his microphone—appears to confess to all three murders. It is, as Greene acknowledges, one of the most "incredible endings in non-fiction history." Certainly, *The Jinx* provides the money shot ending that *Serial* could only dream of—in which the male criminal subject is aurally "caught out" and confesses to his guilt. *The Jinx,* as a televisual experience or a "documentary event" (as HBO trailed the program), provides what the podcast could not: it puts the male criminal subject on *visual* display for viewer evaluation across six episodes. Through its "polygraphic" cinematography, to borrow a notion from Carol Clover (2000b, 116), *The Jinx* strongly compels viewers to "read" or interpret the face of Durst for signs of guilt. The show's denouement and the central character's apparent admission of guilt is therefore the ultimate payoff for our detective work.

Rather than dismissing *The Jinx* as a "bad" or improper documentary, there is a need to understand how it mobilizes certain techniques and practices of documentary as a means of affectively suturing the viewer into its

Fig 4.2. Robert Durst on visual display for the viewer in *The Jinx*

serialized format. It is necessary, that is, to locate *The Jinx* as part of a wider "emotion economy of reality programming" (Grindstaff and Murray 2015, 122), which depends upon the transmedia networked production and circulation of affect. Deploying conventions from documentary, true crime, reality television, and melodrama, *The Jinx* works to interpellate viewers in a series of highly emotive and sensational segments of action—and reaction—that put a premium on affective response. If, as Mareike Jenner has argued, the binge model is a way for the viewing-on-demand industry to bind customers into their products (2017, 305), then *The Jinx* exemplifies the extent to which affective reaction functions as the primary "binding technique" (Dean 2010b, 21) of the binge-able text.

In particular, *The Jinx* deploys what Pier Dominguez (2015) calls the "melodramatic money shot," a common device in reality TV show franchises such as the *Real Housewives*. Taken from pornography, the term "money shot" refers to the moment when male orgasm is made visible through ejaculation. TV theorist Laura Grindstaff uses the term "money shot" to describe the prized moment of emotional outburst on TV talk shows (quoted in Dominguez 2015, 161). Following Grindstaff, Dominguez defines money shots as those moments on reality TV franchises when central characters have dramatic "affective outbursts" of anger, jealousy, or envy (2015, 164). As Dominguez argues, on the long-form reality docu-soap, these money shots are "not stand-alone events. . . . Instead, they are serialized to heighten and extend the thrilling anxiety they provoke throughout a season's episodes and across seasons" (2015, 156). These "intense and explosive money shots" are thus extended across serial time, as they are continually revisited and reconstructed over the course of a series (Dominguez 2015, 157).

Whereas *Serial* is motivated by the attempt to determine whether Adnan Syed is guilty or innocent, the tension of *The Jinx's* narrative, after its initial episode, turns on the question of whether Jarecki can get Durst to admit to murder. Its "gotcha" narrative thrust (Greene 2016) is parceled out over six chapters, of varying lengths, from forty-three minutes to fifty-one minutes long. Viewers are constantly being primed for "money shot" moments through the parceling out of "narrative information in urgent, often melodramatic units that more overtly grab attention" (Williams 2014, 51). As Dominguez concludes of the affective use made of money shots in reality TV: "In this way, viewers are constantly engaged in a potentially never-ending loop of emotions, and consequent interpretations, creating a ratings economy out of an affective one" (2015, 157).

While *The Jinx* moves back and forth between different time lines, the central anchor or through line for viewers is the affective purchase of Jarecki's formal "present-day" interview with Bob Durst. This interview is stretched out and extended across the entirety of the first five chapters of the series. It is significant that the long duration of this interview is presented to viewers in a series of short, sharp, and often melodramatic vignettes (instead of, for example, all at once, in a two-hour-long interview). The presentation of the interview as a series of tonally mixed tableaus, which are sometimes blackly humorous, sometimes thrilling, and sometimes something more sinister, are designed, above all, to maximize the affective experience of watching Bob Durst and his reactions. The interview is thus both extended over the long duration of the series, and yet at the same time chopped up and truncated and presented as a series of set pieces and "money shot" moments of affective reaction that are placed at strategic microtemporal intervals in the narrative.

The call for viewer deliberation and "detection" in *The Jinx* leads not to critical analysis but to a desire for more and more "affective intensity" (Paasonen 2015, 30). Paasonen has discussed how the desire for affective "jolts" and "grabs" is part of networked media, and is what drives user movement "across networks, sites, files, and discussion threads" (30). The success of *The Jinx* and other recent long-form true crime TV docuseries derives from this yearning for affective thrills and speaks to the "interdependence of television and Internet platforms in the new media era" (Grindstaff and Murray 2015, 123). Designed to feed into the affective loops of network culture, *The Jinx* promotes a mode of viewing that is deeply invested in the "rhythm of online exchange and social media use, of constant clicks and shifts from one page, site, video, and image to another, of refreshes and perpetual searches for new documents, images and affective intensities" (Paasonen 2015, 40).

Within its binge-watching economy of cold opens and cliffhangers, the dead female body figures prominently as an affective suturing device. Of the three murder victims in *The Jinx* (one male, two female), one is notably foregrounded above the others for dramatic binge viewing affect/effect: Kathie Durst, Bob Durst's first wife, whose body has never been recovered. A twenty-nine-year-old medical student at the time of her disappearance, Kathie is resurrected for viewers of *The Jinx* through the reenactments staged in the series, through the reading of extracts from her diary, and through the inclusion of numerous family photos. She is described in the synopsis for chapter 2 as a "beautiful girl from a modest background," and Kathie's disappearance and probable murder is central to the show's serialized affective "beats" and rhythms.

Joanne Clarke Dillman writes that in contemporary TV crime thrillers, "a dead beginning—when a dead woman's body is the inciting incident of an episode" (2014, 88) is commonplace. The dead woman "stimulates the interrogatory, seducing the viewer to ask who killed her, how, and why" (84). Dillman is speaking of episodic network television shows such as *CSI* where the "solution" comes about by the end of the episode. Similarly, popular true crime television shows such as *48 Hours Mystery* (CBS, 1988–) include some emotional twists and turns before the murder is "usually solved by the end of the hour" (Murley 2008, 127).

With the postnetwork advent of the long-form true crime series, however, the moment of closure or resolution is extended and prolonged across several episodes or chapters, and a different kind of viewing rhythm is therefore established. While there is little doubt presented in *The Jinx* regarding who killed Kathie Durst, she is nonetheless deployed as an "inciting" object throughout the series. The mystery of what happened to her body is extended across several episodes to produce a strong epistephilic desire (to know more) in viewers and to defer our "affective investment across time" (Dominguez 2015, 162). Kathie Durst is the white female victim (WFV) who functions as what Barbara Klinger (2018a) calls a "gateway body." As Klinger argues, for long-form serial crime TV, which "must be choreographed over hours of episodes," the WFV serves as a "driving force over instalments," a means of both capturing and sustaining attention through the "code's suspenseful tactics of delay and disclosure" (2018a, 8–9).

The fact that her body was never found only makes Kathie Durst a more enticing figure within the show's suspenseful, affects-driven narrative economy. *The Jinx's* deployment of the figure of Kathie Durst relates to the wider media involvement in stories of female disappearance, in which, as Dillman argues, there is a "sense that the media participates in an elaborate form of communal denial, alerting us to the latest woman's disappearance and enjoining members of the community and all within their audience to 'help' in the search, as if this will change the outcome of events" (2014, 134). The serialized format employed by *The Jinx* deliberately suspends—and extends—the broader cultural dynamics of the missing woman narrative in order to encourage viewers to stay locked into its binge-able flow. That is, it maintains "the fiction of the present tense" regarding the mystery of the woman's disappearance for as long as it can in order to suture viewers into the "page-turning" rhythm of its "chapters" (Jenner 2017, 314).

It is instructive to compare the narrative depiction of Kathie Durst to that of Susan Berman, the third murder victim featured in *The Jinx*, who was fifty-five years old at the time of her death in 2000. The death of Berman is reenacted many times in *The Jinx*, and critics have referred to the repeated reenactments of her execution-style murder through a bullet in the back of the head as both aestheticized and "lurid." There is an attempt in *The Jinx* to resurrect Susan's life through the inclusion of family photos and through a brief segment about her life as a middle-aged stepmother in chapter 3, "The Gangster's Daughter," but it is nowhere near on the same scale as the revivification of the young, beautiful, and "lost" Kathie Durst. Tellingly, there is only one shot of Berman in the opening credit sequence of *The Jinx*—from behind, of her being shot and falling to her death. By contrast, images of a young and beaming Kathie abound in the credit sequence, as the newspaper headlines,

"Vanishes: Search for Beautiful Wife" and "Mystery of Missing Beauty," flash across the screen. In its repeated repurposing of visual imagery of Kathie Durst, *The Jinx* plays upon the cultural predominance of the "missing woman narrative," which "requires the woman be young, white and photogenic" (Dillman 2014, 131).

In strikingly similar fashion to *Serial*, the diary segments found in the second chapter of *The Jinx*, "Poor Little Rich Boy," recount the initial heady stages of heterosexual love, through to the eventual deterioration of the relationship and the escalation of domestic violence. Where *Serial* raises a question mark over whether Adnan was a controlling and abusive boyfriend, *The Jinx* makes strong assertions about Bob Durst's abusive behavior. Kathie's diary extracts are voiced over by the actress Chelsea Gonzalez, who also plays her in the reenactments: "Spring of '79: we returned from a party, both drunk, we argued and he slapped me." This entry from Kathie's diary is reinforced visually with a reconstruction of Durst slapping her. *The Jinx* includes such images not only as visual corroboration of domestic violence but, rather, and more significantly, as a means of affectively heightening the viewer's experience of perusing Bob Durst's face for signs of guilt. Thus, when Jarecki quotes Kathie's diary to Bob in his interview, and asks if he remembers hitting her, an imagined reconstruction of the violence is pointedly provided for viewers. This reconstructed scene of violence appears just before the inclusion of a tight reaction "money shot" of Bob's face as he denies remembering the "first time he slapped her or hit her." The response called for here from viewers is a purely affective one: the thrill comes from us knowing the "truth" of Bob's violence, and having the sensation of being involved in catching him out in a lie. This scenario, in which the viewer is encouraged to become involved in catching out the "real" Bob Durst, is the driving motivation of the series and is central to its production of affect.

Similarly, in a crime scene reconstruction, also in chapter 2, viewers are presented with an (imagined) scenario in which the dead body of Kathie Durst, wearing a white winter coat, lies facedown on the living room floor in the home she shared with Durst, blood seeping out of her head. This is immediately followed by Jarecki's most direct interrogation of Durst in the documentary: "Did you have anything to do with the death of your wife?" The camera moves in on a tight "money shot" close-up of Durst's face as he responds with: "I don't know that she's dead." Here, then, an image of Kathie's dead body is presented to viewers in order to heighten the affective impact of the close-up of Bob's face, which viewers are invited to scrutinize "for the smallest twitch, shift of glance, tightening of the mouth" (Clover 2000b, 106). That viewers have just been provided with an image of Kathie Durst's dead body—reconstructed or not—lends an embodied frisson to Bob's denial of her death.

While *The Jinx* shows images of domestic violence through its reconstructions, it never actually *explores* the issue, as sharply demonstrated in an interview with one of Kathie's female friends, when viewers hear Jarecki ask (off camera): "Why didn't she leave?" After a pause, her friend responds, "I don't know. I think she was afraid of him." After Jarecki's uninformed and naïve question regarding why the abused woman might have stayed, the issue of abuse is totally abandoned by the docuseries; as with *Serial*, *The Jinx* does not supply any wider context for understanding the dynamics of domestic violence. Instead, viewers are firmly funneled forward, to the next "chapter," in pursuit of more affective thrills.

Notwithstanding the reconstructed image of her dead body and the "tonally ambiguous" finale where Durst appears to confess to all three murders, *The Jinx* is never able to supply viewers with the official answer to what actually happened to Kathie Durst. What it does offer is a multitude of photos of Kathie for viewers to "mull over" throughout the series. In chapter 5 the attempt to resurrect Kathie as a "lost object" is taken considerably further, culminating in the dramatic appearance of her lookalike niece, Elizabeth McCormack. Born six days after her aunt's disappearance, the niece is now a young woman, who appears (at the time of the filming of the documentary) to be the same age as Kathie Durst when she went missing. The niece is visually presented as angelic, and is wearing a demure white blouse. In an interview, Jarecki shows the niece photos of her aunt Kathie in order to record her reaction: "This could be me, that's incredible. It's chilling for me," she responds. Plaintive nondiegetic music (which is always used in the segments discussing the loss of Kathie) plays as a photo of Kathie Durst is shown to viewers in order to demonstrate the striking resemblance between the two women. Of her aunt Kathie's disappearance, the niece states: "I wish I could say it brought everyone closer but I don't think that would be the truth . . . because there was no closure . . . everything was so shrouded in mystery, there was so much anger and no opportunity to truly grieve."

The melodramatic use made of the niece, who is withheld as a "surprise" from viewers until the penultimate episode (in contrast to all of the other interviewees, whom we see throughout the series), can be understood as an attempt to fulfill a more widespread "wish" in popular culture for the dead woman to have "afterlife agency." Though Kathie Durst is acknowledged as dead, she is shown to "live on" in the figure of the niece, who "channels" her, and is seen to "sustain [her] presence among us . . . metaphorically reanimating [her] in spite of [her] absence" (Dillman 2014, 128). In an interview, Jarecki has said that "the big thing for the audience of 'The Jinx,' I think, is seeing Kathie's niece who looks so much like her and tells how this family has been torn asunder. Getting closure for that family was one of the things that drove us through getting this done" (quoted in O'Connell 2015). Whatever role the family may have played in motivating Jarecki and his production crew, the McCormack family does indeed play a crucial role for the documentary in terms of rhetorically securing a sense of closure for viewers. These interviews with the family, and in particular the lookalike niece, prime the audience for the excitement of the final episode, and heighten the cathartic satisfaction and enjoyment that we take from Durst finally being caught out.

The central contradiction of *The Jinx*, and one it never entirely manages to conceal, despite a shift in "narrative style" in the final episode, when there is an emphasis on Jarecki's attempt to "get justice" (Case Punnett 2018, 71–72), is its celebrification of Durst, and the fact that it turns an alleged murderer into a hugely entertaining public figure for viewer consumption. Although *The Jinx* takes critical aim at the jury that acquitted Durst of Morris Black's murder and dismemberment in Texas, largely on the grounds that they found him a funny and entertaining figure, the series is ultimately guilty of using the very same strategy as the Galveston defense team: it presents Bob Durst as an entertaining, often comical, figure to viewers throughout the series. Laughter is invited in *The Jinx* through the "establishment of a comic modality," which, as Geoff King suggests, "permit(s) the viewer to remain detached, to enjoy the spectacle of violent antics without any feeling of implication, of having to 'care' very much about the consequences" (2004, 130).

As I have suggested, the contemporary serialized true crime format is one where there is a continual interpellation of the viewer into sensational "money shot" displays of affective response and reaction. To this end, *The Jinx* is far more concerned with producing sensational visual *displays* of affect and reaction to "new" evidence than it is with any rational analysis of that evidence. There are many moments during *The Jinx* where "we are spectators of spectators, responding to other people's responses to yet another piece of mediated reality" (Middleton 2014, 113). Most notably, perhaps, the cold open of the final episode begins with the pointed deployment of "surrogate characters" that serve as stand-ins for the audience, as we watch them react to the "new" evidence unearthed by Jarecki and his producers. It is a highly self-conscious and mediated way to begin the finale, and to pick up on the emergence of the thrilling evidence introduced by the cliffhanger of the previous episode, but it sharply illustrates the premium the show places on the physical embodiment of emotion and reaction. The final "hook" of the cold open is when Jarecki shows former Westchester District Attorney Jeanine Pirro the discovery of the envelope from Bob Durst that matches the handwriting from the note sent to police by the killer of Susan Berman. Her dramatic reaction: "Son of a bitch!" cues the opening credit sequence and readies viewers for the show's ultimate money shot ending, where Jarecki and his film crew capture "Bob reacting clean" to the "new" evidence. Durst's reaction provides the most sensational image of embodiment of the entire series, when he begins to burp uncontrollably.

The extent to which viewers are affectively bound to *The Jinx* through their own visceral responses is sharply indicated by the nature of the Twitter feeds dedicated to the show. As Casey McCormick has argued, long-form serials such as *House of Cards* are "social media event(s)" as much as they are "TV shows" (2016, 112). There is a strong "communal element" to binge-viewing, and, as McCormick importantly reminds us, "social media dialogue is not only about what's happening in the narrative but is about what is happening to *us* (physically and emotionally) as we binge the narrative" (112). As confirmation of this observation, it is interesting to note that by far the most dominant Twitter threads on *The Jinx* (apart from those concerning the finale) detail the affective reactions of viewers to Bob Durst's eyes. These remarks strongly echo the YouTube comments on Amanda Knox's eyes, as discussed in the previous chapter, and illustrate how the affective circuits of true crime shows extend to social media networks, where viewers deliberate over, and revel in, their responses to criminal subjects. As one individual tweeted: "Irrelevant tweet timing here but I'd say the biggest sign of Robert Durst's guilt is probably the gaping black death holes he has for eyes?" Other tweets on the subject include:

"I'm no legal expert but Robert Durst's pupils are the same colours as his irises and his eyes look like slick petrol. Horrifying. #TheJinx"; "The verdict is in: Robert Durst's eyes are really a window to his diabolically evil soul. #TheJinx-HBO"; "did the jury not see Robert Durst's creepy dead shark eyes before they found him not guilty, that should have been Exhibit A at his trial"; and "utterly addicted to The Jinx but Bob Durst's black eyes gave me nightmares last night! #TheJinx." Some viewers even pointed out the parallels between *Serial* and *The Jinx*, "Between Adnan's dairy cow eyes and Bob Durst's creepy rodent eyes, I would say the first thing I look for in a man is his smile."[9] In the thousands of tweets on Bob Durst's eyes, viewers are affectively bonding over their shared response to Durst's appearance and the effect/affect that watching the show has on them. These tweets, in other words, are not discussing the vagaries of evidence or worrying about questions of social justice and violence against women. Kathie McCormick and her family are notably not of interest here: it is Bob Durst's eyes that captivate and enthrall.

Hooks and Hypodermic Needles: *Making a Murderer*

The ten-episode-long *Making a Murderer*, promoted by Netflix as a "real life thriller,"[10] is arguably the most grueling of the true crime shows I discuss in this chapter. Whereas both *Serial* and *The Jinx* operate in a "performative mode" of documentary filmmaking (Bruzzi 2006), with Koenig and Jarecki providing a stable, guiding presence for viewers, *Making a Murderer* is filmed in a more traditional observational style, and directors Demos and Riccardi do not appear on camera. What is quite striking, then, is how this long-form true crime documentary about a miscarriage of justice in Wisconsin, USA, captured global audience attention in the way that it did: as a highly addictive, binge-able show. The question of its duration features prominently in both the critical and popular reception of the series. For some viewers, its long duration was a source of complaint: "I find watching it a long and drawn-out affair . . . I . . . dislike how the story is dragged out over several episodes. In my opinion, a maximum of two feature-length episodes would have sufficed," as one Netflix viewer notes.[11] And yet the fact that it was protracted over ten episodes of varying lengths, speeds, and intensities is fundamental to its success. People consumed it avidly—voraciously, in fact—and it was spoken of everywhere as an exemplary binge-watching text.

As with the *Making a Murderer* trailer discussed in the previous chapter, the primary response solicited by the long-form series is one of outrage at the terrible miscarriage of justice against Steven Avery and Brendan Dassey on the part of Manitowac County police and officials. In the wake of its full drop release, much was made in the media of the fact that hundreds of thousands of viewers shared and circulated a petition to then President Obama asking for Steven Avery and Brendan Dassey to be pardoned.[12] The question of a socially active response was also foregrounded by the media reception in more banal, if still revealing, ways. As noted in a headline to a *Daily Mirror* article: "Khloe Kardashian Left Outraged over *Making a Murderer* after Binge Watching Netflix Hit: How Do We Fix This?" (Merriman 2016). This tabloid headline makes plain the way in which the strong sense of outrage induced by *Making a Murderer* was held to be inseparable from the intense experience of binge-watching the series in a short space of time. The small print of the article goes on to detail how "the star spent the weekend getting obsessed with the hit show after being struck down by illness" and immediately began tweeting her concern (Merriman 2016). Celebrity Twittersphere did indeed play a major role in promoting *Making a Murderer*, and though the celebrity response to *Making a Murderer* is not my focus here, I will consider the significant role social media played in celebrifying Steven Avery's white male defense attorneys.

First, however, it is important to examine the nature of the "transaction with the viewer" (Poniewozik 2015) created by binge-watching, something that is explored in the reaction videos to *Making a Murderer* that have emerged on YouTube. One popular *Buzzfeed* video, "17 Thoughts You Had Watching Making a Murderer," which has garnered nearly a million views, pokes fun at the kinds of shared affective responses to the series.[13] The parodic two-minute video features a young white heterosexual couple watching *Making a Murderer* and sharing their experience of being locked into a binge-viewing relationship with it, not leaving the sofa and missing dinner engagements in order to keep watching. The couple share their reactions to the defense lawyers Jerome Buting and Dean Strang: "These guys are so smart"; "They're geniuses"; "Right? And they like look really nice"; "And they wanna help him!" They run through the gambit of emotions experienced while viewing all ten episodes of the series—including the moments of despair evoked in regard to Steven Avery's aging parents and his young nephew Brendan Dassey: "His family deserves a break at this point, right?" "He just wants to go home and watch Wrestle Mania." The video uses its comedic format to reveal how the range of strong emotions aroused by *Making a Murderer* propel the viewer to "play the next goddamn episode."

One of the dominant reactions dramatized throughout this mock reaction video is shock, as indicated through the repeated use of the phrase "are *you kidding* me?" This echoes the reaction to the trailer, but the point here is to show how that kind of shocked, amazed response is extended across the long duration of the series. When the couple finish watching *Making a Murderer* they are shown to be completely drained, and also curiously bereft; they discuss what they will do next ("go outside?"). Finally, they excitedly settle on the option of "rewatching *The Jinx*": "Let's just binge-watch." "It's only eight hours, six hours, we could do that tonight." "Let's do it." It's a conclusion that echoes the widespread circulation of true crime internet listicles that emerged in the wake of *Making a Murderer*. These listicles also imagine a bereft viewer who has finished listening to *Serial* or watching *The Jinx* and *Making a Murderer*, and provide that viewer with a list of *other* true crime programs to binge-watch in order to "Fill The True-Crime Shaped Hole in Your Life," as the title to one listicle put it. Based on what Sidneyeve Matrix elsewhere describes as "all-you-can-eat media models," such listicles as "Obsessed with Serial? You'll Love These Documentaries," "7 amazing true-crime documentaries to cure your 'Jinx' hangover," and "Making a Murderer: 9 similar Netflix shows every fan should watch," indicate a "regime of watching" (Hartley as quoted in Matrix 2014, 134) based on the language of addiction, with words such as "withdrawal" and "craving" continually used.

In the popular reception of *Making a Murderer* and the other true crime series discussed in this chapter, viewers are repeatedly described as "internet sleuths" or "desktop detectives," but they are also, at the same time, talked about as "obsessives" and "addicts." There is a notable tension in the cultural reception of long-form true crime, between the idea of the viewer as a hollow-eyed addict on the search for his or her next true crime "fix" and the notion of the viewer as an eagle-eyed juror-citizen "shaping the outcome" of criminal justice. It is a tension that is keenly captured in one of the epigraphs with which I opened this chapter, from a viewer of *Making a Murderer*: "I was addicted from the start and watched it all in one day. So heart-wrenching, it made me sob. Hope they do indeed continue to film Steven's fight for justice because I was gutted when I ran out of episodes—I'm already planning to re-watch it all over again."[14] In this comment, which is reminiscent of the kind of viewer response to *Dear Zachary* discussed in chapter 1, the emotional investment in true crime is intimately bound up with the activity of binge-watching. The desire to keep watching—to be pleasured by the text and the affective force of its revelations—is inseparable from any attempt to access the "truth" or "fight for justice." What is crucial to emphasize, therefore, is that the delivery mechanisms of these long-form true crime shows and the emotional responses to crime and criminality they encourage and produce are mutually constitutive.

The question of the affective or emotional labor we are being invited to perform in relation to *Making a Murderer* is one of the most compelling questions raised by its success. As illustrated by the *Buzzfeed* video, to "binge-watch" the ten episodes of *Making a Murderer*, which are of varying lengths from forty-seven minutes to just over an hour, is to experience a range of affects and emotions. The filmed interrogation scenes of Brendan Dassey, Avery's then sixteen-year-old nephew, for example, which are focused on in excruciating detail, are deeply agonizing to watch. They appear as painful examples of coerced false confession from a vulnerable minor as explored in other recent crime documentaries such as the *Paradise Lost* films (Berlinger and Sinofsky, 1996, 2000, 2011), *Scenes of a Crime* (Babcock/Hadaegh, US, 2011) and *The Central Park Five* (Burns, US, 2012). When *Making a Murderer* moves on to Steven Avery's trial, and the two charming defense attorneys, Dean Strang and Jerome Buting, it therefore comes as a satisfying relief.

Episode 4, "Indefensible," is the episode in which the teenaged Brendan Dassey, who has learning disabilities, is interrogated by police and coerced into a false confession. It is one of the most punishing and difficult to watch episodes of the entire series, yet it is referred to time and again in user reviews as a turning point, the moment when viewers were well and truly "hooked" or ensnared by the show. According to Netflix data, it is rarely the first episode (what used to be called the pilot) that gets viewers hooked. On its Media Center site, Netflix describes its ongoing research into what it calls "hooked episodes" in the following terms: "The world's leading Internet TV network expanded last year's research to look at more than 30 additional series on a global scale (viewing spanned six continents) to pinpoint the episode that took watchers from casual to committed—that is, the episode that kept 70% of viewers watching through a first season's end" ("You're Still Hooked"

Fig 4.3. Jerry's excited cliffhanger phone call to Dean at the end of episode 4

2016). Netflix confirms that "episode 4 (Brendan Dassey is interrogated)" is the "hooked episode" of *Making a Murderer*, the one where casual viewers become committed ones (ibid.).

Given its successful capture of Netflix's most highly prized commodity—audience attention—it is important to consider the emotional experience produced by episode 4 over the course of its sixty-six minutes. As already noted, the scenes involving Brendan Dassey's interrogation are painful and also enraging: they serve as anxiety-inducing examples of the dysfunctional workings of the justice system and its mistreatment of the vulnerable. But what is most significant about episode 4 is how it rewards viewers who are able to sit through these seemingly interminable, "unwatchable" interrogation scenes. For the 70 percent or more that make it through those scenes, the final minutes of the episode conclude with a thrilling sequence in which defense attorney Jerry Buting details the apparent corruption in the Manitowac County police department before dramatically uncovering a crucial piece of forensic evidence in the form of a tampered-with blood vial. In keeping with the recent true crime emphasis on sensational "money shot" reactions as noted in relation to *The Jinx*, it is telling that this sequence is mediated through Jerry's animated response. The sequence is constructed through rapid crosscutting between Jerry's excited phone call to colleague Dean Strang to tell him about the discovery, and shaky handheld camera footage of the

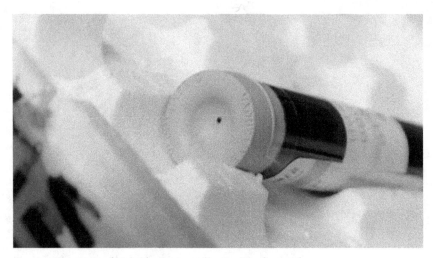

Fig 4.4. Close-up of hypodermic needle at end of episode 4

evidence box and the pinprick hole at the top of the blood vial. As one red-ditor notes, it is clearly presented as a "major Perry Mason moment,"[15] with Jerry's barely contained excitement—"Let me tell you this is a red-letter day for the defense!"—positioning the viewer squarely on the side of the heroic defense team. Jerry's words during the phone call voice-over the images of the allegedly tampered-with evidence box and the discovery of a tiny hole, the size of a "hypodermic needle," as he gleefully declares to Dean (and by extension, the viewer): "Have you fallen on the floor yet, or no? Think about it Dean . . . if Lab Core didn't stick the needle through the top then who did? . . . Game on, game on!"

The reference to a "hypodermic needle" could scarcely be more fitting as a metaphor for how the audience is positioned—or "set up"—by the true crime format here. I would suggest—and Netflix statistics would appear to back up—that this pivotal moment in the series is a perfect demonstration of what is known as the "hypodermic needle theory" of communication, which holds that the mass media influences audiences "directly and uniformly by 'shooting' or 'injecting' them with appropriate messages designed to trigger a desired response" ("Hypodermic" n.d.). While the hypodermic needle theory of media communication has been roundly criticized and problematized for an oversimplification of the relationship between text and audience, it takes on renewed significance for thinking about how binge-able true crime produces such "big data" moments of predictive audience responses and behaviors. As big data theorists Ganaele Langlois, Joanna Redden, and Greg Elmer suggest, "social media corporations are not simply in the business of reflecting on and facilitating the social: they make it possible to orient social processes and feelings, and to modulate responses to social stimuli" (2015, 4). This comment also applies to a corporation such as Netflix: its audience data mining, algorithms, and research on "hooking" is designed to predict—and to shape—a set of very specific affective responses from audiences as part of its commercial enterprise. The question then becomes: where do these engineered affective responses go? If, as I am arguing, critical reflection is discouraged by these true crime shows, what kind of viewer engagement with its serial experience does *Making a Murderer* produce? To answer this question, it is necessary to further consider the role of the heroic defense attorneys, Jerry Buting and Dean Strang.

While the series was not often discussed by the media in terms of race, it is deeply significant that the most talked about twenty-first-century mainstream true crime series to date should center so emphatically on white people—impoverished white people who are disenfranchised and victimized by the system—as well as the good middle-class white people who help them. This is especially meaningful given the fact that *Making a Murderer* emerged in a cultural moment where, as discussed earlier in this book, violence against black bodies was more visible than ever before, with the widespread circulation of online citizen videos of police brutality.[16] I contend that part of what makes *Making a Murderer* so appealing is that it provides a white, middle-class audience with the opportunity to cast themselves in the role of good white citizens. Though it was released before Trump's presidency, and was ten years in the making, *Making a Murderer* holds striking resonance for a post-Trump era in so far as it speaks to a sense of white disgruntlement and alienation at the same time as it tries to ameliorate it. The corrupt Manitowac police and prosecutors are revealed as "bad" whites that are shown to be ignorant and immoral. Jerry Buting and Dean Strang are the "good" middle-class whites of the documentary, our idealized guides to morality and social justice.

Episode 8, "The Great Burden," includes an image of Jerry Buting and Dean Strang on their laptops perusing the social media responses to their trial performances and media appearances. It is a "meta" moment that gestures toward the kind of fandom that greeted Buting and Strang, or Jerry and Dean, as some fans prefer to call them, after the success of *Making a Murderer*. The pair emerged as internet heartthrobs; *Elle* fashion magazine, for example, whose demographic is women aged eighteen to forty-nine, devoted a spread to Dean Strang titled: "Deconstructing Your Sexual Attraction to Dean Strang in 13 Steps." Fans of Dean Strang became known as "strangers": "For a while I thirsted in shameful solitude, until the Internet showed me I was not alone. I am just one of many #strangers." There was an outpouring of affection for the two middle-aged lawyers on Twitter, where "I love Jerry Buting and Dean Strang" tweets proliferated. Indicative examples include: "Do hero lawyers Dean Strang and Jerome Buting realize all the fan girls they have on Twitter? #makingamurderer" and "I want a Jerry Buting in the streets and a Dean Strang in the sheets ;) #makingamurderer." There was also a Tumblr page devoted to the "early to mid-2000s normcore style of Dean Strang."[17] The page waxed lyrical over Strang's sartorial choices from his "dad jeans" and jumpers to his argyle socks. A Google search of Dean Strang in February 2016 was also illuminating. When I typed in "Dean Strang is" on the Google search engine, this is what appeared: "Dean Strang is awesome"—"Dean Strang is he married?" Numerous GIFS and memes circulated of Dean and Jerry's wise and noble speeches about the law and social justice. "Jerry Buting in the streets, Dean Strang in the sheets" T-shirts and other items of merchandise were sold. Finally, following the success of *Making a Murderer,* Buting and Strang went on a sold-out North American and European tour called "A Conversation on Justice," in which they spoke of their experiences working the Avery trial to a rapturous reception from audiences.

This kind of celebrification of white male law officials is a significant feature of the contemporary true crime entertainment phenomenon. Recently, Paul Holes, the fifty-year-old police detective credited with finally catching the "Golden State Killer" after twenty-four years of investigation has become a fully fledged internet sex symbol. The hashtag #hotforholes has gone viral, there is an ever-expanding "Hot for Holes/Holerinos Facebook group (a subset of the now archived My Favourite Murder "Murderinos" Facebook group), and the podcast *My Favorite Murder*, which played a key role in spreading the internet fandom of Holes, has devoted an episode to celebrating him as a new kind of "superhero" (episode 122, "Surprise! It's Paul Holes").

In a news article on how Holes has "become an unlikely internet obsession for thousands of mostly-female true crime fans," female fans are quoted explaining their admiration for the middle-aged detective: "Literally, he's like

Murderer's Dean Strang in 13 Steps

Defender of justice, keeper of my heart.

BY DIANA BRUK   JAN 5, 2016   26K   f   ⌑   ✉

Fig 4.5. The celebrification of Dean Strang and Jerome Buting in *Elle* magazine

a detective out of central casting to me," said fan Teri Smith, fifty, of Utah. "If you were putting an ad in *Variety* for open casting, he would be who you pick out for smooth, handsome, unflappable detective" (quoted in Chabria 2018). Although, as already noted, contemporary true crime is often considered to be more critical of law enforcement than previous predigital iterations, the internet adoration for the white male police officers and lawyers from these true crime shows suggests a more conservative impulse may underlie the recent cultural elevation of the genre. Indeed, in the *My Favorite Murder* podcast on Holes, the valorization of the heroic individual law enforcement figure is seen to harken back to an earlier age: Holes is likened to a digital-era Jack Webb— the central character of *Dragnet* (NBC, 1951–59, 1967–70), a crime series that famously shored up public belief and trust in the police (Jenner 2016, 76–79; Mittell 2004, 121–52). This cult of the (white) (male) *individual* would seem to be in tension with Demos and Riccardi's stated aim of wanting people to come away from their long-form series being critical of the criminal justice system as a *system* (Smith 2016).

It is important to also note here that the fandom surrounding Buting and Strang goes hand in hand with the widespread vilification of prosecuting attorney Ken Kratz and defense attorney Len Kachinsky (who represented Brendan Dassey before being removed from the case), both of whom were inundated with messages of hate after the series' release. Ken Kratz has been described as "Twitter's Most Hated Man," and online click bait articles include lists of the "50 Best Ken Kratz Mean Tweets," which include: "in a documentary about a 'murderer' the scariest thing shouldn't be the prosecutor's creepy feminine voice" #kenkratz #makingamurderer (Emerson 2016). In addition, viewers of *Making a Murderer* flooded the Yelp business pages of Kratz and Kachinsky with bad reviews, saying they shouldn't be allowed to practice law anymore (Loughrey 2015).

Kratz (unsurprisingly) has come out in strong protest against *Making a Murderer*, accusing it of a biased approach and suggesting that it leaves out key prosecutorial evidence: "This is not a documentary. It's a . . . defense advocacy piece. . . . Their bias . . . what they spoon feed the viewers, what they pick and choose by way of facts . . . causes only one reaction: that Mr. Avery was innocent" (quoted in Egan 2016). In response, *Making a Murderer*'s directors, Moira Demos and Laura Ricciardi, stated that it was impossible for them to include all of the evidence: "That's called a trial. What we made was a documentary" (quoted in Egan 2016). But despite Demos and Ricciardi's claims to the contrary, scholars such as Carol Clover, Jennifer Mnookin, and Kristen Fuhs have pointed to the strong "structural affinity between trials and documentaries" (Mnookin 2005, 158). In terms of user participation, the digital-era privileging of interaction greatly heightens the sense of a documentary as a "trial." The long-form digital streaming text extends the transmedia appeal of the documentary true crime format, as viewers feel involved in a "collective criminal investigation" (Little 2015) and are compelled to dispense "justice" in an internet "trial" of public opinion.

The affective responses to "Jerry and Dean" and "Ken and Len" emerge out of the adversarial US justice system and its "point and counterpoint" structure (Fuhs 2014, 787), but they also strongly feed into the post-truth culture of "liking" and "disliking" in the age of social media networks, as discussed throughout this book. Such affective networks are constructing new frameworks for responding to real-crime stories and, as Jennifer Petersen has argued elsewhere, the pressing issue is what such "public displays of affect" enable—or disable—as the case may be (2011, 165). One of the things that most noticeably goes missing in the effusive displays of emotional response—both positive and negative—toward the central white male figures in *Making a Murderer* is the dead female victim.

As with the other long-form true crime texts discussed in this chapter, but in a much starker fashion, the female murder victim is a spectral presence in *Making a Murderer*. The only access viewers have to any sense of Teresa Halbach as a person is from the inclusion of a video diary, which appears at two strategic moments in the series. The first inclusion of the video diary is in the cold open to episode 2, "Turning the Tables." The episode begins with an audio recording of Halbach leaving a voice message for Steven Avery, followed by a first-person reconstruction from inside a vehicle as the docuseries recreates the drive she would have taken to Avery's Salvage Yard on the day she went missing. We are then shown a video diary segment, in which Halbach speaks directly to the camera: "So let's say I die before I'm thirty-one. Or let's say I die tomorrow. I don't think I will—I think I have a lot more to do. I just want to know whenever I do die, I just want people I love to know whenever I die, that I was happy. That I was happy with what I did with my life." This video footage is strangely decontextualized. The only bit of orienting information provided is a printed message identifying the woman in the video as "Teresa Halbach" and locating the time of the video as "three years earlier." The video is used to cue the opening credit sequence and is then completely abandoned as the show resumes its extraordinarily detailed account of the wrongdoings of the justice system and legal processes. *Making a Murderer* never tells us where this video diary comes from or why it might be significant; it operates primarily as a sensational means of piquing viewers' curiosity and suturing them into the flow of the episode and the series. The imagery of Halbach here functions as an example of Klinger's "gateway body," in which "the white female victim's body, often presented through abject imagery, as both attention grabber and holder" serves as "an audio-visual, narrative, and generic *apparatus of capture*" (2018a, 7).

It is important to consider what the deployment of the video in the extended narrative of *Making a Murderer* has to tell us about the problematic gender dynamics of this immersive true crime series. The video diary can be read in the context of other "haunting" video footage that circulates through the internet, of dead women who have fallen victim to violent crimes. As Janine Mary Little writes of the much-watched CCTV footage of Jill Meagher, an Australian woman who was murdered in 2012: she "appears *like* a ghost" because of viewer's knowledge of her rape and murder (2015, 402, her emphasis). Part of the "phenomenal pulling power" (401) of such videos, which are often exhibited on YouTube, is that they show us women who are about to die and who, at the time of watching, are already dead.

There is a similar ghostly, morbid quality to Halbach's video diary, another excerpt of which is shown in the penultimate episode of *Making a Murderer*, "A Lack of Humility." This time, the video appears in the context of the courtroom, at Steven Avery's sentencing hearing, which is presented at the end of the episode. Played for the courtroom on a big screen, the video shows Teresa Halbach speaking to camera about how she loves "hugs and making people laugh." She states: "I love my sisters, my mum, my whole family of course. I don't hate anyone. I love a lot of people. I feel loved." When the video ends, Teresa's younger brother, Mike Halbach, makes a victim statement. While the context in which the video was made—for a school project—was apparently acknowledged in the courtroom, the documentary never specifies its origin or meaning.

The video diary, which presents a decontextualized, idealized depiction of the dead woman, needs to be read in relation to the documentary's inclusion of the sensational press conference led by Ken Kratz, which details a lurid account of Teresa Halbach's death. *Making a Murder* takes advantage of the serial form to include footage of this press conference *twice*—in episode 3 and in episode 6, when it is replayed as the cold open to the episode. Kratz begins his highly performative, dramatic recounting of the crime, culled from various segments of Brendan Dassey's coerced confessions, with a warning that no one under the age of fifteen should be watching. The press conference is indeed extremely graphic and recounts in excessive, grotesque detail the harm that was done to Halbach's body as she was raped and murdered. As Dean Strang notes in his closing arguments: the press conference was a "horror story . . . It was a fable, an ugly, horrific fable but a fable all the same, belied by the physical evidence."

While the docuseries is critical of Kratz's horror show press conference,[18] it is significant that during its earlier inclusion in episode 3, the documentary goes beyond mere observation of Kratz's prosecutorial recounting, with first-person camera footage that takes viewers down the corridor of Avery's trailer into the bedroom where the crime allegedly occurred. This may be done to counteract the notion of the grotesque bloodbath generated by Kratz's lurid descriptions of the crime (we see an untidy room with clothes strewn everywhere rather than a killing chamber), but it also evokes a kind "of horror film lexicon of camera movement," (Biressi 2001, 405), which encourages viewers to imagine the unimaginable horrors done to the woman. Innocent or defiled: this is the binary opposition through which "lost girls" are so often presented in popular culture.[19]

While the gender politics of true crime have long been problematic, with the genre keeping "most of its victims unknown and unnarrated" (Murley 2008, 136), the serialization of the story through Netflix's binge-able format brings true crime's affective dynamics into sharp relief. *Making a Murderer* is interesting for how it provides viewers with a very intensive and detailed account of the processes of the justice system over the course of a number of episodes of varying lengths and emotional intensities. However, in the final analysis, this buildup of information over episodes does not automatically lead to greater critical thinking. Instead, the appeal is more profoundly emotional: we are invited to respond to a cast of predominantly white male characters based on their "likeability (or lack thereof) . . . as cultural heroes or villains" (Konkle 2018).

While it may be an overstatement to assert that "cold-blooded killers are using Netflix to scam their way out of jail," as American legal commentator, TV presenter, and victim rights advocate Nancy Grace claimed in a thundering denouncement of "that Netflix documentary," as she refers to *Making a Murderer*,[20] there are nonetheless important discussions to be had about the affective imbrication of TV, social media, crime, and the law that is currently happening. The engine of the contemporary true crime format is propelled by what Christoph Lindner calls the "serial drive," which has newfound importance and dominance in a digital culture "where traditional and (often technological) boundaries between media are rapidly changing and, in some cases, even dissolving" (2014, x).

True crime lends itself to the cultural obsession with binge-watching through its stock conventions, including "the creation of mystery, drama and suspense and . . . such techniques as withholding information and rearranging the structure of events to fit a recognized pattern" (Murley 2008, 146–47). As I have shown, the long-form rhythm of these true crime series is actually very dependent upon the "short" beats of its spectacular vignettes, the modus operandi of which is to constantly "grab" viewer attention, whether through a video-game logic, through "money shots," or through "hooking." Building on the wider drive of media networks to create opportunities for constant stimulation, docuseries such as *Serial, The Jinx,* and *Making a Murderer* are part of a culture of compulsive communication, in which critical reflection is often submerged beneath the "injunction to get connected and participate" (Jodi Dean as quoted in Wolters, 2013).

"The Case Isn't Over": *Making a Murderer Part 2*

On October 19, 2018, Netflix dropped the ten-episode-long *Making a Murderer Part 2,* which explores the postconviction process for Steven Avery and Brendan Dassey: "The case isn't over. Making a Murder Part 2. Now streaming, only on @netflix," ran the tagline on Twitter. While the first series was filmed by Demos and Ricciardi over the course of a ten-year period, and was begun in a time before the widespread use of social media (and before Netflix started streaming its own original content), *Making a Murderer Part 2* is very clearly—and overtly—part of a fully fledged social media network culture. If Demos and Ricciardi could, in 2015 and 2016, express some surprise at how *Making a Murderer Part 1* was taken up as a cause by people on the internet,[21] there can be no such astonishment with the second series. Indeed, the meta-opening of *Making a Murderer Part 2* illustrates how the first Netflix series exploded on Twitter, igniting widespread social uproar, turning lawyers Dean Strang and Jerry Buting into "rock stars," and drawing the attention of celebrities ("celebrities have been tweeting like crazy," as one broadcaster is shown saying). Later in the series, we hear a media outlet describe Steven Avery as "the star of the Netflix documentary," and we meet a new character, a woman named Lynn Hartman, who becomes engaged to Steven after writing letters to him in prison. In a statement that crystallizes the extent to which the Steven Avery case is now mediated through the Netflix machine, Hartman states to the camera: "I knew that if there was another series of the documentary that I was going to be in it as Steven's girlfriend."

Just as the *Paradise Lost* trilogy of documentaries on the case of the West Memphis Three became "instrumental in shaping its legal developments" and "in shifting and revising assertions of guilt and culpability" (Watson 2014, 202), so, too, the *Making a Murderer* documentaries are now irrefutably a major part of the criminal case(s) they are documenting. "Don't let Netflix tell you what to think!" screams one angry man as he heckles protestors against Manitowac County in scenes included in the pre–credit sequence of *Making a Murderer Part 2*. "We want justice! We want justice!" the protestors cry as Part 2's revamped title sequence begins, and it is this quest for justice, and the outrage over the workings of the American criminal justice system, that continues to be the driving impetus behind the second series.

One of the most notable differences from the first series to the second is just how prominently new media technologies and social media networks figure throughout *Part 2*, with the Avery and Dassey families routinely pictured with their smartphones, regularly checking Facebook updates and counting the number of "likes" on posts that update their followers about Steven's and Brandon's attempt to get their convictions overturned. "Two hundred forty-two likes!" Brendan's mom, Barb, exclaims of a social media post about going to visit her son in prison. "I can't wait to tell him (Steven) how many comments there are!" remarks Sandy Greenman, Steven's ex-girlfriend and longtime advocate, of another post.

In the second series, Demos and Ricciardi address much of the criticism directed against the first, including that which I have discussed in this chapter: the elision of Teresa Halbach from the story. They interview some of Halbach's friends and, through montage sequences of photos, home videos, archive footage, and interviews, make an attempt to give more of a sense of what the loss of her life meant to her grieving friends and family (although her family still declines to be interviewed). To a large extent, however, I would argue that these sequences are tokenistic gestures: as one of Teresa's friends states at one point, the fact remains that she is gone and there's nothing to be done about that. Acknowledging this bare fact, and suggesting that Teresa Halbach's memory would best be served by uncovering the real killer, the affective energies of the second series are largely given over to further fomenting the social outrage initiated by *Making a Murderer Part 1*. The figure of the lawyer again plays a central role in stirring up this outrage, and in a new twist, explicitly utilizes the tools of social media to do so.

One of the most interesting developments is that the "stars" of the first series—Dean Strang and Jerry Buting—have now been dethroned, and a new star has emerged: Kathleen Zellner, described by Netflix as the "powerhouse lawyer" who takes on Steven Avery's postconviction case. Demos and Ricciardi give Strang and Buting the chance to respond to claims (voiced by Zellner) that their defense was not up to par, but these moments are lackluster and it is striking the extent to which the docuseries has moved on and detached itself from Part 1's defense team. It is Zellner's scathing assessment of the ineptitude of the cast of characters involved in the case (especially Ken Kratz but also many others), delivered through a series of "money shot," pithy sound bites, that is most satisfying, and that the entire second series is organized around. There are two other new lawyers, too, Laura Nirider and Steven Drizin, who are Brendan Dassey's postconviction lawyers, but they are secondary to Zellner, who is the undisputed star of the series. In a perceptive review of the new series for *Variety*, Daniel D'Addario suggests that Zellner:

> pitches her advocacy at the level of WWE [World Wrestling Entertainment]-style displays of power; over the course of the second season, she seems at times to be running a double game, seeking first to get Avery freed from prison and second, and more zealously, to convince the public to rise up in outrage. She's fluent in the language of swaying public opinion these days, tweeting missives directed, in her words, at "all the skeptics, doubters & haters." (2018)

Twitter is indeed central to Zellner's public relations strategy, and she uses the #makingamurder2 hashtag as a central part of her advocacy for Steven Avery.[22] With 596,000 followers on Twitter (as of December 1, 2018), she has engaged in a postrelease *Making a Murderer* Q and A under the hashtag #askzellner, and she routinely tweets to keep up public interest in the case. Her pinned tweet as of November 20, 2018, is a handwritten note from Steven Avery, thanking people for their support and urging them to watch *Making a Murderer Part 2*.

Zellner has already accrued a solid fan base on social media and has received a rapturous reception on Twitter.[23] The fact that it is now a white woman who is the object of fan adoration would seem to complicate some of the claims made earlier in this chapter regarding the veneration of white male legal officials in contemporary true crime. Certainly, *Making a Murderer Part 2* is interesting for how it puts women center stage: in addition to Zellner and Nirider, there are Steven's mom and Brandon's mom, both of whom are given a great deal of screen time and who emerge as beleaguered, tragic figures deserving of viewer sympathy. But despite the newfound emphasis on women, and

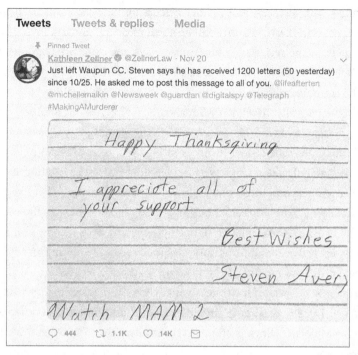

Inside the tweet image:

Tweets   Tweets & replies   Media

📌 Pinned Tweet

Kathleen Zellner ✅ @ZellnerLaw · Nov 20

Just left Waupun CC. Steven says he has received 1200 letters (50 yesterday) since 10/25. He asked me to post this message to all of you. @lifeafterten @michellemalkin @Newsweek @guardian @digitalspy @Telegraph #MakingAMurderer

Happy Thanksgiving

I appreciate all of your support

Best Wishes

Steven Avery

Watch MAM 2

💬 444   🔁 1.1K   ♡ 14K   ✉

Fig 4.6. Kathleen Zellner's pinned tweet from November 20, 2018

despite the prominence given to the two female lawyers, the affective dynamics of *Making a Murderer Part 2* are ultimately very similar to the first series in terms of how its binge-watching modus operandi revolves around the production of heroes, villains, and "fans." As D'Addario notes in his review, "The show exists to educate viewers about the real disadvantages defense attorneys face in the justice system, but also to thrill with a morality play about good and bad lawyers and the civilians whose lives they throw into disarray" (2018). The docuseries generates real sadness for the Avery and Dassey families, with close-ups of their anguished, aging faces, but this is tempered by the moments of "pure enjoyment" (D'Addario 2018) provided by the second series and its exciting forensic and legal discoveries and thrills. Episode 1, "Number 18," for example, ends with a leather-clad Zellner in a parking garage with a group of male forensic experts and a mannequin that stands in for Teresa Halbach's dead body, in the first of a series of rather gruesome, fascinating, and highly entertaining reenactments designed to reveal the "gross, extreme, egregious prosecutorial misconduct" in the original case against Avery. The episode concludes with a close-up of Zellner discussing how she plans to dismantle the prosecution's case: "So, that will be a real pleasure, unmasking Mr. Kratz," she drawls, as the series' signature music plays, the extensive list of names of those who declined to participate in the second series is shown on-screen,[24] and the countdown to episode 2 (in 5, 4, 3, 2, 1 seconds) begins.

Problematically, *Making a Murderer Part 2* singles out another suspect: Bobby Dassey, Brendan Dassey's brother. The penultimate episode, "Friday Nite," concludes with Zellner firmly pointing the finger at Dassey as a suspect: "Why is Bobby Dassey lying? Why does Bobby Dassey have all of this deviant porn on his computer?" she asks. This is reminiscent of what happens in *Paradise Lost 2*, when directors Berlinger and Sinofsky identify the eccentric John Mark Byers, the stepfather of one of the young boys who was murdered, as a suspect.[25] Byers, as it turns out, was innocent and *Paradise Lost 2* has been strongly criticized for suggesting his guilt (Watson 2014, 208–11), which was subsequently believed (for a time) by many fans of the documentary series.

As of December 4, 2018, Brendan Dassey and Steven Avery remain in prison. Kathleen Zellner is still actively involved in the case and continues to tweet, and Laura Nirider and Steven Drizin are now doing speaking tours in the United Kingdom.[26] There is no question that *Making a Murderer* is keeping the Dassey and Avery cases in the spotlight and highlighting serious flaws in the criminal justice system. But, as this chapter has suggested, it is important to consider what else the series is doing as it shapes viewer interaction with the narrative through the Netflix interface. In her discussion of the likeness between documentary films and trials, Kristen Fuhs suggests that the juridical documentary serves as an "alternative 'public' trial for their subjects and a meta-trial on the legitimacy of the actual trials" (2014, 784). The binge-worthy long-form true crime docuseries is similarly influential in shaping public understandings of, and engagement with, questions of law and social justice. For this reason, it is crucial that future research continue to interrogate the cultural work performed by long-form true crime series across a range of digital media platforms.

Afterword

Feminist True Crime

> It is hopeful and exciting to imagine a true crime that, instead of trading in the spectacle and sensation that generates impotent emotional responses directed at a small number of depraved individuals, could actually weave a narrative that attempts to understand the social causes of crime, violence, and abuse.
>
> —Jean Murley (2008, 142)

ONE OF THE CHALLENGES of writing this book has been keeping pace with the extraordinary explosion of true crime images and texts circulating on the internet. In addition to new true crime series and shows emerging on a monthly basis, there has been a dramatic rise in digitally based crimes—from "revenge porn"[1] to "upskirting"[2] and "sextortion."[3] During the last year of writing and revising this book, the Harvey Weinstein story broke, and the #metoo movement emerged.[4] The horrific depth and reach of rape culture was suddenly being acknowledged in mainstream culture in a way that would have seemed unimaginable previously.

When Harvey Weinstein finally turned himself in at a New York police station on May 25, 2018, I watched the ABC livestream on Twitter (along with millions of others), and followed the actress Asia Argento's tweets: "Live from NYC #Weinstein perp walk."[5] To watch Argento's response—in real time—to Hollywood producer Weinstein finally being held legally accountable for his alleged crimes against women, felt deeply significant. It came soon after her powerful speech at Cannes in which she recounted her rape by Weinstein and warned other predators that they, too, would be held responsible for their actions. As I sat transfixed in front of my laptop screen, watching the livestream of Weinstein's arrest, other high-profile actresses who survived his alleged abuse, including Rose McGowan and Mira Sorvino, added to the chorus of voices on Twitter.

Fig 5.1. Rose McGowan tweet on Harvey Weinstein arrest, May 25, 2018

Fig 5.2. Mira Sorvino tweets on Harvey Weinstein arrest, May 25 and May 24, 2018

Such moments matter, and are hugely important in both real and symbolic terms for how they give survivors of sexual abuse a voice, and build a sense of collective resistance to endemic sexualized violence. However, as Tarana Burke, black feminist activist and founder of the original me too campaign, cautioned in a public Facebook post on May 26, 2018, not all sexual abuse victims can have the satisfaction of seeing their attackers brought to justice in this public a way, and it is crucial not to lose sight of the wider collective struggle to eradicate sexual violence as a systemic problem, not one reduced to individual "monsters." Indeed, a stark reminder of the risks involved in making the #metoo movement about individuals occurred when Asia Argento was herself accused of sexual assault by actor Jimmy Bennett in a *New York Times* article in August 2018.[6] It is important to note that the allegations against Argento do not invalidate the claims of her own victimization, nor do they discredit the wider #metoo movement (O'Malley 2018; North 2018; Burke as quoted in Strause 2018), but the incident does point to the need for a nuanced and systemic understanding of shifting relationships between power, privilege, and violence.

In this afterword, I want to offer a few reflections on what a feminist version of true crime—one that captures the social, collective, and intersectional dimensions of crime—might look like, and how it might intervene in public discourses of violence and social justice in the streaming era. To what extent can the true crime format be deployed in the service of a critical interrogation of systemic crime and violence?

On May 19, 2017, Netflix released all seven episodes of *The Keepers*, a series that was immediately praised for being "more respectful to the victims than other true crime stories" (D'Addario 2017). Directed by Ryan White, *The Keepers*, like other recent long-form true crime serials, centers on a mystery: who killed Sister Cathy Cesnick? Pitched as a docuseries for those who liked *Making a Murderer*, *The Keepers* is marketed as a real-life whodunnit, with the blurb on its website reading "Two former students launch a dogged investigation into the cold case of Sister Catherine Cesnick, a nun who was slain in Baltimore in 1969." The two former students turned amateur investigators are Gemma Hoskins and Abbie Schaub, both in their sixties—described by one blogger as "*Cagney and Lacey* with a dash of *Murder She Wrote*" ("Netflix's 'The Keepers'" 2017). Hoskins and Schaub serve as our on-screen surrogates, leading the pursuit for justice through their meticulous research and their tenacity in tracking leads, many of which arise from their public Facebook page, which was originally founded in 2013 and which is now called "The Keepers Official Group: Justice for Catherine Cesnik and Joyce Malecki."[7]

As viewers soon discover, however, the focus of *The Keepers* is not the murder of Sister Cesnick but the story of systemic sexual abuse by a male

Catholic priest, Father Joseph Maskell, who ran Archbishop Keough, the school where Sister Cesnick worked and where his abuse of teenaged girls took place. These details are noticeably kept out of the promotional blurbs for *The Keepers*, and are held back in the first episode, in which "The Murder," as the episode is titled, is used as the narrative hook. It is only in episode 2, "The School," that there is a shocking reveal of the grotesque sexual abuse that was inflicted on young female students at Archbishop Keough. In this episode, the central female survivor, Jean Haragon Wehner, is dramatically unveiled: it is her story of abuse, survival, and resistance that forms the emotional core of the series. While Jean, known initially as "Jane Doe," anchors the story, many other women (and one man), all now in late middle age, also give testimony of their abuse; indeed, the final episode of *The Keepers* concludes with a montage sequence of each of the survivors' faces in repose as Jean talks about the possibility of their collective voices "shattering" the wall of silence erected by the Catholic Church.

Although the docuseries continually circles back to Sister Cathy's murder, and who might have committed it, to a large extent Sister Cathy functions as the "gateway body" of the series. As discussed in the previous chapter, although the gateway, as argued by Klinger, "may lead to other bodies that displace its centrality," it is a necessary "driving force" for the long-form TV serial and offers a "compelling means of capturing and maintaining attention" (Klinger 2018a, 8). In the case of *The Keepers*, the mystery of "who killed Sister Cathy" is a Trojan horse for the story of systemic sexual abuse enabled by the white patriarchal structures of the Catholic Church, the police, and the local government in Baltimore. *The Keepers* uses many of the same devices of the long-form true crime blockbusters already analyzed in this book, including "a wow moment at the end of every episode" (Seale 2017), opening "hooks," and the withholding of key information in order to maximize entertainment value. But where the true crime serials discussed in the previous chapter use the dead female body as a lure, only to then turn away from the issue of gendered violence, *The Keepers* maintains its focus on the victims and the wider societal structures at work in Baltimore in the late 1960s and early 1970s that allowed such widespread violence to occur. While Father Maskell emerges as the main villain of *The Keepers*, the series nevertheless works to expose sexual violence as a wider social problem, one that is enabled by systems of power and is therefore not simply attributable to the actions of individual "bad men" (Mendes, Ringrose, and Keller 2018, 238).[8]

The Keepers follows the lead of other recent true crime texts in generating strong emotions in its viewers; however, what is notable is that these emotions become the occasion for "building networks of solidarity" (Mendes, Ringrose, and Keller 2018, 238) and are not simply the occasion for personal catharsis or individual judgment. *The Keepers* foregrounds images of Gemma and Abbie in front of computer screens as they deploy the tools of social media to build alliances and to help survivors forge connections with one other. As Mendes, Ringrose, and Keller suggest in their important research on hashtag activism, the kind of solidarity built up among digital feminist activists is significant, and "often transforms into a feminist consciousness amongst hashtag participants, which allows them to understand sexual violence as a structural rather than personal problem" (238). Recent scholarship has shown that what needs to be at the forefront of feminist investigations into digital violence is the "importance of wider cultural contexts" (Ging and Siapera 2018, 517), which acknowledge how violence against women intersects with racism and other forms of abuse. Moving ahead, it's important to consider how the surge of public interest in true crime can be seized upon as a way of bringing meaningful attention to forms of violence against women, and, more specifically, to what extent true crime can be repurposed and reframed in the service of an intersectional approach to crime and violence.

Missing and Murdered: Intersectional True Crime

Connie Walker's podcast "Missing and Murdered," produced by the Canadian Broadcasting Corporation (CBC), is an extraordinary example of how true crime can be reframed for political purposes in a digital multimedia environment. "Missing and Murdered" so far consists of two series, *Who Killed Alberta Williams?* (2016) and *Finding Cleo* (2018), both of which, on the surface, are true crime mysteries of the kind encountered throughout this book, but which, on closer analysis, are significantly different for how they center the female victim and insist upon showing the ways in which violence against indigenous women in Canada is part of a wider history of systemic racist and gendered oppression.

Tanya Horeck
13 April · CBC · 👥 ▾

Today I finished listening to the ten episode long Finding Cleo, a podcast by Connie Walker for CBC. I urge everyone - and especially all Canadians - to listen to it. This is incredible journalism. This is what feminist true crime sounds like. I listened through almost constant tears - it is unbearably moving in places, so much so that I often had to stop to pause it. But this is such compassionate and intelligent reporting that I want to shout about it from the rooftops. Walker provides the most politically astute and sensitive recounting of the horror of the sixties scoop and residential schools in Canada I have ever heard. She reinvents the 'lost girl' true crime narrative by focusing attention on the story of missing indigenous girl Cleo and putting her story in the context of the violent uprooting of indigenous children from their families and communities. She contextualizes and performs intersectional analysis in a way that is seldom heard in public culture. An important piece of work.

Fig 5.3. My personal Facebook post on *Finding Cleo*, April 13, 2018

The critical impetus to humanize the forgotten and ignored victims of violent crime is also apparent in the CBC's creation of a database, started in 2015, of unsolved cases of missing and murdered indigenous women, which includes a profile for each missing or murdered girl or woman (including Alberta Williams).[9] There is a graph that details "the stark and staggering" statistics on the hundreds of cases of missing and murdered indigenous girls and women in Canada, and a Case Explorer that enables people to "explore the cases of these women" through various filters, including their age and their last sighting.

This interactive CBC database is part of a wider movement to acknowledge the history of violence against the indigenous people of Canada, following the Truth and Reconciliation Commission into the history of Indian residential schools, which concluded in 2015. In September 2016, the Government of Canada launched an independent $53.8-million national inquiry into Missing and Murdered Indigenous Women and Girls (http://www.mmiwg-ffada.ca). As noted on the official website for the Inquiry: "The Commissioners' mandate is to examine and report on the *systemic causes* of all forms of violence against Indigenous women and girls and 2SLGBTQ individuals in Canada by looking at patterns and underlying factors" ("National Inquiry" n.d., my emphasis). It is the focus on the systemic causes and patterns of violence that stands out here, as the National Inquiry emphasizes the interlocking and "devastating impacts of colonization, racism and sexism—aspects of Canadian society that many Canadians are reluctant to accept" ("National Inquiry" n.d.). The National Inquiry has been hindered by various obstacles,[10] and, as noted in a *Globe and Mail* editorial, the challenge is how to not only commemorate and honor these missing girls and women and their families but make connections between these various cold cases ("Globe Editorial" 2017).

I want to suggest that Connie Walker's podcasts meet that challenge and that they do so through a strategic deployment of the narrative devices of long-form true crime. Walker, who is herself an Indigenous woman of Cree origin, is open about how she has sought to capitalize upon the recent interest in true crime in order to "examine the bigger picture" of violence against indigenous people (quoted in Green 2018). Walker provides a context for understanding the brutal realities of life for Indigenous people in Canada (quoted in Green 2018) through exploring both the tragic history of residential schools in Canada, in which indigenous children were removed from their homes and communities with the intent of assimilating them into dominant white Christian culture (*Who Killed Alberta Williams?*), and the Sixties Scoop, in which children were placed in state-run welfare facilities or removed from their families and placed for adoption in white families in Canada and the United States (*Finding Cleo*).

For Walker, the "hooks" and lures of true crime are crucial to securing audience attention and involvement in these long-ignored stories of violence against indigenous girls and women and serve as a means to an end. As she explains of her strategic deployment of true crime: "We're giving people the medicine alongside the treat. I think there's such an appetite right now for true crime podcasts. It just seems insatiable. I'm not actually interested in true crime. I don't listen to other true crime podcasts. I am mostly interested in the context" (quoted in Green 2018). Thus, while Walker supplies audiences with the appeal of a "mystery" over several episodes, what she is really interested in exploring is the "effects of colonization on Indigenous women and girls" (quoted in Green 2018). It is an approach to true crime that keeps the female victims at the center of the story. As Walker states of her first podcast, *Who Killed Alberta Williams?*:

> Obviously with these podcasts, there are so many twists and turns and it's easy to get caught in the true crime aspect of it, but we want people to keep in mind Alberta was a 24-year-old woman who was loved by her family and community, and there are so many families out there just like hers who are still searching for the truth and looking for justice. (quoted in Ciobanu 2016)

The question of how the single, individual story relates to the broader, collective struggle to illuminate the causes of violence against indigenous women in Canadian history and culture resonates with discussions that have emerged in the #metoo era about how the problem of gendered violence "goes beyond individuals and instead relates to wider cultural forces" (Donegan 2018).

In episode 4 ("The Brothers") of *Who Killed Alberta Williams?* Walker's narration makes manifest the pressing need to make connections between individual cases and to ask "bigger questions":

> We started this story looking for answers about Alberta Williams' unsolved murder. But the deeper we got into the story the more I thought about the bigger questions. Why are there over 1,200 cases of missing and murdered Indigenous women in Canada? Why are we more likely to be physically and sexually assaulted? Why are we more likely to be killed? What is at the root of this horrific violence? My hope in telling Alberta's story is to begin to connect the dots. That by telling a single story we can help illuminate something bigger.

The long-form true crime structure is used to reveal "patterns in the violence" (*Who Killed Alberta Williams?* episode 4, "The Brothers") and to explore the painful legacy of residential schools. The temptation to cast crime in relation to individual good guys and bad guys is resisted at every turn, and what emerges instead is a thoughtful, multilayered account of the intergenerational trauma that emerges from systemic societal oppression.

In episode 6 ("Little Pine") of *Finding Cleo*, we learn that Cleo was not raped and murdered, as her family long believed, but that she took her own life at the age of thirteen. Although this is treated as a moment of revelation and plot "twist" on a par with other true crime texts examined in this book (such as *Dear Zachary*, discussed in chapter 1), what is significant is how Walker deploys this device in order to suture audiences into an in depth sociopolitical analysis of systemic racism against indigenous people in North America. Walker makes it clear that "Cleo's death is not an anomaly" and that "death by suicide is all too common for children who were taken during the sixties scoop" (episode 6, "Little Pine"). She is emphatic about the social causes behind Cleo's suicide, which are a "direct result of a system of oppression" in which indigenous children are "seven times more likely to live in impoverished circumstances" and to "take their own lives" (episode 6, "Little Pine"). Opening Cleo's death onto its wider social dimensions, Walker delves into the trauma of how Cleo was separated from her mother and family at such a young age and the effect such cultural and familial dislocation would have had on her. She asks: "What were the government decisions that led to her being adopted by a white family in the United States?" (episode 7, "Lillian"). The podcast also examines the traumatic history of Cleo's mother, Lillian, who had her six children taken away from her; in the absence of Lillian's own testimony about her experiences in residential school, Walker brings in the voices of other indigenous people who spoke at the Truth and Reconciliation commission about the horrific racialized abuse they faced in the schools and the lasting effects on their lives.

In the long-form true crime series I examined in the previous chapter, audiences were funneled forward through a series of microtemporal affective thrills organized around the desire to issue judgment over individual men accused of violent crimes. In the case of *Serial*, listeners are positioned in relation to a series of sharply polarized and comforting binary oppositions that foreclose more critical reflection. In the case of *The Jinx*, viewers are offered a satisfying payoff for our "detective" work through the final dramatic confession of Robert Durst. Finally, in the case of *Making a Murderer*, viewers are steered into a position of moral outrage, which is bolstered by an identification with on-screen surrogates in the form of legal representatives. However, the aim of *Missing and Murdered* is significantly different: Walker states that she wants people to "feel the weight" of what both Cleo and Lillian went through (episode 8, "Salesperson of the Year"). As she asserts at the end of episode 8, it is about learning to see the "ripple effects across families and generations" and about "how women and girls in particular have borne the brunt of the violence of colonization and residential schools and racism." Furthermore, and crucially, Walker makes listeners consider the wider web of societal forces that led to the deaths of Alberta and Cleo and that allowed them to be ignored for so long. Walker makes it painfully clear that this is a crisis that is far from over: there remains an overrepresentation of indigenous children in care, and indigenous families continue to struggle with the effects of residential schools and the "racism that still divides us" (*Finding Cleo*, episode 8, "Salesperson of the Year"). In keeping its intersectional analysis of crime and violence in the foreground, *Missing and Murdered* shows the possibilities for a form of true crime that urgently attends to the raced, classed, and gendered dimensions of violence.[11] Instead of encouraging an aimless internet "sleuthing"—of chasing down "clues" and endlessly debating questions of guilt and innocence—Walker invites a form of critical listening that "connects the dots" of systemic institutionally sanctioned violence.

In this book, I have examined the cultural turn to true crime in early twenty-first-century digital culture with a view to interrogating the nature of the affective investment in the genre. My focus has been on "networked affect" (Paasonen, Hillis, and Petit 2015) and specifically the kinds of affective attachments engendered through engagement with the online circulation of true crime images. In particular, I've been interested in how true crime has come to serve as an exemplary genre for the new modes of listening and watching media in the streaming era, including, for example, the so-called distracted viewing of YouTube and wider clip culture and the more apparently immersive viewing solicited by Netflix and binge-watching. If, as I have asserted, true crime comes into its own in a digital network culture that privileges the notion of internet sleuthing, then it is imperative to look at the kinds of audience participation that are promoted through recent popular true crime texts. While I have been skeptical about some of the claims that are made for digital-era true crime, especially those regarding the potential of audience interactivity to effect social change, the above examples suggest that the current cultural moment may be ripe for a feminist rearticulation of the genre. In addition to the examples just considered, ongoing true crime series such as *My Favorite Murder*, discussed in the introduction to this book, are working to debunk many problematic assumptions and stereotypes of the genre. Episodes of *MFM*, for example, often begin with "corrections corner," in which mistakes and errors from previous weeks are dealt with and Twitter feedback is discussed. In one of the most talked about early examples of how the podcast adapts and revises itself, Karen and Georgia changed their use of the term "prostitute" to "sex worker," in response to platform feedback that "prostitute" is an outmoded and derogatory term. More recently, Georgia referenced her problematic use of the dated term "transvestite" in response to feedback from a listener and acknowledged the importance of using the term "trans" instead. Such self-conscious adjustments and efforts to rethink the problematic tropes of true crime emerge as part of *MFM*'s attempt to continually update itself and can be viewed as part of a wider drive in contemporary networked media culture to respond to feedback and keep up with the "new." Given that women have long been acknowledged as the core audience for true crime texts (see, for example, Biressi 2001; Browder 2006; 2010; Murley 2008; and Jermyn 2007), there is a need to open up further debate about the potential for a feminist revision of true crime in contemporary convergence culture.

In addition to the recent explosion of true crime podcasts investigating the disappearances and murders of girls and women,[12] there has been a steady rise in crowdsourced, fan-based websites such as Websleuths.com (https://www.websleuths.com/forums/). Criminologists are beginning to explore the significance of digital websleuthing as a more diverse and varied activity than has previously been imagined, with websleuths investigating a "wide variety of cases, including homicide, missing persons, terrorism, property offences and sexual offences" (Yardley et. al 2018a, 104).[13] A striking, if bittersweet, example of a recent websleuth success story centers around American writer Michelle McNamara's *I'll Be Gone in the Dark: One Woman's Obsessive Search for the Golden State Killer* (2018). Published after her untimely death in 2016 (it was completed by a close colleague and her researcher), the book is based on years of her painstaking research, both online and offline, into the serial rapist and murderer she dubbed the "Golden State Killer." Two months after the publication of McNamara's posthumous work, on April 24, 2018, police officers arrested seventy-two-year-old Joseph James DeAngelo on the basis of DNA evidence that linked him with the rapes and murders of the "Golden State

Killer," committed in the 1970s and 1980s in California. McNamara's copious research and dedicated investigation, as outlined on her true crime blog and website, *True Crime Diary* (http://truecrimediary.com), is largely credited with keeping the case at the forefront of public consciousness (Rosenberg 2018).

While there is a definite need for further research on the complexities of websleuthing in a networked era, what is equally important to examine, as I have suggested throughout this book, are the more mundane kinds of affective attachments to crime and violence engendered by the sociotechnical platforms through which true crime texts are now exhibited. *Justice on Demand: True Crime in the Digital Streaming Era* has sought to examine the cultural currency of true crime in networked culture and to look at the particular ways in which certain popular examples of the genre attempt to capture—and to shape—audience attention and involvement. The popularity of true crime shows no signs of abating, and it is therefore necessary to continue to think about its new iterations and the different forms of multimedia engagement it solicits. To understand the cultural importance of digital-era true crime, it is crucial to consider how its networked protocols are shaping our affective responses to issues of crime and criminality. Social justice still does not come on "demand," however much the immediacy and accessibility of social media networks might give us a sense that it does; what therefore matters most is that we think critically about the kinds of sociopolitical connections and formations that are produced through our interaction with true crime images in the digital streaming era.

Notes

Introduction

1. *My Favorite Murder* launched its first episode in 2016 with Feral Audio. In 2017, it moved to Midroll Media.
2. This is from the description of the series found on iTunes and elsewhere: https://itunes.apple.com/gb/podcast/my-favorite-murder-karen-kilgariff -georgia-hardstark/id1074507850?mt=2
3. Women have long been acknowledged as the core audience for true crime but *My Favorite Murder* makes this explicit in a way that few true crime texts have done previously. See Deborah Jermyn (2007) and Jean Murley (2008) for a discussion of the pleasures of true crime for its predominantly female audiences.
4. The term was coined by a member of the Facebook fan page for *My Favorite Murder*. One self-confessed "murderino," Jessica Hullinger, defines the term as: "Person with a borderline obsessive interest in true crime, and the specific nature and details of disturbing murders" (2016). As of December 1, 2018, 149 episodes plus 99 minisodes of the podcast have aired.
5. As Michael Salter writes, "Facebook is currently the largest and most high-profile social media platform in the world. Since its launch in 2004, it has evolved from a website for Harvard College students to a global internet behemoth, reporting 1.49 billion monthly active users in 2015" (2017, 8). *MFM* had a thriving Facebook page with 235, 099 members until Karen and Georgia shut it down on August 17, 2018. In episode 135 of the podcast, "The Multiverse Trajectory," released on August 23, 2018, the hosts explain their decision to archive the Facebook page because of a racist post and their recognition that they could no longer manage or be responsible for the kind of negativity sometimes presented on the Facebook group.
6. Yardley, Kelly, and Robinson-Edwards provide the following succinct definition of the podcast: "Podcasts are digital audio files which can be downloaded by users onto personal devices like MP3 players, smartphones or computers to listen to at their convenience" (2018, 2).

7. Since the release of the wildly popular podcast *Serial* in 2014, there has been a wave of true crime podcasts. In addition to *MFM*, other popular examples include, but are not limited to: *S-Town, Missing and Murdered, Someone Knows Something, True Crime Garage, Crime Town, Dirty John, In the Dark, Up and Vanished, Atlanta Monster, Accused, Last Podcast on the Left*, and *Casefile True Crime*. For further examples, consult one of the numerous true crime listicles available online, such as Hillary Nelson's "52 Great True-Crime Podcasts: The post-*Serial* boom" in *Vulture*.

8. It is important to remember, of course, that not everyone in the world has access to the internet. As Venessa Garcia and Samantha Arkerson note, although "we are in a digital age when everyone can link to the media and to each other . . . not everyone can afford the electronic devices needed to make these connections" (2018, 4).

9. Ann Rule's true crime books were part of a wider boom in true crime publishing in the 1970s and 1980s (Murley 2008, 44). Rule is most famous for her debut book, *The Stranger Beside Me* ([1980] 2000), about serial killer Ted Bundy.

10. It gestures toward it but it also attempts to conceal it, through its female author and through its use of a gender neutral second-person address.

11. In 2014 the Stockton Police Department in California posted a mug shot on their Facebook page of a thirty-year-old man called Jeremy Meeks who was arrested on felony weapons charges; the image immediately went viral because of Meeks's "photogenic" looks. As the BBC reports, Meeks's mug shot generated "95,000 likes and 25,000 comments" on Facebook ("Mug-shot" 2014). Referred to as the "hot felon," Meeks is now an international top model managed by White Cross Management and has a child with Chloe Green, the heiress to the Top Shop billionaire fortune. I have discussed Meeks's mug shot and the wider implications of the online mug shot industry in a paper, "Celebrity Mugshots and the Digital Celebrification of Crime," presented at the Celebrity Studies conference in Rome in June 2018.

12. As Michael Salter describes it, "Twitter is an influential 'micro-blogging' social media site. Launched in 2006, it recorded 310 million monthly active users in 2015" (2017, 8). On Twitter, people post and interact with one another via "tweets," which were originally 140 characters long but as of November 7, 2017, have expanded to 280 characters.

13. There is a growing body of important research by cultural criminologists that investigates how social media networks are transforming understandings of crime and justice-seeking. See, for example: Salter (2017); Hayes and Luther

(2018); Garcia and Arkerson (2018); Yardley, Lynes, Wilson, and Kelly (2018); Yardley, Kelly, and Robinson-Edwards (2018); and Martin (2018).

14. Criminologists Elizabeth Yardley, Adam Lynes, David Wilson, and Emma Kelly use the term "websleuthing" to describe the increasing numbers of people who flock "to networked spaces to analyse a wide range of cases" (2018, 82). In their recent essay on websleuthing in *Crime, Media, Culture*, Yardley et al. (2018) begin to develop a critical framework for understanding this phenomenon, including an empirical study on how the media depicts websleuths.

15. As Laura Browder suggests, "true crime literature first flourished during the Elizabethan era in the form of simple pamphlets detailing the exploits of local murderers" (2010, 122) and has gone on to have a long and varied history. Murley notes that: "Although murder narratives and nonfiction crime writing have a history that spans centuries, modern true crime made its earliest appearance in the pages of *True Detective Magazine* during the 1940s and 1950s, as a new way of narrating and understanding murder—one more sensitive to context, more psychologically sophisticated, more willing to make conjectures about the unknown thoughts and motivations of killers—emerged" (2008, 2). For detailed historical discussions of true crime as a genre see Anita Biressi (2001); Jean Murley (2008); Laura Browder (2010); and Ian Case Punnett (2018).

16. See "True Crime" at https://en.wikipedia.org/wiki/True_crime, accessed July 18, 2018.

17. Twitter reportedly took the videos down within ten minutes of them being uploaded, but not before they had been shared hundreds of times. Facebook apparently took longer to remove the video (Rawlinson 2015).

18. See Jennifer Malkowski's *Dying in Full Detail: Mortality and Digital Documentary* (2017) for an excellent discussion of witnessing and the recording of death in the digital era. As Malkowski notes of Flanagan's video: "During the window in which a fated-to-be-removed death video is still accessible, it is not only shareable but downloadable (through any number of free and easily accessed programs online). . . . Thus, despite the swift removal of Flanagan's video by Facebook and Twitter, anyone can still watch it today on LiveLeak or TheYNC, two sites that form end points on a spectrum of respectability for 'death porn' websites" (2017, 162).

19. See Caetlin Benson-Allott for a fascinating discussion of Reynolds's Facebook Live video and the possibilities it raises for "liveness as a participatory media practice rather than merely a spectatorial mode" (2016, 62).

20. It is important to acknowledge here that there is a growing body of feature-length crime documentaries that explore miscarriages of justice against African Americans and the indifference to black death, including, for example, *David and Me* (Klonsky and Lamy, Canada/USA, 2014); *A Murder in the Park* (Rech and Kimber, USA, 2014); *3½ Minutes, Ten Bullets* (Silver, USA, 2015); *Time Simply Passes* (Flowers, USA, 2016); *Strong Island* (Ford, USA/Denmark, 2017); *Marvin Booker Was Murdered* (Gardner, USA, 2017); *Bad Henry* (Palmer, USA, 2018); and *Stray Bullet* (Delaloye, USA, 2018).

21. Although the focus of a true crime documentary such as ESPN's *O.J.: Made in America* is on the question of race, the dominant narrative focus, as Rachel Alicia Griffin argues, is nonetheless aligned with a white gaze and with whiteness as "the normative racial frame" (Griffin 2018, 360).

22. Reality TV tabloid crime shows such as *Cops* (1989–present) are notorious for demonizing African Americans as criminals. See Rapping (2003, 60–66).

23. As this book was going to press, Ava DuVernay's four-part Netflix true crime drama series, *When They See Us*, was released (on May 31, 2019). The series is a dramatization of the "Central Park Jogger" rape case from 1989; it explores the wrongful conviction of five young black and Hispanic boys: Kevin Richardson, Antron McCray, Yusef Salaam, Korey Wise, and Raymond Santana. The series is significant for exposing the racism of the criminal justice system and marks an important turning point for mainstream true crime drama. *When They See Us* is an important companion piece to DuVernay's documentary *13th* (Netflix, 2016), as both works insist upon a critical and systemic analysis of social injustice, which, as I discuss in the afterword to this book, must be central to any critical intervention in public discourses of crime and violence in the streaming era.

24. See Annalee Newitz (1997) for an excellent discussion of the processes by which "White trash, by occupying the position of 'bad' Other, offer a perspective from which 'good' whites can see themselves as a racial and classed group" (136).

25. The documentary *Kony 2012* (Russell, 2012) is a significant, if controversial, example of a viral documentary. Produced by the American charity Invisible Children, *Kony 2012* details the crimes and abuses of Ugandan militia leader Joseph Kony, and was part of the charity's "Stop Kony" campaign. Released online on March 5, 2012, the video spread rapidly via social media networks, including Facebook and Twitter, and reached 100 million views in six days. As of November 9, 2018, the video has had over 102 million views on YouTube. While the video sparked global outrage, it has also been criticized

for its simplistic take on a complex problem and for its overly slick styling of social action as a form of social media consumption, through shares and "likes." For an interesting discussion of *Kony 2012*, see Sharma and Tygstrup (2015).

26. The "West Memphis Three"—Damon Echols, Jessie Misskelley, and Jason Baldwin—eventually agreed to take an "Alford plea," which, as explained in a *New York Times* article on the case (Robertson 2011), allows "people to maintain their innocence and admit frankly that they are pleading guilty because they consider it in their best interest." This was less than ideal in light of the lack of evidence of their involvement in the crime and was particularly resisted by Baldwin, who did not want to plead guilty.

27. For further scholarship on the *Paradise Lost* trilogy, see, for example, Mnookin (2005); Opel (2005); Adkins (2008); Watson (2014), and Aguayo (2014).

28. My thinking here is informed by Caetlin Benson-Allott's influential scholarship on platforms, in which she examines how "innovations in motion picture *exhibition* have changed the way filmmakers imagine and address the spectator" (2013, 12).

29. During the course of its long run, *Crimewatch* (1984–2017) typically aired once a month on the BBC, Britain's public service broadcaster. Nick Ross and Sue Cook hosted the program for the first eleven years. Cook was replaced by Jill Dando, who cohosted the program until her tragic murder in 1999. Ross hosted the program alone until news presenter Fiona Bruce joined in 2000. Kirsty Young and Matthew Amroliwala took over as presenters in 2007 and stayed until 2015. In the final incarnation of the show, Jeremy Vine and Tina Daheley hosted the show until it was canceled in 2017. There is a spin-off daytime show called *Crimewatch Roadshow* that airs on BBC One (2009–).

30. Adam Walsh is the host and creator of *America's Most Wanted*. Walsh turned to anticrime activism after the murder of his son, Adam Walsh, in 1981. After its run on Fox, Walsh's *America's Most Wanted* moved to the Lifetime network in 2011, where it ran until 2013.

31. In his recent book, *Toward a Theory of True Crime Narratives*, Ian Case Punnett points out that true crime has, in fact, always been strongly intertextual with a typical "mixture of written text, diagrams, illustrations and crime scene photography" (2018, 4). The inherent intertextuality of the genre in part explains true crime's success in a multiplatform, media convergence culture. Punnett's informative book examines the relationship

between journalism and true crime, and provides a "meta-theory" of the genre through an analysis of its "most common, consistent elements" (2, 3). Punnett takes ten true crime texts as his case studies, from magazine articles, books, TV shows, and a podcast; the texts he discusses include Truman Capote's *In Cold Blood* (1966), Sarah Koenig's *Serial* (2014), and Moira Demos and Laura Ricciardi's *Making a Murderer* (2015). Punnett defines true crime as an "occasionally controversial multi-platform genre that is most often associated with murder narratives, and shares some common ancestral heritage with journalism, but always has been driven by different impulses" (2018, 3).

32. Any discussion of *MFM*'s feminism needs to take into account the trend toward the popularization of feminism in the social networks of twenty-first-century media culture. As several feminist scholars have argued (Banet-Weiser and Portwood-Stacer 2017; Banet-Weiser 2018; Gill 2016; Ging and Siapera 2018), the newfound attention to feminist issues enabled by the internet and social media is not without its contradictions and tensions. *MFM* often displays certain characteristics of what Rosalind Gill calls a distinctly "postfeminist sensibility" (2007). There is a "championing" of women on the podcast in which the term "feminism" is used as a kind of "cheer word" (Gill 2016, 619), and its assertive defiance of male violence and toxic masculinity is often expressed through phrases of the "fuck you!" and the "You go girl!" variety.

Chapter 1

1. For an interesting discussion regarding documentary's growth in popularity in the first decade of the twenty-first century, please see the Special Issue of *Cineaste* on "American Documentary Today" (2005); in particular, see Paul Arthur (2005) and Patricia Aufderheide (2005).

2. This observation is based on my analysis of the customer reviews of *The Imposter* on amazon.com. Several viewers expressed surprise upon discovering it was a documentary, with one customer declaring, "It's a documentary!!! . . . thought it was a movie, movie, but it is a documentary." Another viewer noted, "Just to clear it up, this is not a film as such, it's a documentary with re-enactments and interview footage etc." For full customer reviews, please see http://www.amazon.co.uk/The-Imposter-DVD-Frederic-Bourdin/dp/B008VTXTL4/ref=sr_1_1?ie=UTF8&qid=1398156918&sr=8-1&keywords=the+imposter.

3. Founded in 2005, Reddit describes itself as "the front page of the internet."

It functions as a discussion board where registered members can create their own "subreddits" on topics they wish, and where other "redditors" can vote content "up" or "down," pushing the most popular discussions to the top of the board (Salter 2017, 10). For a detailed discussion of the dynamics of Reddit please see Adrienne Massanari (2015; 2017).

4. What sparked my initial interest in *Dear Zachary* was the intense emotional response to the documentary on open access sites. My main analysis of audience response to *Dear Zachary* is based on the user reviews of the film found on amazon.com and IMDb.com.

5. Despite its popularity among viewers, there is surprisingly little critical work on *Dear Zachary*, especially when compared to the wealth of literature on *Capturing the Friedmans* (Arthur 2005; Bruzzi 2006; Bell 2008; van Dijck 2008; Druick 2008). In part, I believe this might have something to do with its low-budget, personal rendering of trauma. The strong attachment that spectators have to *Dear Zachary*, as expressed in online forums, captures and exemplifies the wider cultural investment in the true crime documentary as an affective object in early twenty-first-century culture.

6. See the HBO DVD of *Capturing the Friedmans* and the Warp Films DVD of *Paradise Lost: The Child Murders at Robin Hood Hills* and *Paradise Lost 2: Revelations*. Please also see the trailer for *The Imposter*, available at: https://www.youtube.com/watch?v=yDjpnpzw4GY.

7. This quotation is from the trailer for *Dear Zachary*. See http://www.youtube.com/watch?v=dZXatzQ1kzg.

8. Please see the imdb.com user reviews at http://www.imdb.com/title/tt1152758/?ref_=fn_al_tt_1 and the amazon.com customer reviews on http://www.amazon.com/Dear-Zachary-Letter-About-Father/dp/B002FOCXJA/ref=sr_1_1?ie=UTF8&qid=1379334384&sr=8–1&keywords=Dear+Zachary.

9. For more details on the life and mental health history of Shirley Turner, see the Turner Review and Investigation (2006), available online.

10. While individual crime documentaries such as *Capturing the Friedmans* and *Standard Operating Procedure* are referred to in articles on reenactment by Bill Nichols (2008) and Jonathan Kahana (2009), there has not, to my knowledge, been a substantive analysis of how true crime documentaries as a subgenre bring key questions to the fore regarding the operation of reenactment in documentary.

11. As Bill Nichols has suggested, reenactments, and their complex rendering of the "experience of temporality," primarily "fulfill an affective function" (2008, 74).

12. There is a distinction to be made here between emotion and affect, which is crucial for affect theorists. As Grusin, helpfully paraphrasing Deleuze, explains, affects are "uncontained bodily intensities," whereas emotions are "limited and contained expressions of affects first felt by the body, and only afterwards recognized as emotional states" (2010, 81).

13. See Ron Wilkinson (2008), who argues that *Dear Zachary* is a "remembrance" for those who knew the victims and "means nothing to the rest of us."

14. In his review of *The Act of Killing*, Slavoj Zizek has suggested that the Hollywood-style reenactments performed by the murderers are revealing of the increasing trend toward the "privatization of public space." Countering the notion that in the digital media age it is "private space that is disappearing," Zizek argues that it is actually "the public space proper that is disappearing. The person who displays on the web his or her naked images or intimate data is not an exhibitionist: exhibitionists intrude into the public space, while those who post their naked images on the web remain in their private space and are just expanding it to include others" (2013).

15. In addition to being widely publicized on Canadian print and broadcast news, as well as internationally, there was also a bestselling book written by Andrew's father, David Bagby, *Dance with the Devil: A Memoir of Murder and Loss* (Key Porter Books, 2007).

Chapter 2

1. *TMZ* stands for "thirty-mile zone," which delineates the historic and legal boundaries of Hollywood, otherwise known as the "studio zone."

2. Available at http://www.tmz.com/videos/0_6lrpg6kh/

3. Available at http://www.tmz.com/videos/0_ekaflcqq/

4. "Celebrity Justice" was the name of a 2002 television show produced by Harry Levin, the founder and executive producer of *TMZ*. But I use the notion of "celebrity justice" here to describe the self-declared ethos of *TMZ* to expose and indict celebrities.

5. This is also the title to a *New Yorker* feature on *TMZ*. See Schmidle (2016).

6. It is revealing, in this regard, how the two separate elevator incidents appear to contain the other in their very staging—almost in anticipation of one another—in terms of the different coordinates of racialized and gendered violence they imagine: a black man is being beaten (by an "angry black woman")/a black woman is being beaten (by a "violent black man"). In the toxic, racist, and misogynist comments that accompany the respective videos on YouTube, viewers wonder what might have happened had Jay-Z

hit Solange or, in respect to the Ray Rice video, they speculate what would have happened if it had been a woman punching a man, thus indicating the extent to which the content of the videos was somehow already closely linked in the public imagination.

7. On February 15, 2014, both Janay Palmer Rice and Ray Rice were arrested and charged with assault. The charges against Palmer Rice were eventually dropped, and Rice's charges were increased to aggravated assault. The charges against Rice were officially dismissed on May 21, 2015, when he was spared prosecution by agreeing to enter a twelve-month counselling program (Clark 2016).

8. On February 26, 2012, Trayvon Martin, an unarmed seventeen-year-old African American, was shot dead in Florida as he walked home from a convenience store by police officer George Zimmerman. Zimmerman claimed self-defense and was later acquitted. On July 17, 2014, forty-three-year-old African American Eric Garner was put in a choke hold by police officer Daniel Pantaleo and died from suffocation. The entire incident was captured on a smartphone and circulated widely online. On August 9, 2014, Michael Brown was shot repeatedly and killed by police officer Darren Wilson in Ferguson, Missouri, after he was suspected of robbing a convenience store. His death led to widespread protests.

9. See blacklivesmatter.com for an account of how the deaths of black citizens led to the founding of Black Lives Matter.

10. See Lartey (2016) for a discussion of the "targeting" of people who record police and the group of filmmakers who are demanding an inquiry into their unjust treatment.

11. According to an ESPN report, Rice's legal team took issue with the video on the grounds it is a "cleaned up, whittled-down and condensed version" (Sanchez 2014). For *TMZ*'s response, see "Ray Rice Will Reportedly Claim TMZ Edited Tape . . . Dumbest Defense Ever" (2014),

12. This presentation of the video is available at: http://www.tmz.com/2014/05/ 12/jay-z-solange-fight-elevator-video-beyonce-met-gala/ (accessed August 28, 2016).

13. This "autoplay" presentation of the video is available at: http://www.tmz .com/videos/0_6lrpg6kh/ (accessed August 28, 2016).

14. Dubbed versions of the video also rapidly appeared on YouTube, which jokingly depicted what "really" occurred in the elevator, including one by the rapper 50 Cent where he supplied the voices to both Jay-Z and Solange. Thousands of parodies emerged across various media forms, including a

skit on Saturday Night Live, in which it turns out that Solange Knowles was merely helping to get a spider off an arachnophobic Jay-Z.

15. See Sharma for an important discussion of the problematics of internet research that tries to discern the ethnic identity of social media users from their profile pictures (2013, 53).

16. Since the elevator incident, Beyoncé's star image has become increasingly politicized, and the currency of her fame has risen even further. On April 23, 2016, Beyoncé released her critically acclaimed visual album *Lemonade*—a searing political indictment of violence against black Americans, as well as a poetic tribute to the suffering and endurance of black women. Following the release of the video for her single "Formations," there have been a series of politically charged blockbuster performances, including her much discussed, controversial halftime Super Bowl act in August 2017, which referenced Black Lives Matter and paid tribute to the 1960s Black Panther Movement, and her "history-making turn as the first black woman to headline" the Coachella Festival (Taylor 2018) in April 2018. As public discussion focuses ever more intently on the relationship between Beyoncé's publicly avowed politics and her status as a black female megastar, people continue to post comments beneath the Jay-Z/Solange "fight video" on YouTube. In the initial period after the release of *Lemonade* in 2016, for example, viewers returned to rewatch it, armed with apparently new information gleaned from Beyoncé's lyrics, particularly the suggestion that *Lemonade* is an album about Jay-Z cheating on Beyoncé: "Lemonade makes sense now," declared one fan. For others, and more commonly, it was *Lemonade* that helped to make sense of the "fight video." As another fan agreed: "Everything makes sense now! You go Solange!" On this reading, Solange is the protective little sister defending Beyoncé from Jay-Z and his allegedly disrespectful, cheating ways.

17. It is an increasingly prevalent and controversial cultural practice to use GIFS and memes of black people "reacting" online as a form of "digital blackface." As Ellen E Jones (2018) suggests, memes of black people reacting "disseminat(e) old racist stereotypes with a contemporary pop-cultural twist." See cultural critic Lauren Michele Jackson (2017) for an important discussion of how images of black people (over) reacting are a staple of internet culture and run alongside the disturbing images of black "death, looped over and over."

18. See Susan Berridge and Laura Portwood-Stacer (2015) for a good introduction to feminist hashtag activism and violence against women and girls.

19. See Rosemary Clark (2016) for an informative analysis of #WhyIStayed and how it reframed public discourse on sexual violence and domestic abuse.

Chapter 3

1. The lack of scholarship on nonfiction trailers is partly to do with the fact that there are not as many examples of theatrical documentary trailers in a predigital age. As Keith Johnston notes, "major cinematic releases of documentaries were few and far between in previous decades." The earliest trailers for theatrical documentaries, as Johnston explains, could "be more accurately described as trailers for concert movies such as *Woodstock* (1970), *ABBA: The Movie* (1977), or compilation films such as *That's Entertainment* (1974) and its sequels." While, as Johnston suggests, "the trailer format has been used for decades on television, to advertise television documentaries (among many other programmes)," it is difficult to find examples because of the ephemerality of TV trailers (Keith Johnston, email correspondence, August 17, 2016).

2. Netflix itself has acknowledged the significance of long-form true crime as "one of its most bankable genres" (Heritage 2017) by inventing its own parody of the form with *American Vandal* (Yacenda 2017), the first series of which revolves around the mystery of who is vandalizing a small-town school with penis drawings. Described by the *Guardian* as "basically a four-hour dick joke," the eight-episode-long first series parodies *Making a Murderer* (and other shows like it) and "is rammed with cleverly paced twists and the stock characters that a true-crime doc requires" (Heritage 2017). To date, there are two series of *American Vandal*. On October 26, 2018, Netflix announced it was canceling the series.

3. This chapter examines the trailer for the first series of *Making a Murderer*. On October 9, 2018, Netflix released the trailer for *Making a Murderer Part 2*, which is available on YouTube at https://www.youtube.com/watch?v=Nu4GgQ1LWiI. This second trailer, which has already accrued 687, 054 views as of December 4, 2018, makes similar discursive moves to the first, and is designed to rouse similar emotions in viewers; its tagline is: "The convictions were only the beginning. The worldwide phenomenon contin-ues October 19, only on Netflix." This new trailer introduces the figure of postconviction attorney Kathleen Zellner, whom I will discuss further in the postscript to chapter 4, and deploys the familiar rhetoric of the "secret": "When everything is questioned . . . what will be uncovered?"

4. It re-aired on ABC during the 1959–60 season at 7:30 p.m. on Wednesdays.

5. See the back-of-book blurb for the 2017 edition of *The Court of Last Resort* (Open Road Integrated Media).

6. *The Court of Last Resort* TV show followed a formula whereby the opening to each episode invited the audience to decide upon the guilt or innocence of the accused or convicted.

7. Journalist Kathryn Schulz has also made the case for the renewed significance of *The Court of Last Resort* in light of the remarkable popularity of recent long-form series such as *Serial* and *Making a Murderer*. As Schulz suggests in a 2016 article for the *New Yorker*, "Although it subsequently faded from memory, 'The Court of Last Resort' stands as the progenitor of one of today's most popular true-crime subgenres, in which reporters, dissatisfied with the outcome of a criminal case, conduct their own extrajudicial investigations" (Schulz 2016).

8. The *Making a Murderer* trailer is available on YouTube at https://www.youtube.com/watch?v=qxgbdYaR_KQ&t=4s.

9. All of the user comments discussed in this chapter can be found on YouTube trailer site at https://www.youtube.com/watch?v=qxgbdYaR_KQ&t=4s, accessed July 18, 2018.

10. In his fascinating analysis of viewer responses to *Making a Murderer* on Reddit, Liam Kennedy makes a similar finding and notes that several redditors made explicit connections between *Making a Murderer* and the racializing killings of citizens in America by police officers that were widespread in the context of the Netflix series release. For example, Kennedy quotes one redditor who asserted that "If Steven Avery were black he would have been dead by now" (2018, 402). Kennedy's analysis of viewers' affective responses to *Making a Murderer* on Reddit "demonstrates the value of looking to user-generated content on social media platforms to understand how we think and feel about crime-related matters" (391). My use of a qualitative methodology of viewer response to the *Making a Murderer* trailer on YouTube is similarly concerned with the importance of online viewer response for understanding the relationship between emotions, judgments, beliefs, and criminal justice.

11. The Netflix trailers for the *Amanda Knox* documentary are available on YouTube. For the "Believe Her" trailer go to: https://www.youtube.com/watch?v=NueLjUNB-GM&t=6s and for the "Suspect Her" trailer go to: https://www.youtube.com/watch?v=9r8LG_lCbac. The YouTube comments I discuss in this chapter were accessed from these sites on July 15, 2018.

12. In reading the reviews of the *Amanda Knox* documentary, it is striking

just how many reviewers complained about its length. It was criticized for its "brevity" and for its "too-short run time." *Empire* magazine, for example, argued that: "in a post-*Serial* world, where *The Jinx* and Netflix's own *Making a Murderer* have become media sensations, *Amanda Knox's* 90-minute running time feels rushed. . . . Expectations of this type of true-crime documentary have changed, and this speedy tour through eight years of Italian justice (or lack of) fails to fully satisfy" (Pile 2016). Reviewer Katie Erbland makes a similar complaint, suggesting that the documentary is "hobbled by its short shrift feature-length" and leaves viewers "wanting more." She writes: "As a 92-minute commercial for a deeper look at the case, 'Amanda Knox' is unquestionably intriguing; as a standalone offering, it makes one hell of an airtight case for something bigger and better" (2016). I would argue that such complaints are less about the need for more information or evidence regarding the case, and more about the desire to be held longer in the affective experience of the long form.

Chapter 4

1. Research company Symphony Advanced Media claims that, as the hype around *Making a Murderer* grew, within in its first few weeks over 19.3 million viewers had watched the series (Nededog 2016).

2. For an excellent discussion of the cold open in long form serial TV drama please see Coulthard (2010).

3. Ultimately, the appeals court upheld Brendan Dassey's conviction, and as of December 2018, he remains in jail. *Making a Murderer Part 2* outlines the legal decisions that led to Dassey remaining in jail.

4. Robert Durst has been in prison since his March 2015 arrest. In October 2018, Los Angeles Country Superior Judge Mark Windham ruled that there is enough evidence to try Durst for the murder of Susan Berman in 2000.

5. As of December 2018, Adnan Syed remains in jail and has not yet had his new trial.

6. *Saturday Night Live* performed a parody skit of a podcast awards show, "The Poddy," on its November 10, 2018, episode and included an award for "Best Nervous White Girl in a Place She Doesn't Belong," with Sarah Koenig (Cecily Strong) as one of the presenters. The skit pokes fun at the emotional charge of social justice podcasts featuring white women who "brazenly" venture into "dangerous," unfamiliar territory—as well as to the white women who serve as eager listeners ("Thanks to the thousands of women who chose to listen to gruesome confessions of neo Nazis while walking on

their treadmills.") Thanks to Mareike Jenner for drawing my attention to this skit.

7. See Julie Carrie Wong (2014) for a good account of the Asian stereotyping in *Serial*. As Wong argues, both Adnan and Hae "receive the model minority treatment" and are stereotyped as good, hardworking, and "responsible" students in comparison to the African American, Jay, who serves as "their 'thuggish' black foil."

8. On June 2018, Netflix announced that they had "repackaged and revamped [*The Staircase*] for a streaming audience," adding three new episodes to heighten its binge-ability at thirteen episodes long (Zafar 2018).

9. These tweets are all found through a search of the phrase "Robert Durst's eyes" on Twitter. Please see https://twitter.com/search?q=robert%20durst's %20eyes&src=typd, accessed July 18, 2018.

10. Ian Case Punnett suggests that *Serial, The Jinx,* and *Making a Murderer* did not present themselves specifically as "true crime" texts (2018, 2, 26), but I would argue that they were strongly promoted, discussed, and understood in these terms in their popular media reception.

11. This quotation is from the Member Reviews for *Making a Murderer*, which I accessed on Netflix UK in March 2016. Netflix has since archived its member reviews and stopped allowing viewers to post reviews as of July 30, 2018.

12. See Harnick (2016) for an account of this petition and the White House response to it: "Since Steven Avery and Brendan Dassey are both state prisoners, the President cannot pardon them. A pardon in this case would need to be issued at the state level by the appropriate authorities."

13. This Buzzfeed video is available at https://www.youtube.com/watch?v =dqXAmMCR9lQ.

14. This quotation is from the Member Reviews for *Making a Murderer* on Netflix UK, which I accessed in March 2016. Netflix has since archived its member reviews and stopped allowing viewers to post reviews as of July 30, 2018.

15. See https://www.reddit.com/r/MakingaMurderer/comments/4201p7/the _evidence_box_with_the_blood_vial_tampered/.

16. As Case Punnett notes, true crime is notable for its failure to reference "the black crime experience in America at all, either as victims or perpetrators" (2018, 43). Case Punnett also refers to Murley's observation that "True crime's intense focus on the intersection of whiteness and violence is at odds with statistical reality, where in 2006, African Americans made up 12.5

percent of the total United States population, but 49.5 percent of its murder victims" (Murley 2008, 20).

17. See https://strangcore.tumblr.com.

18. *Making a Murderer Part 2* revisits Kratz's 2006 press conference yet again, and voices sharp criticism of it through lawyer Kathleen Zellner (who I discuss in the final part of this chapter). Part 2 also includes a TV segment in which Kratz says he regrets doing the press conference.

19. See Rebecca Wanzo (2008) on the "Lost Girl Event" in popular culture. As Wanzo writes: "The Lost Girl Event is always about innocent girls, inexplicable violence, and villainy. Ironically, tales about the missing and murdered girls lost through unnatural occurrences make cozy bedfellows of psychological comfort and cultural anxiety" (100).

20. See https://www.youtube.com/watch?v=tiuqGf8T_So.

21. In interviews following the release of the first series of *Making a Murderer*, Demos and Ricciardi said they could not have anticipated the kind of social media reaction they received. As Laura Ricciardi notes: "We always hoped that there would be viewer engagement, we just had no idea that people would become amateur sleuths" (quoted in Yamato 2016).

22. Some of Zellner's tweets on the case are included in *Making a Murderer Part 2*. At the beginning of episode 3, "A Legal Miracle," one of Teresa Halbach's friends questions why Zellner uses Twitter to try to get Avery out of jail.

23. For an example of Kathleen Zellner fan tweets, please see: https://twitter .com/search?f=tweets&q=kathleen%20zellner%20and%20making%20a %20murderer%202&src=typd.

24. The inclusion of the list of names of those who declined to participate at the end of every episode of Series 2 is a strong retort to those who accused Series 1 of "bias." By including this list of names, Demos and Ricciardi are powerfully demonstrating their attempt to include other voices—and highlighting the force of their silence and refusal to participate. However, I would argue that it remains an unintended consequence of both Part 1 and Part 2 that the family of Teresa Halbach come across as somehow negative in their portrayal (in Part 2 we see them at various moments in archival footage and in scenes in which they arrive for postconviction hearings), as they are depicted as being on the other side of the series' strong affective backing of the postconviction attorneys and the Dassey and Avery families.

25. Bobby Dassey did not agree to be interviewed on camera for *Making a Murderer Part 2*, whereas John Mark Byers is an enthusiastic participant throughout *Paradise Lost 2: Purgatory*.

26. For details of Nirider's and Drizin's speaking tour, please see https://www
    .seetickets.com/tour/making-a-murderer-laura-nirider-and-steven-drizin.

Afterword

1. "Revenge porn" is the term for sharing nonconsensual images of another
   person in a way intended to cause them distress (see "Revenge Porn: The
   Facts" n.d.). The sharing and distribution of "revenge pornography" has
   been made a criminal offense in the United Kingdom and in a number of
   states in America, although it still remains difficult to prosecute. The term
   "revenge porn" is itself problematic, as it implies the victim is to somehow
   be blamed for the crime, and feminists have argued instead for the terms
   "image-based sexual abuse" (McGlynn n.d.); "non-consensual pornography"
   (Cyber Civil Rights Initiative n.d.); and "technologically facilitated sexual
   violence" (Henry and Powell 2017, 4).

2. As defined by Katie O'Malley in an article for the British newspaper the
   Independent, upskirting is "a term used to describe the act of taking a
   photograph up someone's skirt without their permission" (2019). The photos
   are generally taken with a smartphone and are sometimes circulated online
   through social media networking sites.

3. "Sextortion" is when people—often young men—allow themselves to be
   filmed, by digital webcams, carrying out sex acts. They are then extorted by
   criminal gangs who threaten to share the explicit images with employers and
   family members. In May 2018 in the United Kingdom, the National Crime
   Agency reported that cases of "sextortion" are on the rise, with "1,304 cases
   reported in 2017, up from 428 in 2015—although the real number of victims
   is thought to be much higher" (Whitworth 2018).

4. For a discussion of #metoo, see Cobb and Horeck (2018).

5. Asia Argento has since deleted her Twitter account.

6. In a *New York Times* article (Severson 2018) it was alleged that Argento paid
   $380,000 to actor Jimmy Bennett, who claimed that she sexually assaulted
   him when he was seventeen years old (the age of consent in California is
   eighteen) and she was thirty-seven years old, in a hotel room. The pair were
   working on a film together at the time.

7. Joyce Malecki was a twenty-year-old woman who went missing four days
   after Sister Catherine Cesnik. She was found murdered on November 13,
   1969. *The Keepers* briefly examines Malecki's story and the possible connection to the murder of Sister Cathy, though she does not appear in any of the
   marketing materials for the series.

8. Please see Karen Boyle's important work (2018, 1) on the need to identify "specifically gendered patterns of violence and experience" in public accounts of male violence.

9. Please see http://www.cbc.ca/missingandmurdered/.

10. Various staff members have left the national inquiry into missing and murdered indigenous women, and most recently, the commissioner has said she may quit as well after the Canadian government offered only a limited time extension. Please see Barrera (2018) for further details.

11. Intersectionality is a term coined by Kimberlé Crenshaw (1989) to refer to how race and gender interact together to subordinate black women. As Crenshaw has recently stated: "Intersectionality is a lens through which you can see where power comes and collides, where it interlocks and intersects" (Crenshaw 2017).

12. There is not the space here to list all the true crime podcasts that have emerged in the last decade, but see, for example, *Up and Vanished* (2016–17), a US podcast that investigated the 2005 disappearance of beauty queen Tara Grinstead from her home in Georgia and that is credited with reigniting interest in the case, resulting in the arrest of two new suspects.

13. Yardley et al. note that, even as criminal justice officials "draw upon information that websleuths provide, it seems that they often label websleuths as problematic: doing more harm than good; opening rather than closing cases; lacking understanding of procedural constraints; harming the criminal justice process; and having the potential to negatively affect suspects, victims and others affected by cases" (2018a, 105). Michelle McNamara's friends and families, for instance, felt that legal officials unfairly downplayed her critical involvement in the wake of the dramatic capture of the Golden State Killer (Rosenberg 2018).

Works Cited

"Accolades for 'Dear Zachary.'" 2008. NBC News, May 12, 2008. http://www
.nbcnews.com/id/28074909/ns/msnbc-documentaries/t/accolades-dear
-zachary/#.XGgu6SonhPM.

Adams, Sam. 2016. "Making a Murder and True Crime in the Binge-Watching
Era." *Rolling Stone*, January 13, 2016. http://www.rollingstone.com/tv/news/
making-a-murderer-and-true-crime-in-the-binge-viewing-era-20160113.

Adkins, King. 2008. "Paradise Lost: Documenting a Southern Tragedy." *Journal
of Film & Video* 60 (1): 14–22.

Aguayo, Angela. 2014. "*Paradise Lost* and Found: Popular Documentary, Collective Identification and Participatory Media Culture." *Studies in Documentary
Film* 7 (3): 233–48.

Ahmed, Sara. 2004. *The Cultural Politics of Emotion.* Edinburgh: Edinburgh
University Press.

Andrejevic, Mark. 2007. *iSpy: Power and Surveillance in the Interactive Era.* Lawrence: University of Kansas Press.

———. 2016. "The *Jouissance* of Trump." *Television & New Media* 17 (7): 651–55.

Arnold, Sarah. 2016. "Netflix and the Myth of Choice/Participation/Autonomy."
In *The Netflix Effect*, edited by Kevin McDonald and Daniel Smith-Rowsey,
49–62. New York: Bloomsbury.

Arthur, Paul. 2003. "True Confessions, Sort of: *Capturing the Friedmans* and the
Dilemma of Theatrical Documentary." *Cineaste* (Fall) 28 (4): 4–7.

———. 2005. "Extreme Makeover: The Changing Face of Documentary." *Cineaste*
30 (3): 18–23.

Atkinson, Sarah. 2014. *Beyond the Screen: Emerging Cinema and Engaging Audiences.* New York: Bloomsbury.

Aufderheide, Patricia. 2005. "The Changing Documentary Marketplace." *Cineaste* 30 (3): 24–28.

———. 2016. "Mainstream Documentary since 1999." In *American Film History:
Selected Readings, 1960 to the Present*, edited by Cynthia Lucia, Roy Grund-
mann, and Art Simon, 376–92. Chicester, West Sussex: Wiley-Blackwell.

Austin, Thomas. 2007. *Watching the World: Screen Documentary and Audiences.* Manchester: Manchester University Press.

Banet-Weiser, Sarah. 2018. *Empowered: Popular Feminism and Popular Misogyny.* Durham: Duke University Press.

Banet-Weiser, Sarah, and Laura Portwood-Stacer. 2017. "The Traffic in Feminism: An Introduction to the Commentary and Criticism on Popular Feminism." *Feminist Media Studies* 17 (5): 884–88.

Banks, David. 2012. "Trial by Twitter." *Guardian,* August 14, 2012. https://www .theguardian.com/law/2012/aug/14/court-reporters-twitter.

Barker, Cory, and Myc Wiatrowski. 2017. *The Age of Netflix: Critical Essays on Streaming Media, Digital Delivery and Instant Access.* Jefferson, NC: McFarland.

Barnard, Linda. 2012. "The Imposter Review: Doc Thriller Deserves Oscar Nod." *Star,* October 11, 2012. https://www.thestar.com/entertainment/movies/ 2012/10/11/the_imposter_review_doc_thriller_deserves_oscar_nod.html.

Barrera, Jorge. 2018. "MMIWG Inquiry Commissioner May Quit After Ottawa Grants Limited Extension." *CBC News,* June 5, 2018. https://www.cbc.ca/ news/indigenous/inquiry-extension-ottawa-1.4691903.

Barthes, Roland. 1993. *Camera Lucida.* London: Vintage.

Bauder, David. 2015. "The Jinx Documentary Is Made for the Binge Watcher." *Star,* February 6, 2015. https://www.thestar.com/entertainment/television/ 2015/02/06/the-jinx-documentary-is-made-for-the-binge-watcher.html.

Bell, Vikki. 2008. "The Burden of Sensation and the Ethics of Form: Watching *Capturing the Friedmans.*" *Theory, Culture and Society* 25 (3): 89–101.

Bennett, James, and Tom Brown. 2008. *Film and Television After DVD.* London: Routledge.

Benson-Allot, Caetlin. 2013. *Killer Tapes and Shattered Screens: Video Spectatorship from VHS to File Sharing.* Berkeley: University of California Press, 2013.

———. 2016. "Learning from Horror." *Film Quarterly* 70 (2): 58–62.

———. 2017. "Whose Horror? Digital Violence and White Spectatorship." Keynote address, Digital Violence Symposium, Anglia Ruskin University, November 4.

Berridge, Susan. 2013. "Teen Heroine TV: Narrative Complexity and Sexual Violence in Female-Fronted Teen Drama Series." *New Review of Film and Television Studies* 11 (4): 477–96.

Berridge, Susan, and Laura Portwood-Stacer. 2015. "Introduction: Feminism, Hashtags and Violence against Women and Girls." *Feminist Media Studies* 15 (2): 341.

Betters, Elyse. 2016. "Facebook Reactions Explained: Here's the Scoop on Those New Smileys." *Pocket-lint*, February 24, 2016. https://www.pocket-lint.com/apps/news/facebook/136870-facebook-reactions-explained-here-s-the-scoop-on-those-new-smileys.

Bird, Steve. 2017. "BBC Axes Crimewatch After 33 Years on Air." *Telegraph*, October 17, 2017. https://www.telegraph.co.uk/news/2017/10/17/bbc-axes-crimewatch-33-years-air/.

Biressi, Anita. 2001. *Crime, Fear and the Law in True Crime Stories*. Houndsmill, Basingstoke: Palgrave Macmillan.

Black Lives Matter. n.d. "What We Believe." Accessed July 8, 2018. https://blacklivesmatter.com/about/what-we-believe.

Boland, Hannah. 2018. "Netflix Shares Pop as It Hits 125 Million Subscribers." *Telegraph*, April 16, 2018. https://www.telegraph.co.uk/technology/2018/04/16/netflix-shares-pop-hits-125-million-subscribers/.

Boyle, Karen. 2018. "What's in a Name? Theorising the Inter-Relationships of Gender and Violence." *Feminist Theory*, first published online February 20. https://doi.org/10.1177/146470011875495: 1–18.

Bradshaw, Peter. 2012. "The Imposter—Review." *Guardian*, August 23, 2012. http://www.theguardian.com/film/2012/aug/23/the-imposter-review.

Browder, Laura. 2006. "Dystopian Romance: True Crime and the Female Reader." *Journal of Popular Culture* 39 (6): 928–53.

———. 2010. "True Crime." In *The Cambridge Companion to American Crime Fiction*, edited by Catherine Nickerson, 121–34. Cambridge: Cambridge University Press. Accessed November 17, 2018. https://scholarship.richmond.edu/english-faculty-publications/64/.

Brown, Tom. 2008. " 'The DVD of Attractions?': *The Lion King* and the Digital Theme Park." In *Film and Television After DVD*, edited by James Bennett, and Tom Brown, 81–100. London: Routledge.

Bruzzi, Stella. 2006. *New Documentary*. 2d ed. London: Routledge.

———. 2012. Keynote presentation at The Powers of the False Symposium, Cine Lumière, Institut Francais, London, May 18–19, convened by Steven Eastwood and Catherine Wheatley.

Buchanan, Jason. n.d. Review of Dear Zachary: A Letter to a Son About His Father. *TV Guide*. Accessed July 16, 2009. http://movies.tvguide.com/dear-zachary-letter-son-father/review/295382.

Butler, Isaac. 2016. "What Errol Morris Thinks of *Making a Murderer*." *Slate*, January 27, 2016. http://www.slate.com/articles/arts/culturebox/2016/01/errol_morris_q_a_on_the_thin_blue_line_and_making_a_murderer.html.

Butler, Judith. 1993. "Endangered/Endangering: Schematic Racism and White Paranoia." In *Reading Rodney King, Reading Urban Uprising*, edited by Robert Gooding-Williams, 15–22. New York: Routledge.

———. 2004. *Precarious Life: The Powers of Mourning and Violence*. London: Verso.

———. 2009. *Frames of War: When Is Life Grievable?* London: Verso.

Capehart, Jonathan. 2014. "What Jay Z Could Teach Ray Rice." *Washington Post*, September 10, 2014. https://www.washingtonpost.com/blogs/post-partisan/wp/2014/09/10/what-jay-z-could-teach-ray-rice/.

Capote, Truman. (1966) 2000. *In Cold Blood: A True Account of Murder and Its Multiple Consequences*. Penguin Modern Classics. London: Penguin.

Case Punnett, Ian. 2018. *Toward a Theory of True Crime Narratives: A Textual Analysis*. New York: Routledge.

Cavender, Gray, and Mark Fishman. 1998. *Entertaining Crime: Television Reality Programs*. New York: Aldine De Gruyter.

Chabria, Anita. 2018. "'He's Just a Babe': Detective in East Area Rapist Case Has Become an Unlikely Sex Symbol." *Sacramento Bee*, May 9, 2018. https://www.sacbee.com/latest-news/article210665984.html.

Charjan, Mahesh. 2018. "Netflix to Try Out AI to Craft Personalized Trailers for Movies." *D Zone/AI Zone*, May 1, 2018. https://dzone.com/articles/netflix-to-try-out-ai-to-craft-personalised-traile.

Childress, Erik. n.d. Review of *Dear Zachary: A Letter to a Son About his Father*. Oscilloscope DVD.

Chun, Wendy Hui Kyong. 2016. *Updating to Remain the Same: Habitual New Media*. Cambridge: Massachusetts Institute of Technology.

Ciobanu, Mădălina. 2016. "Why CBC News Produced Its First Investigative Podcast." Journalism.co.uk, October 27, 2016. https://www.journalism.co.uk/news/why-cbc-news-produced-its-first-investigative-podcast/s2/a686762/.

Clark, Rosemary. 2016. "'Hope in a Hashtag': The Discursive Activism of #WhyIStayed." *Feminist Media Studies* 16 (5): 788–804.

Clarke Dillman, Joanne. 2014. *Women and Death in Film, Television, and News: Dead but Not Gone*. New York: Palgrave Macmillan.

Clover, Carol. 2000a. "Judging Audiences: The Case of the Movie Trial." In *Reinventing Film Studies*, edited by Christine Gledhill and Linda Williams, 244–64. London: Arnold.

———. 2000b. "Law and the Order of Popular Culture." In *Law in the Domains of Culture*, edited by Austin Sarat and Thomas R. Kearns, 97–119. Ann Arbor: University of Michigan Press.

Cobb, Shelley, and Tanya Horeck. 2018. "Post Weinstein: Gendered Power and Harassment in the Media Industries." *Feminist Media Studies* 18 (3): 489–508.

Cochran, Amanda. 2013. "*America's Most Wanted* Host John Walsh on Cancellation: Show Needs to Be on TV." *CBS This Morning,* May 7, 2013. https://www.cbsnews.com/news/americas-most-wanted-host-john-walsh-on-cancellation-show-needs-to-be-on-tv/.

Collins, Patricia Hill. 2000. *Black Feminist Thought: Knowledge, Consciousness and the Politics of Empowerment.* 2nd ed. London: Routledge, 2000.

Corner, John. 2009. "Performing the Real: Documentary Diversions." In *Reality TV: Remaking Television Culture,* edited by Susan Murray and Laurie Ouellette, 44–64. New York: New York University Press, 2009.

Coscarelli, Joe. 2013. "All the Mistakenly Identified 'Suspects' in the Boston Bombing Investigation." *New York Magazine,* April, 19, 2013. http://nymag.com/daily/intelligencer/2013/04/wrongly-accused-boston-bombing-suspects-sunil-tripathi.html.

Coulthard, Lisa. 2010. "The Hotness of Cold Opens: *Breaking Bad* and the Serial Narrative as Puzzle." November 12, 2010. https://www.flowjournal.org/2010/11/the-hotness-of-cold-opens/.

Covert, James. 2015. "Users Rage After On-Air Murder Autoplays on Social Media." *New York Post,* August 28, 2015. http://www.news.com.au/finance/business/media/users-rage-after-onair-murder-autoplays-on-social-media/news-story/d8f21e88715bfaea5d0a3575443c3d93.

Cowie, Elizabeth. 1997. *Representing the Woman: Cinema and Psychoanalysis.* Houndmills, Basingstoke: Macmillan.

Crary, Jonathan. 2013. *24/7: Late Capitalism and the Ends of Sleep.* London: Verso.

Crenshaw, Kimberlé. 1989. "Demarginalizing the Intersection of Race and Sex: A Black Feminist Critique of Antidiscrimination Doctrine, Feminist Theory and Antiracist Politics." University of Chicago Legal Forum. Vol. 1989: Issue 1, Article 8. http://chicagounbound.uchicago.edu/uclf/vol1989/iss1/8.

———. 2017. "Kimberlé Crenshaw on Intersectionality, More than Two Decades Later." Columbia Law School, June 8, 2017. https://www.law.columbia.edu/pt-br/news/2017/06/kimberle-crenshaw-intersectionality.

Cyber Civil Rights Initiative. n.d. Accessed June 15, 2018. https://www.cybercivilrights.org.

D'Addario, Daniel. 2017. "*The Keepers* Avoids True Crime's Ghastliest Pitfalls." *Time,* May 25, 2017. http://time.com/4793893/the-keepers-review.

———. 2018. "TV Review: 'Making a Murderer: Part 2.'" *Vulture,* October 19,

2018. https://variety.com/2018/tv/reviews/making-a-murderer-part-2-review
-netflix-1202982874/.

Dean, Jodi. 2002. *Publicity's Secret: How Technoculture Capitalizes on Democracy.*
New York: Cornell University Press.

———. 2010a. *Blog Theory: Feedback and Capture in the Circuits of Drive.* Cambridge: Polity Press.

———. 2010b. "Affective Networks." *Media Tropes* 2 (2): 19–44.

"Dear Zachary: A Letter to a Son About His Father." n.d. Subreddit. Accessed
July 11, 2018. https://www.reddit.com/r/Documentaries/comments/67gp3y/
dear_zachary_a_letter_to_a_son_about_his_father/.

Desta, Yohana. 2016. "Chilling Trailers for Netflix's Amanda Knox Doc Capture
Both Sides of Her Story." *Vanity Fair,* September 8, 2016. https://www.vanity
fair.com/hollywood/2016/09/amanda-knox-netflix-doc-trailers.

Doane, Bethany, Kaitlin McCormick, and Guiliana Sorce. 2017. "Changing Methods for Feminist Public Scholarship: Lessons from Sarah Koenig's Podcast
Serial." *Feminist Media Studies* 17 (1): 119–21.

Dominguez, Pier. 2015. " 'I'm Very Rich, Bitch!': The Melodramatic Money Shot
and the Excess of Racialized Gendered Affect in the *Real Housewives* Docusoaps." *Camera Obscura* 30, no. 1 (88): 155–83.

Donegan, Moira. 2018. "How #MeToo Revealed the Central Rift within Feminism Today." *Guardian,* May 11, 2018. https://www.theguardian.com/
news/2018/may/11/how-metoo-revealed-the-central-rift-within-feminism
-social-individualist.

Driscoll, Margarette. 2016. "Terribly Wronged, or a Devil with an Angel Face?
Inside Netflix's 'Sympathetic' Amanda Knox Documentary." *Telegraph,* September 25, 2016. https://www.telegraph.co.uk/women/life/terribly-wronged
-or-a-devil-with-an-angel-face-inside-netflixs-s/.

Druick, Zoë. 2008. "The Courtroom and the Closet in *The Thin Blue Line* and
Capturing the Friedmans." *Screen* 49 (1): 440–49.

Dubrofsky, E. Rachel, and Megan M. Wood. 2015. "Gender, Race, and Authenticity: Celebrity Women Tweeting for the Gaze." In *Feminist Surveillance Studies,* edited by Rachel E. Dubrofsky and Shoshana Amielle Magnet, 93–106.
Durham: Duke University Press.

Durham, Alexis M., H. Preston Elrod, and Patrick T. Kinkade. 1995. "Images of
Crime and Justice: Murder and the 'True Crime' Genre." *Journal of Criminal
Justice* 23 (2): 143–52.

Dyer, Richard. 2015. *Lethal Repetition: Serial Killing in European Cinema.* London: BFI/Palgrave.

Egan, Leigh. 2016. "'Making a Murderer': Filmmakers Respond to Deleting Key Evidence From Documentary." *Inquisitr*, January 20, 2016. https://www.inquisitr.com/2724976/making-a-murderer-filmmakers-respond-to-deleting-key-evidence-from-documentary/

Elias, Justine. 2014. "More on That Later: The Truth about 'Serial.'" *Balder and Dash*, December 18, 2014. https://www.rogerebert.com/balder-and-dash/more-on-that-later-the-truth-about-serial.

Ellis, John. 2009. "What Are We Expected to Feel? Witness, Textuality and the Audiovisual." *Screen* 50 (1): 67–76.

Emerson, Brian. 2016. "50 Best Ken Kratz Mean Tweets." *BaeDaily,* January 8, 2016. https://baedaily.com/entertainment/ken-kratz-meantweets/.

Eppink, Jason. 2014. "A Brief History of the GIF (So Far)." *Journal of Visual Culture* 13 (3): 298–306.

Erbland, Katie. 2016. "'Amanda Knox': Netflix Documentary Makes Case for Larger Look at Enthralling Crime Story—TIFF Review." *IndieWire*, September 10, 2016. https://www.indiewire.com/2016/09/amanda-knox-review-netflix-documentary-tiff-1201725361/.

Finn, Ed. 2017. *What Algorithms Want: Imagination in the Age of Computing.* Cambridge: MIT Press.

Friend, Stacie. 2007. "The Pleasures of Documentary Tragedy." *British Journal of Aesthetics* 47 (2): 184–98.

Frosh, Paul, and Amit Pinchevski. 2014. "Media Witnessing and the Ripeness of Time." *Cultural Studies* 28 (4): 594–610.

Fuhs, Kristen. 2014. "The Legal Trial and/in Documentary Film." *Cultural Studies* 28 (5–6): 781–808.

———. 2017. "'The Dramatic Idea of Justice': Wrongful Conviction, Documentary Television, and *The Court of Last Resort*," *Historical Journal of Film, Radio and Television* DOI: 10.1018/01439685.2016.125845: 1-19.

Gaines, Jane M. 1999. "Political Mimesis." In *Collecting Visible Evidence*, edited by Jane M. Gaines and Michael Renov, 84–102, Minneapolis: University of Minnesota Press.

Garcia, Stephen, and Chris Jaffe. 2016. "New Netflix TV Experience Includes Video Previews that Speed Your Next Selection." December 6, 2016. https://media.netflix.com/en/company-blog/new-netflix-tv-experience-includes-video-previews-that-speed-your-next-selection.

Garcia, Venessa, and Samantha G. Arkerson. 2018. *Crime, Media, and Reality: Examining Mixed Messages about Crime and Justice in Popular Media.* Lanham, MD: Rowman & Littlefield.

Gardner, Erle Stanley. (1952) 2017. *The Court of Last Resort*. New York: Open Road Integrated Media.

———. 1957a. Memo to "ALL members of the Court of Last Resort," June 10, 1957, Erle Stanley Gardner Collection, Harry Ransom Center, Boxes 56–58.

———. 1957b. Gardner to Jules Goldstone, June 17, 1957, Erle Stanley Gardner Collection, Harry Ransom Center, Boxes 56–58.

———. 1957c. Gardner to Gail Jackson, August 13, 1957, Erle Stanley Gardner Collection, Harry Ransom Center, Boxes 56–58.

———. 1957d. "The Court of Last Resort: The Darlene Fitzgerald Tag." Correspondence. September 10, 1957, Erle Stanley Gardner Collection, Harry Ransom Center, Boxes 56–58.

———. 1957e. Gardner to Jules Goldstone, October 4, 1957, Erle Stanley Gardner Collection, Harry Ransom Center, Boxes 56–58.

Gill, Rosalind. 2007. "Post-Feminist Media Culture: Elements of a Sensibility." *European Journal of Cultural Studies* 10 (2): 147–66.

———. 2016. "Post-Postfeminism? New Feminist Visibilities in Postfeminist Times." *Feminist Media Studies* 16 (4): 610–30.

Ging, Debbie. 2017. "Alphas, Betas and Incels: Theorizing the Masculinities of the Manosphere." *Men and Masculinities*. First published online May 10, 2017.

Ging, Debbie, and Eugenia Siapera, eds. 2018. "Special Issue on Online Misogyny." *Feminist Media Studies* 18 (4): 515–24.

Giorgis, Hannah. 2014. "Don't Watch the Ray Rice Video. Don't Ask Why Janay Palmer Married Him. Ask Why Anyone Would Blame a Victim." *Guardian,* September 8, 2014. https://www.theguardian.com/commentisfree/2014/sep/08/ray-rice-domestic-violence-video-janay-palmer-victim-blaming.

Glassman, Amanda. 2015. "How 'Serial' and 'The Jinx' Have Changed Everything." *Huffington Post*, March 19, 2015. https://www.huffingtonpost.com/amanda-glassman/how-serial-and-the-jinx-h_b_6898970.html.

Glebatis Perks, Lisa. 2015. *Media Marathoning: Immersions in Morality*. Lanham, MD: Lexington Books.

"Globe Editorial: Inquiry into Missing and Murdered Indigenous Women Can Still Make a Difference." 2017. *Globe and Mail*, November 3, 2017. https://www.theglobeandmail.com/opinion/editorials/globe-editorial-inquiry-into-missing-and-murdered-indigenous-women-can-still-make-a-difference/article36827702/.

Godwin, Richard. 2015. "Serial Thriller: Are True Crimes Dramas Turning Us into a Nation of Armchair Detectives?" *Evening Standard*, September 3, 2015. https://www.standard.co.uk/lifestyle/esmagazine/serial-thriller-how

-true-crimes-dramas-have-turned-us-into-a-nation-of-armchair-detectives
-a2925946.html.

"Goodell: NFL Wasn't Given Tape." 2014. *ABC13: Eyewitness News*, September 10, 2014. http://abc13.com/sports/goodell-nfl-wasnt-given-tape/301606/.

Gooding-Williams, Robert. 1993. "'Look, a Negro!'" In *Reading Rodney King, Reading Urban Uprising*, edited by Robert Gooding-Williams, 157–77. New York: Routledge.

Grainge, Paul. 2011. "Introduction: Ephemeral Media." In *Ephemeral Media: Transitory Screen Culture from Television to YouTube*, edited by Paul Grainge, 1–19. London: BFI.

Gray, Jonathan. 2010. *Show Sold Separately: Promos, Spoilers, and Other Media Paratexts*. New York: New York University Press.

Green, Elon. 2018. "Using True Crime to Teach Indigenous History: Reporter Connie Walker on 'Finding Cleo.'" *Columbia Journalism Review*, July 5, 2018. https://www.cjr.org/q_and_a/finding-cleo.php.

Greene, Robert. 2016. "The Jinx: Not My Documentary Renaissance." *Sight and Sound*, November 22, 2016. http://www.bfi.org.uk/news-opinion/sight
-sound-magazine/reviews-recommendations/tv/jinx-not-my-documentary
-renaissance.

Griffin, Rachel Alicia. 2018. "The Spectacularization and Serialization of White-ness: Theorizing 50+Years of O.J. Simpson's Contentious Notoriety." *Communication, Culture and Critique* 11: 359–77.

Grindstaff, Laura, and Susan Murray. 2015. "Reality Celebrity: Branded Affect and the Emotion Economy." *Public Culture* 27 (1): 109–35.

Grusin, Richard. 2010. *Premediation: Affect and Mediality after 9/11*. London: Palgrave MacMillan.

———. 2016. "DVDs, Video Games, and the Cinema of Interactions." In *Post-Cinema: Theorizing 21st Century Film*, edited by Shane Denson and Julia Leyda. Falmer: Reframe Books. http://reframe.sussex.ac.uk/post-cinema/.

Gunning, Tom. 1999. "Embarrassing Evidence: The Detective Camera and the Documentary Impulse." In *Collecting Visible Evidence*, edited by Jane M. Gaines and Michael Renov, 46–64. Minneapolis: University of Minnesota Press.

Gye, Lisa, and Jeremy Weinstein. 2011. "*Docummunity* and the Disruptive Poten-tial of Collaborative Documentary Filmmaking." In *Expanding Documen-tary 2011: Conference Proceedings* vol. 1, no. 2.

Hamad, Hannah. 2015. "Eddie Murphy's Baby Mama Drama and Smith Family Values: The (Post-) Racial Familial Politics of Hollywood Celebrity Couples."

In *First Comes Love: Power Couples, Celebrity Kinship and Cultural Politics*, edited by Shelley Cobb and Neil Ewen, 116–32. New York: Bloomsbury.

Harnick, Chris. 2016. "*Making a Murderer* Petitions Call for President Obama to Pardon Steven Avery." *EOnline*, January 7, 2016. https://www.eonline.com/uk/news/727818/making-a-murderer-petitions-call-for-president-obama-to-pardon-steven-avery.

Hawkes, Rebecca. 2017. "Netflix's Choose Your Own Adventure Experiment: Are Multiple Endings the Future of TV?" *Wired YA*, March 23, 2017. http://cplwchoya.blogspot.com/2017/03/netflixs-choose-your-own-adventure.html.

Hayes, Rebecca M., and Kate Luther. 2018. *#Crime, Social Media and the Criminal Legal System*. Cham, Switzerland: Palgrave Macmillan.

Henderson, Lesley. 2007. *Social Issues in Television Fiction*. Edinburgh: Edinburgh University Press.

Henry, Nicola, and Anastasia Powell. 2017. *Sexual Violence in a Digital Age*. Basingstoke: Palgrave Macmillan.

Heritage, Stuart. 2017. "American Vandal Review: Netflix Sends Itself Up with a Four-Hour Penis Joke." *Guardian*, September 21, 2017. https://www.theguardian.com/tv-and-radio/2017/sep/21/american-vandal-review-netflix-sends-itself-up-with-a-four-hour-penis-joke.

Hillyer, Minette. 2010. "Labours of Love: Home Movies, Paracinema, and the Modern Work of Cinema Spectatorship." *Continuum: Journal of Media and Cultural Studies* 24 (5): 763–74.

Holt, Jennifer, and Kevin Sanson, eds. 2014. *Connected Viewing: Selling, Streaming, and Sharing Media in the Digital Era*. New York: Routledge.

Hooton, Christopher. 2016. "Making a Murderer, Serial and the Rise of the Blood-Boiling True Crime Story." *Independent*, January 5, 2016. https://www.independent.co.uk/arts-entertainment/tv/features/making-a-murderer-serial-and-the-rise-of-the-blood-boiling-true-crime-story-a6797836.html.

Hughes, Sarah. 2015. "We're Gripped, but Is 'True Crime' on TV Playing Fast and Loose with Facts?" *Observer*, March 21, 2015. https://www.theguardian.com/theobserver/2015/mar/22/murder-most-gripping-we-are-becoming-obsessed-with-real-life-crime.

Hullinger, Jessica. 2016. "I Am a Murderino." *The Week*, October 21, 2016. http://theweek.com/articles/654473/murderino.

Humanick, Rob. 2009. Review of *Dear Zachary: A Letter to a Son About His Father*. *Slant*, February 26, 2009. http://www.slantmagazine.com/dvd/review/dear-zachary-a-letter-to-a-son-about-his-father/1481.

Hussan, Huda. 2015. "The Angry Black Woman Must Die." *Buzzfeed*, July 31, 2015. https://www.buzzfeed.com/hudahassan/the-twilight-of-the-angry-black -woman?utm_term=.rdyNzKgAj#.vwPb10BP7.

"Hypodermic Needle Theory." n.d. University of Twente, Communication Studies Theories. Accessed July 18, 2018. https://www.utwente.nl/en/bms/ communication-theories/sorted-by-cluster/Mass%20Media/Hypodermic _Needle_Theory/.

IMDb User Reviews of *Dear Zachary: A Letter to a Son About His Father*. n.d. Accessed May 10, 2012. http://www.imdb.com/title/tt1152758/.

"IndieWire Interview: 'Dear Zachary' Director Kurt Kuenne." 2008. *Indiewire*, October 28, 2008. https://www.indiewire.com/2008/10/indiewire-interview -dear-zachary-director-kurt-kuenne-71494/.

Jackson, Lauren Michele. 2017. "We Need to Talk About Digital Blackface in Reaction Gifs." *Teen Vogue*, August 2, 2017. https://www.teenvogue.com/ story/digital-blackface-reaction-gifs.

Jacobsson Purewal, Sarah. 2013. "Be an Internet Super-Sleuth: Everybody Stalks So You May as Well Do It Right. Here Are the Key Tactics You Can Use to Gather Intel on Others—and Yourself." *Men's Health*, November 25, 2013. http://www.menshealth.com/techlust/internet-super-sleuth.

James, Robin. 2015. *Resilience and Melancholy: Pop Music, Feminism, Neoliberalism*. Winchester: Zero Books.

Jameson, Angela. 2016. "Netflix Share Prices Soar after Making a Murderer Boosts Subscriber Numbers." *Independent*, January 20, 2016. https://www .independent.co.uk/news/business/news/netflix-share-price-surges-after -making-a-murderer-helps-boost-subscriber-numbers-a6822331.html.

Jeltsen, Melissa. 2014. "Why Didn't You Just Leave? Six Domestic Violence Survivors Explain Why It's Never That Simple." *Huffington Post*, September 12, 2014. http://www.huffingtonpost.com/2014/09/12/why-didnt-you-just-leave _n_5805134.html.

Jenkins, Henry. 2006. "Welcome to Convergence Culture." *Confessions of an ACA Fan* (blog). June 19, 2006. http://henryjenkins.org/blog/2006/06/welcome _to_convergence_culture.html.

Jenkins, Henry, Sam Ford, and Joshua Green. 2013. *Spreadable Media: Creating Value and Meaning in a Networked Culture*. New York: New York University Press.

Jenkins, Nash. 2016. "Watch the Trailers for Netflix's Upcoming Amanda Knox Documentary." *Time*, September 9, 2016. http://time.com/4485063/amanda -knox-meredith-kercher-netflix/.

Jenner, Mareike. 2016a. *American TV Detective Dramas: Serial Investigations.* Houndsmill, Basingstoke: Palgrave Macmillan.

———. 2016b. "Is This TVIV? On Netflix, TVIII and Binge-Watching." *New Media and Society* 18 (2): 257–73.

———. 2017. "Binge-Watching: Video-on-Demand, Quality TV and Mainstreaming Fandom." *International Journal of Cultural Studies* 20 (3): 304–20.

Jensen, Charlotte Sun. 2014. "Reduced Narration, Intensified Emotion: The Film Trailer," *Projections: The Journal for Movies and Mind* 8, no. 1 (Summer): 105–25.

Jermyn, Deborah. 2004. "'This *Is* about Real People! Video Technologies, Actuality and Affect in the Television Crime Appeal." In *Understanding Reality Television*, edited by Su Holmes and Deborah Jermyn, 71–90. London: Routledge.

———. 2007. *Crime Watching: Investigating Real Crime TV.* London: I.B. Tauris.

Johnson, Catherine. 2012. *Branding Television.* Abingdon: Routledge.

Johnston, Keith. 2008. "The Coolest Way to Watch Movie Trailers in the World: Trailers in the Digital Age," *Convergence: The International Journal of Research into New Media Technologies* 14 (2): 145–60.

Jones, Ellen E. 2018. "Why Are Memes of Black People Reacting So Popular Online?" *Guardian,* July 8, 2018. https://www.theguardian.com/culture/2018/jul/08/why-are-memes-of-black-people-reacting-so-popular-online.

Jones, Nate. 2015. "*Making a Murderer* Directors on Bringing Steven Avery's Story to Netflix." *Vulture,* December 18, 2015. http://www.vulture.com/2015/12/making-a-murderer-directors-on-steven-avery-case.html.

Joy, Stuart. 2017. "Sexual Violence in Serial Form: *Breaking Bad* habits on TV." *Feminist Media Studies,* published online November 20, 2017, https://doi.org/10.1080/14680777.2017.1396484.

Juhasz, Alexandra. 2016. "How Do I (Not) Look? Live Feed Video and Viral Black Death," *JSTOR Daily,* July 20, 2016. https://daily.jstor.org/how-do-i-not-look/.

Kahana, Jonathan. 2009. "Introduction: What Now? Presenting Reenactment." *Framework* 50 (1 & 2): 46–60.

Kendall, Tina. 2016a. "Affect and the Ethics of Snuff in Extreme Art Cinema." In *Snuff: Real Death and Screen Media*, edited by Neil Jackson, Shaun Kimber, Johnny Walker, and Thomas Joseph Watson, 257–75. New York: Bloomsbury.

———. 2016b. "Staying on, or Getting off (the Bus); Approaching Speed in Cinema and Media Studies." *In Focus: Speed, Cinema Journal* 55, no. 2 (Winter): 112–18.

Kennedy, Liam. 2018. "'Man I'm All Torn up Inside': Analyzing Audience Responses to Making a Murderer." *Crime, Media, Culture* 14 (3): 391–408.

Kernan, Lisa. 2004. *Coming Attractions: Reading American Movie Trailers*. Austin: University of Texas Press.

Kiernan, Louise. 2014. "'Serial' Podcast Producers Talk Storytelling, Structure and If They Know Whodunnit." NiemanStoryboard, October 30, 2014. http://niemanstoryboard.org/stories/serial-podcast-producers-talk-story telling-structure-and-if-they-know-whodunnit/.

King, Geoff. 2004. "'Killingly Funny': Mixing Modalities in New Hollywood's Comedy-With-Violence." In *New Hollywood Violence*, edited by Steven Jay Schneider, 126–43. Manchester: Manchester University Press.

Kissell, Rick. 2015. "Ratings: HBO's 'The Jinx' Finale Draws Over 1 Million Viewers on Sunday." *Variety*, March 17, 2015. https://variety.com/2015/tv/ news/ratings-hbos-the-jinx-finale-draws-over-1-million-viewers-on-sunday -1201454423/.

Klinger, Barbara. 1989. "Digressions at the Cinema: Reception and Mass Culture." *Cinema Journal* 28, no. 4 (Summer): 3–19.

———. 2018a. "Gateway Bodies: Serial Form, Genre and White Femininity in Imported Crime TV." *Television & New Media*. First published April 27, 2018: 1–20.

———. 2018b. "Streaming." CFP: Themed Section of Particip@tions: Journal of Audience and Reception Studies. https://networks.h-net.org/node/14467/ discussions/1999112/journal-audience-and-reception-studies>

Konkle, Amanda. 2018. "Docudrama in the Post-Truth Era." In Media Res, May 25, 2018. http://mediacommons.org/imr/2018/05/25/docudrama-post -truth-era.

Korte, Gregory. 2014. "Obama on Ray Rice: Domestic Violence Is 'Contempt-ible.'" *USA Today*, September 8, 2014. https://eu.usatoday.com/story/theoval/ 2014/09/08/obama-ray-rice-statement/15315989/.

Kuenne, Kurt. 2006. "Dear Zachary: Statement from the Filmmaker." Original Statement, November 2006. http://dearzachary.com/statement/.

———. 2010. "Dear Zachary: Statement from the Filmmaker." Addendum, December 16, 2010. http://dearzachary.com/statement/.

Kuntsman, Adi, and Rebecca L. Stein. 2015. *Digital Militarism: Israel's Occupation in the Social Media Age*. Stanford: Stanford University Press.

Langlois, Ganaele, Joanna Redden, and Greg Elmer, eds. 2015. *Compromised Data: From Social Media to Big Data*. New York: Bloomsbury.

Larson, Sarah. 2014. "'Serial': The Podcast We've Been Waiting For." *New Yorker*,

October 9, 2014. https://www.newyorker.com/culture/sarah-larson/serial
-podcast-weve-waiting.

Lartey, Jamiles. 2016. "Film-Makers Demand Inquiry into 'Targeting' of People
Who Record Police." *Guardian*, August 11, 2016. https://www.theguardian
.com/film/2016/aug/10/filmmakers-citizen-journalists-justice-department
-investigation.

Lawson, Mark. 2015. "Serial Thrillers: Why True Crime Is Popular Culture's Most
Wanted." *Guardian*, December 12, 2015. https://www.theguardian.com/culture/
2015/dec/12/serial-thrillers-why-true-is-popular-cultures-most-wanted.

Lebeau, Vicky. 2008. *Childhood and Cinema*. London: Reaktion Books.

Lee, Benjamin. 2016. "Amanda Knox Review—Slick Documentary Excels
with Unprecedented Access." *Guardian*, September 15, 2016. https://www
.theguardian.com/film/2016/sep/15/amanda-knox-review-documentary
-netflix-meredith-kercher.

Lindner, Christoph. 2014. "Foreword: The Serial Drive." In *Serialization in Popular Culture*, edited by Rob Allen and Thijs van den Berg, ix–xi. New York:
Routledge.

Little, Janine Mary. 2015. "Jill Meagher CCTV." *Feminist Media Studies* 15 (3):
397–410.

Longworth, Karina. 2008. "Dear Zachary Review." SpoutBlog. https://web
.archive.org/web/20081105034851/http://blog.spout.com/.

Lotz, Amanda. 2017. *Portals: A Treatise on Internet-Distributed Television*. Ann
Arbor: Michigan Publishing.

Loughrey, Clarisse. 2015. "Making a Murderer: Fans Flood Prosecutor's Yelp
Page with Negative Reviews." *Independent*, December 30, 2015. https://www
.independent.co.uk/arts-entertainment/tv/news/making-a-murderer-fans
-flood-prosecutors-yelp-page-with-negative-reviews-a6790911.html.

Macatee, Rebecca. 2014. "Janay Palmer Supports Ray Rice After Shocking
Video Surfaces, Blames Media for Husband's NFL Suspension." *Eonline.
com*, September 9, 2014. Accessed June 15, 2018. https://www.eonline.com/
news/577262/janay-palmer-supports-ray-rice-as-shocking-video-surfaces
-blames-media-for-husband-s-nfl-suspension.

Malkowski, Jennifer. 2017. *Dying in Full Detail: Mortality and Digital Documentary*. Durham: Duke University Press.

Martin, Greg. 2018. *Crime, Media and Culture*. New York: Routledge.

Massanari, Adrienne. 2015. *Participatory Culture, Community, and Play: Learning
from Reddit*. New York: Peter Lang.

———. 2017. "#Gamergate and The Fappening: How Reddit's Algorithm,

Governance and Culture Support Toxic Technocultures." *New Media and Society* 19 (3): 329–46.

Massumi, Brian. 2012. "Affective Attunement in a Field of Catastrophe: A Conversation between Erin Manning, Brian Massumi, Josef Fritsch and Bodil Marie Stavning Thomsen." *Peripeti*, June 6, 2012. http://www.peripeti.dk/2012/06/06/affective-attunement-in-a-field-of-catastrophe/.

Matrix, Sidneyeve. 2014. "The Netflix Effect: Teens, Binge Watching and On-Demand Digital Media Trends." *Jeunesse: Young People, Texts, Cultures* 6 (1): 119–38.

McCormick, Casey. 2016. " 'Forward is the Battle Cry': Binge-Viewing Netflix's *House of Cards*." In *The Netflix Effect*, edited by Kevin McDonald and Daniel Smith-Rowsey, 101–16. New York: Bloomsbury.

McGlynn, Clare. n.d. "Image-based Sexual Abuse: Quick Reads." Accessed June 15, 2018. https://claremcglynn.com/imagebasedsexualabuse/revenge-pornography-quick-reads/.

McIntyre, Lee. 2018. *Post Truth*. Cambridge: MIT Press.

McKay, Sally. 2018. "The Affect of Animated GIFS (Tom Moody, Petra Cortright, Lorna Mills)." *ArtFCity*, July 16, 2018. http://artfcity.com/2018/07/16/the-affect-of-animated-gifs-tom-moody-petra-cortright-lorna-mills/

McNamara, Mary. 2015a. "If We Watch the Virginia TV Shooting Is the Suspected Shooter 'Winning'?" *Los Angeles Times*, August 26, 2015. https://www.latimes.com/entertainment/tv/la-et-st-critics-notebook-virginia-shooting-20150827-53-column.html.

———. 2015b. " 'Making a Murderer' Probes a True-Crime Puzzler." *Los Angeles Times*, December 18, 2015. https://www.latimes.com/entertainment/tv/la-et-st-making-a-murderer-20151217-column.html?outputType=amp.

McNamara, Michelle. 2018. *I'll Be Gone in the Dark: One Woman's Obsessive Search for the Golden State Killer*. London: Faber & Faber.

Mendes, Kaitlynn, Jessica Ringrose, and Jessalyn Keller. 2018. "#MeToo and the Promise and Pitfalls of Challenging Rape Culture through Digital Feminist Activism." *European Journal of Women's Studies* 25 (2): 236–46.

Merriman, Rebecca. 2016. "Khloe Kardashian Left Outraged over *Making a Murderer* after Binge-Watching Netflix Hit: 'How Do We Fix This?' " *Mirror*, March 21, 2016. https://www.mirror.co.uk/3am/celebrity-news/khloe-kardashian-left-outraged-over-7601626.

Middleton, Jason. 2014. *Documentary's Awkward Turn: Cringe Comedy and Media Spectatorship*. New York: Routledge.

Miller, Jenni. 2008. "Dear Zachary: A Letter to a Son About His Father." *Premiere*

November 18, 2008. https://web.archive.org/web/20090607132247/http://
www.premiere.com/Review/Movies/Dear-Zachary-A-Letter-to-a-Son
-About-His-Father.

Miller, Laura. 2015. "'Killed Them All, Of Course': The Astonishing Finale of HBO's
'The Jinx' Redeems the True-Crime Series' Many Weaknesses." *salon.com*,
March 16, 2015, https://www.salon.com/2015/03/16/killed_them_all_of_
course_robert_durst_arrested_in_shocking_coda_to_hbos_the_jinx_finale/.

Milner, Ryan. 2013. "Hacking the Social: Internet Memes, Identity Antagonism,
and the Logic of Lulz." *Fibreculture Journal* issue 22. http://twentytwo
.fibreculturejournal.org/fcj-156-hacking-the-social-internet-memes-identity
-antagonism-and-the-logic-of-lulz/.

Minor, Laura. 2015. "Hybridity, Extratextuality and the Docudrama: Re-
evaluating 'Spoilers' in *The Jinx*." *Flow*, November 21, 2015. https://www
.flowjournal.org/2015/11/re-evaluating-spoilers-in-the-jinx/.

Mittell, Jason. 2004. *Genre and Television: From Cop Shows to Cartoons in American Culture*. New York: Routledge.

———. 2015. *Complex TV: The Poetics of Contemporary TV Storytelling*. New
York: New York University Press.

Mnookin, Jennifer L. 2005. "Reproducing a Trial: Evidence and Its Assessment
in Paradise Lost." In *Law on the Screen*, edited by Austin Sarat, Lawrence
Douglas, and Martha Merrill Umphrey, 153–200. Palo Alto: Stanford University Press.

Morozov, Evgeny. 2009. "Foreign Policy: Brave New World of Slacktivism."
NPR, May 19, 2009. http://www.npr.org/templates/story/story.php?storyId
=104302141.

Morris, Errol. 2008. "Play It Again, Sam (Re-enactments, Part One)." *New York
Times*, April 3, 2008. http://opinionator.blogs.nytimes.com/2008/04/03/play
-it-again-sam-re-enactments-part-one/?_php=true&_type=blogs&_r=0.

"Mugshot Gains 95,000 Likes on Police Facebook Page." 2014. *BBC Newsbeat*,
June 23, 2014. http://www.bbc.co.uk/newsbeat/article/27936265/mugshot
-gains-95000-likes-on-police-facebook-page.

Mulvey, Laura. 2006. *Death 24x a Second: Stillness and the Moving Image*. London: Reaktion Books.

Murley, Jean. 2008. *The Rise of True Crime: 20th-Century Murder and American
Popular Culture*. Westport, CT: Praeger.

Musser, Charles. 1996. "Film Truth, Documentary and the Law: Justice at the
Margins." *University of San Francisco Law Review* 30 (4): 963–84.

Nakumara, Lisa. 2014. "'I WILL DO EVERYthing That Am Asked': Scambaiting,

Digital Show-Space, and the Racial Violence of Social Media." *Journal of Visual Culture* 13 (3): 257–74.

———. 2015. "Blaming, Shaming, and the Feminization of Social Media." In *Feminist Surveillance Studies*, edited by Rachel E. Dubrofsky and Shoshana Amielle Magnet, 221–28. Durham: Duke University Press.

National Inquiry into Missing and Murdered Indigenous Women and Girls. n.d. Accessed July 10, 2018. http://www.mmiwg-ffada.ca.

Nededog, Jethro. 2016. "Here's How Popular Netflix's 'Making a Murderer' Really Was According to a Research Company." *Business Insider UK*, February 14, 2016. https://www.businessinsider.com.au/netflix-making-a-murderer -ratings-2016-2.

Nelson, Hillary. n.d. "52 Best True-Crime Podcasts: The Post-*Serial* Boom." *Vulture*. Accessed November 16, 2018. https://www.vulture.com/article/52-best -true-crime-podcasts.html.

"Netflix Announces New Original Documentary Series *Making a Murderer.*" 2015. Netflix Media Center, November 9, 2015. https://media.netflix.com/ en/press-releases/netflix-announces-new-original-documentary-series -making-a-murderer.

"Netflix's 'The Keepers' is a Rallying Cry for Those Suffering in Silence (REVIEW)." 2017. For All Nerds. May 23, 2017. fanbros.com, https://forall nerds.com/review-netflixs-the-keepers/.

Newitz, Annalee. 1997. "White Savagery and Humiliations, or A New Racial Consciousness in the Media." In *White Trash: Race and Class in America*, edited by Matt Wray and AnnaLee Newitz, 131–54. New York: Routledge.

Nichols, Bill. 2001. *Introduction to Documentary*. Bloomington: Indiana University Press.

———. 2008. "Documentary Reenactment and the Fantasmatic Subject." *Critical Inquiry* 35 (Autumn): 72–89.

———. 2010. *Introduction to Documentary.* 2nd ed. Bloomington: Indiana University Press.

Noble, Safiya Umoja. 2018. *Algorithms of Oppression: How Search Engines Reinforce Racism*. New York: New York University Press.

North, Anna. 2018. "The Sexual Assault Allegations Against #MeToo Advocate Asia Argento, Explained." *Vox,* August 23, 2018. https://www.vox.com/ 2018/8/20/17758714/asia-argento-jimmy-bennett-harvey-weinstein-me-too -movement-sexual-assault-allegations.

Nti-Asare, Anna. 2015. "When People Say Ray Rice = Solange Knowles."

Huffington Post, US edition, March 19, 2015. http://www.huffingtonpost. com/anna-ntiasare/when-people-say-ray-rices_b_6880192.html.

Nussbaum, Emily. 2015. "What About Bob? The Strange Allure of Robert Durst and 'The Jinx.'" *New Yorker*, March 23, 2015. https://www.newyorker.com/ magazine/2015/03/23/what-about-bob.

O'Connell, Michael. 2015. "Emmys: The Jinx Creators Break Silence, Call Robert Durst Not Just 'Random Killer. He's a Strategic Killer.'" *Hollywood Reporter*, June 10, 2015. https://www.hollywoodreporter.com/news/emmys -jinx-creators-break-silence-801240

O'Gorman, Daniel. 2012. "Empathy After 9/11." *Alluvium: 21st Century Writing, 21st Century Approaches*, June 1, 2012. http://www.alluvium-journal.org/ author/daniel-o-gorman/.

O'Meara, Jennifer. n.d. "'Like Movies for Radio': Media Convergence and the *Serial* Podcast Sensation." *Frames Cinema Journal*, issue 8. Accessed December 6, 2018. http://framescinemajournal.com/article/like-movies-for-radio -media-convergence-and-the-serial-podcast-sensation/.

Opel, Andy. 2005. "Paradise Lost I & II: Documentary, Gothic, and the Monster of Justice." *Jump Cut* 47. http://www.ejumpcut.org/archive/jc47.2005/goth/ text.html.

Orgeron, Marsha, and Devin Orgeron. 2007. "Familial Pursuits, Editorial Acts: Documentaries after the Age of Home Video." *Velvet Light Trap* 60 (Fall): 47–62.

Otterson, Joe. 2016. "'Amanda Knox' Ratings Are No Killer on Netflix, Firm Says." *Wrap*, October 6, 2016. https://www.thewrap.com/amanda-knox -ratings-are-no-killer-on-netflix-firm-says/.

Paasonen, Susanna. 2015. "A Midsummer's Bonfire: Affective Intensities of Online Debate." In *Networked Affect*, edited by Ken Hillis, Susanna Paasonen, and Michael Petit, 27–42. Cambridge: MIT Press.

———. 2017. "Time to Celebrate the Most Disgusting Video Online." *Porn Studies*. 4 (4): 463–67.

Paasonen, Susanna, Ken Hillis, and Michael Petit. 2015. "Introduction: Networks of Transmission: Intensity, Sensation, Value." In *Networked Affect*, edited by Ken Hillis, Susanna Paasonen, and Michael Petit, 1–24. Cambridge: MIT Press.

Panse, Silke. 2014. "The Judging Spectator in the Image." In *A Critique of Judgment in Film and Television*, edited by Silke Panse and Dennis Rothermel, 33–70. Basingstoke: Palgrave Macmillan.

Panse, Silke, and Dennis Rothermel. 2014. "Judgment between Ethics and

Aesthetics: An Introduction." In *A Critique of Judgment in Film and Television,* edited by Silke Panse and Dennis Rothermel, 1–30. Basingstoke: Palgrave Macmillan.

Papacharissi, Zizi. 2015. *Affective Publics: Sentiment, Technology, and Politics.* Oxford: Oxford University Press.

Patterson, John. 2016. "From Serial to Making a Murderer: Documentaries Renew Hope for Justice." *Guardian,* August 13, 2016. https://www .theguardian.com/culture/2016/aug/13/making-murderer-serial-jinx-crime -documentaries-brendan-dassey.

Perren, Alisa. 2001/2002. "Sex, Lies, and Marketing: Miramax and the Development of the Quality Indie Blockbuster." *Film Quarterly* Winter 55 (2): 30-39.

Petersen, Jennifer. 2011. *Murder, the Media, and the Politics of Public Feelings: Remembering Matthew Shepard and James Byrd Jr.* Bloomington: Indiana University Press.

Petersen, Anne Helen. 2010. "Smut Goes Corporate: *TMZ* and the Conglomerate, Convergent Face of Celebrity Gossip." *Television and New Media* 11 (1): 62–81.

Pettman, Dominic. 2016. *Infinite Distraction.* Cambridge: Polity Press.

Pile, Jonathan. 2016. "Amanda Knox Review." *Empire,* October 3, 2016. https:// www.empireonline.com/movies/amanda-knox/review/.

Plantinga, Carl. 2013. " 'I'll Believe It When I Trust the Source': Documentary Images and Visual Evidence." In *The Documentary Film Book,* edited by Brian Winston, 40–47. London: British Film Institute/Palgrave Macmillan.

Poniewozik, James. 2015. "Streaming TV Isn't Just a New Way to Watch: It's a New Genre," *New York Times,* December 16, 2015. http://www.nytimes.com/ 2015/12/20/arts/television/streaming-tv-isnt-just-a-new-way-to-watch-its-a -new-genre.html.

"Proper Use of Tags: 4 Tips to Grow Your Audience." 2015. *Grapevine,* March 26, 2015. http://blog.grapevinelogic.com/proper-use-of-tags-4-tips-to-grow -your-youtube-audience/.

Proud, Amelia. 2014. "Beyoncé's Enraged Sister Solange Kicks and Throws Punches at Jay Z in Violent Attack after Met Gala." *Daily Mail,* May 12, 2014. http://www.dailymail.co.uk/tvshowbiz/article-2626389/Jay-Z-ATTACKED -Beyonces-sister-Solange.html.

Rafter, Nicole. 2006. *Shots in the Mirror: Crime Films and Society.* Oxford: Oxford University Press.

Rapping, Elayne. 2003. *Law and Justice as Seen on TV.* New York: New York University Press.

Rawlinson, Kevin. 2015. "Virginia Shooting: Facebook and Twitter Told to Rethink Autoplay Video." *BBC News,* August 27, 2015, http://www.bbc.co.uk/news/technology-34073206.

"Ray Rice Will Reportedly Claim TMZ Edited Tape . . . Dumbest Defense Ever." 2014. *TMZ,* September 21, 2014. http://www.tmz.com/2014/09/21/ray-rice-tape-elevator-video-tmz-sports-edited-defense/.

Rayns, Tony. 2013. "Review: The Act of Killing." *Sight and Sound* July 2013. http://www.bfi.org.uk/news-opinion/sight-sound-magazine/reviews-recommendations/review-act-killing.

"Revenge Porn: The Facts." n.d. Accessed December 6, 2018. https://assets.publishing.service.gov.uk/government/uploads/system/uploads/attachment_data/file/405286/revenge-porn-factsheet.pdf.

Rich, Katey. 2008. "Exclusive Interview: Dear Zachary Director Kurt Kuenne." *Cinemablend.com,* October 31, 2008. http://www.cinemablend.com/new/Exclusive-Interview-Dear-Zachary-Director-Kurt-Kuenne-10733.html.

Richman, Darren. 2014. "Why Serial Is the Greatest Podcast Ever Made," *Telegraph,* November 14, 2014. https://www.telegraph.co.uk/men/the-filter/11230770/Why-Serial-is-the-greatest-podcast-ever-made.html.

Robertson, Campbell. 2011. "Deal Frees 'West Memphis Three' in Arkansas." *New York Times,* August 19, 2011. https://www.nytimes.com/2011/08/20/us/20arkansas.html?pagewanted=all&_r=0.

Ronson, Jon. 2015. *So You've Been Publicly Shamed.* London: Picador.

Rosenberg, Alyssa. 2014. "Why We Watch Awful Things Like Solange Knowles's Attack on Jay Z." *Washington Post,* May 12, 2014. https://www.washingtonpost.com/news/act-four/wp/2014/05/12/why-we-watch-awful-things-like-solange-knowles-attack-on-jay-z/?utm_term=.e51dda13d048.

Rosenberg, Eli. 2018. "She Stalked the Golden State Killer until She Died. Some Think Her Work Led to the Suspect's Arrest." *Washington Post,* April 26, 2018. https://www.washingtonpost.com/news/true-crime/wp/2018/04/26/she-stalked-the-golden-state-killer-until-she-died-some-think-her-work-led-to-the-suspects-arrest/?utm_term=.62ff2a554358.

Rule, Ann. (1980) 2000. *The Stranger Beside Me.* New York: Norton.

Ryan, Erin Gloria. 2016. "Pantsuit Nation Is the Worst: Why a Book of Uplifting Facebook Posts Won't Heal America." *Daily Beast,* December 21, 2016. http://www.thedailybeast.com/pantsuit-nation-is-the-worst-why-a-book-of-uplifting-facebook-posts-wont-heal-america.

Salter, Michael. 2017. *Crime, Justice and Social Media.* London: Routledge.

Sanchez, Mark. 2014. "Ray Rice: That Elevator Tape Was Unfairly Edited." *New York Post*, September 21, 2014. http://nypost.com/2014/09/21/ray-rice-that -elevator-tape-was-unfairly-edited/.

Sartin, Hank. 2008. "Dear Zachary: A Letter to a Son About His Father." *Time Out Chicago*, Issue 193: November 6–12.

Schmid, David. 2005. *Natural Born Celebrities: Serial Killers in American Culture*. Chicago: University of Chicago Press.

Schmidle, Nicholas. 2016. "The Digital Dirt: How *TMZ* Gets the Videos and Photos that Celebrities Want to Hide." *New Yorker*, February 22, 2016. http:// www.newyorker.com/magazine/2016/02/22/inside-harvey-levins-tmz.

Schulz, Kathryn. 2016. "Dead Certainty: How 'Making a Murderer' Goes Wrong." *New Yorker*, January 25, 2016. https://www.newyorker.com/magazine/2016/ 01/25/dead-certainty.

Sciretta, Peter. 2012. "The Imposter Is This Year's 'Catfish' (Sundance 2012)," *Slashfilm* (blog). January 25, 2012. http://www.slashfilm.com/the-impostor -years-catfish-sundance-2012/.

Seale, Jack. 2017. "Who Murdered Sister Cathy: Netflix Takes True Crime to the Next Level." *Guardian*, May 18, 2017. https://www.theguardian.com/ tv-and-radio/2017/may/18/the-keepers-netflix-nun-murder-baltimore-true -crime-documentary.

Seitz, Matt Zoller. 2015. "I've Never Seen Anything Like the End of *The Jinx*." *Vulture*, March 16, 2015. http://www.vulture.com/2015/03/ive-never-seen -anything-like-the-jinxs-ending.html.

Selby, Jenn. 2014. "What Jay Z Really Said to Solange . . . According to the Internet." *Independent*, May 13, 2014. http://www.independent.co.uk/news/ people/what-jay-z-really-said-to-solange-according-to-the-internet-9361169 .html.

Seltzer, Mark. 2007. *True Crime: Observations on Violence and Modernity*. New York: Routledge.

Serial Reddit. n.d. Accessed May 5, 2016. https://www.reddit.com/r/serial podcast/.

Serjeant, Jill. 2016. "Americans Become Judge and Jury in True Crime TV Obsession." Reuters, January 12, 2016. https://www.reuters.com/article/us -television-truecrime-idUSKCN0UQ2Q320160112.

Severson, Kim. 2018. "Asia Argento, a #MeToo Leader, Made a Deal with Her Own Accuser." *New York Times*, August 19, 2018. https://www.nytimes.com/ 2018/08/19/us/asia-argento-assault-jimmy-bennett.html.

Sharma, Devika, and Frederik Tygstrup. 2015. "Introduction." In *Structures of*

Feeling: Affectivity and The Study of Culture, edited by Devika Sharma and Frederik Tygstrup, 1–25. Berlin: De Gruyter.

Sharma, Sanjay. 2013. "Black Twitter? Racial Hashtags, Networks and Contagion." *New Formations* 78: 46–64.

Sharma, Sudeep. 2016. "Netflix and the Documentary Boom." In *The Netflix Effect*, edited by Kevin McDonald and Daniel Smith-Rowsey, 143–54. New York: Bloomsbury.

Shaviro, Steven. 2010. *Post-Cinematic Affect*. Ropley: Zero Books, 2010.

Shifman, Limor. 2013. "Memes in a Digital World: Reconciling with a Conceptual Troublemaker." *Journal of Computer-Mediated Communication* 18: 362–77.

———. 2014. "The Cultural Logic of Photo-Based Meme Genres." *Journal of Visual Culture* 13 (3): 340–58.

Smaill, Belinda. 2010. *The Documentary: Politics, Emotion, Culture*. Houndsmill, Basingstoke, Hampshire: Palgrave Macmillan.

Smith, Nigel. 2016. "Making a Murderer Directors Defend Series: 'Of Course We Left Out Evidence.'" *Guardian*, January 17, 2016. https://www.theguardian .com/culture/2016/jan/17/making-a-murderer-netflix-steven-avery.

Snead, James. 1994. *White Screens/Black Images: Hollywood From the Dark Side*. New York: Routledge.

Snickars, Pelle. 2009. "The Archival Cloud." In *The YouTube Reader*, edited by Pelle Snickars and Patrick Vonderau, 292–313. Stockholm: National Library of Sweden.

Snickars, Pelle, and Patrick Vonderau. 2009. "Introduction." In *The YouTube Reader*, edited by Pelle Snickars and Patrick Vonderau, 9–21. Stockholm: National Library of Sweden.

Spangler, Todd. 2018. "Netflix's New 30-Second Mobile Previews Look Like Snapchat and Instagram Stories." *Variety*, April 19, 2018. https://variety.com/ 2018/digital/news/netflix-mobile-previews-trailers-snapchat-instagram -stories-1202758403/.

Srnicek, Nick. 2016. *Platform Capitalism*. Cambridge: Polity Press.

Steimatsky, Noa. 2017. *The Face on Film*. Oxford: Oxford University Press.

Strause, Jackie. 2018. "Tarana Burke Responds to Asia Argento Report: 'There Is No Model Survivor.'" *Hollywood Reporter,* August 20, 2018. https://www .hollywoodreporter.com/news/me-founder-tarana-burke-responds-asia -argento-report-1135904.

Surowiecki, James. 2013. "The Wise Way to Crowdsource a Manhunt." *New Yorker*, April 23, 2013. https://www.newyorker.com/news/daily-comment/ the-wise-way-to-crowdsource-a-manhunt.

"The Tag." n.d. *TV Tropes*. Accessed May 29, 2018. http://tvtropes.org/pmwiki/pmwiki.php/Main/TheTag.

Taylor, Alex. 2018. "The Iconography behind Beyonce's 'Iconic' Coachella Sets." *BBC News*, April 23, 2018. https://www.bbc.co.uk/news/entertainment-arts-43783861.

Thain, Alanna. 2009. "Insecurity Cameras: Cinematic Elevators, Infidelity and the Crime of Time." *Intermédialités* 14 (Autumn): 51–66.

"The Thin Blue Line: Harvey Letter." Accessed March 20, 2016. Errolmorris.com, http://www.errolmorris.com/film/tbl_harveyletter.html.

Thomas, Sarah. 2014. "Celebrity in the 'Twitterverse': History, Authenticity and the Multiplicity of Stardom Situating the 'Newness' of Twitter." *Celebrity Studies* 5 (3): 242–55.

Tomasulo, Frank. 1996. " 'I'll See It When I Believe It': Rodney King and the Prison-House of Video." In *The Persistence of History: Cinema, Television, and the Modern Event*, edited by Vivian Sobchack, 69–88. New York: Routledge.

Torchin, Leshu. 2012. *Creating the Witness: Documenting Genocide on Film, Video, and the Internet*. Minneapolis: University of Minnesota Press.

Tryon, Chuck. 2013. *On-Demand Culture: Digital Delivery and the Future of Movies*. New Brunswick: Rutgers University Press.

Tsai, Martin. 2008. "*Dear Zachary: A Letter to a Son About His Father* Is a Lifetime in the Making." *Village Voice* October 29, 2008. https://www.villagevoice.com/2008/10/29/dear-zachary-a-letter-to-a-son-about-his-father-is-a-lifetime-in-the-making/.

Turner Review and Investigation. 2006. Office of the Child and Youth Advocate, Province of Newfoundland and Labrador. https://www.childandyouthadvocate.nl.ca/pdfs/turner-v1.pdf.

van der Bijl, Hanno. 2015. "Whites Only: Segregated Elevators during Jim Crow." *Elevator World Unplugged (blog)*, January 19, 2015. http://www.elevatorworld.com/blogs/2015/01/.

van der Meulen, Emily, and Robert Heynen. 2016. "Gendered Visions: Reimagining Surveillance Studies." In *Gender and The Politics of Surveillance*, edited by Emily van der Meulen and Robert Heynen, 1–32. Toronto: University of Toronto Press.

van Dijck, José. 2008. "Future Memories: The Construction of Cinematic Hindsight." *Theory, Culture and Society* 25 (3): 71–87.

Vernallis, Carol. 2013. *Unruly Media: YouTube, Music Video, and the New Digital Cinema*. Oxford: Oxford University Press.

Wadhwa, Tarun. 2013. "Lessons from Crowdsourcing the Boston Bombing Investigation." *Forbes.com,* April 22, 2013. https://www.forbes.com/
sites/tarunwadhwa/2013/04/22/lessons-from-crowdsourcing-the-boston
-marathon-bombings-investigation/#3cb94fd04424.

Wanzo, Rebecca. 2008. "The Era of Lost (White) Girls: On Body and Event."
Differences: A Journal of Feminist Cultural Studies 19 (2): 99–126.

Warren, Rossalyn. 2014. "Ray Rice Abuse Video Sparks a Powerful #WhyIStayed
Conversation about Domestic Violence." *Buzzfeed.* September 9, 2014.
https://www.buzzfeednews.com/article/rossalynwarren/ray-rice-abuse
-video-sparks-powerful-twitter-hashtag.

Watson, Thomas Joseph. 2014. "Rethinking History Through Documentary:
Paradise Lost and the Documented Case of the West Memphis Three." In
Cinema, Television and History: New Approaches, edited by Laura Mee
and Johnny Walker, 200–220. Newcastle upon Tyne: Cambridge Scholars
Publishing.

West, Kelly. n.d. "Unsurprising: Netflix Survey Indicates People Like to Binge-
Watch TV." *CinemaBlend.* Accessed July 12, 2018. https://www.cinemablend
.com/television/Unsurprising-Netflix-Survey-Indicates-People-Like-Binge
-Watch-TV-61045.html.

Wheatley, Helen. 2001. "Real Crime Television in the 8–9 Slot: Consuming Fear."
In "Factual Entertainment on British Television: The Midlands TV Research
Group 8–9 Project." *European Journal of Cultural Studies* 4 (1): 29–62.

Whittaker, Richard. 2013. "Making a 'Killing': Joshua Oppenheimer on the
Half-Decade He Spent Filming for 'The Act of Killing.'" *Austin Chronicle,*
August 9, 2013. http://www.austinchronicle.com/screens/2013-08-09/making
-a-killing/.

Whitworth, Dan. 2018. "Sextortion: Big Rise in Victims with 'Tens of Thousands
at Risk.'" *BBC News,* May 24, 2018. https://www.bbc.co.uk/news/newsbeat
-43433015.

Wilkinson, Ron. 2008. "Dear Zachary: A Letter to His Son About His
Father." *M & C Movies,* December 7, 2008. https://web.archive.org/
web/20081210081634/http://www.monstersandcritics.com/movies/reviews/
article_1447047.php/Dear_Zachary_A_Letter_to_a_Son_About_His_Father
_-_Movie_Review.

Williams, Linda. 1993. "Mirrors without Memories: Truth, History, and the New
Documentary." *Film Quarterly* 46 (3): 9–21.

———. 2014. *On the Wire.* Durham: Duke University Press.

Winfrey Harris, Tamara. 2014. "Precious Mettle: The Myth of the Strong Black

Woman." *Bitch Media,* May 13, 2014. https://www.bitchmedia.org/article/
precious-mettle-myth-strong-black-woman.

Wolters, Eugene. 2013. "Jodi Dean and Andrew Feenberg Debate the Inter-
web." *Critical-Theory.com,* April 21, 2013. http://www.critical-theory.com/
jodi-dean-and-andrew-feenberg-debate-the-interweb/.

Wong, Julie Carrie. 2014. "The Problem with 'Serial' and the Model Minority
Myth." *Buzzfeed News,* November 16, 2014. https://www.buzzfeednews.com/
article/juliacarriew/the-problem-with-serial-and-the-model-minority-myth.

Wood, Helen. 2018. "The Magaluf Girl: A Public Sex Scandal and the Digital
Class Relations of Social Contagion." *Feminist Media Studies,* April 11,
2018. https://www.tandfonline.com/doi/full/10.1080/14680777.2018.1447352
?needAccess=true&instName=Anglia+Ruskin+University.

Yamato, Jen. 2016. "How We Made 'Making a Murder': Filmmakers Moira
Demos and Laura Ricciardi Pull Back the Curtain." *Daily Beast,* March 1,
2016. https://www.thedailybeast.com/how-we-made-making-a-murderer
-filmmakers-moira-demos-and-laura-ricciardi-pull-back-the-curtain.

Yardley, Elizabeth, Adam George Thomas Lynes, David Wilson, and Emma Kelly.
2018. "What's the Deal with 'Websleuthing?' News Media Representations
of Amateur Detectives in Networked Spaces." *Crime, Media, Culture* 14 (1):
81–109.

Yardley, Elizabeth, Emma Kelly, and Shona Robinson-Edwards. 2018. "Forever
Trapped in the Imaginary of Late Capitalism? The Serialized True Crime
Podcast as a Wake-Up Call in Times of Criminological Slumber." *Crime,
Media, Culture,* September 11, 2018. https://journals.sagepub.com/doi/pdf/
10.1177/1741659018799375.

Young, Alison. 2010. *The Scene of Violence: Cinema, Crime, Affect.* Oxon:
Routledge-Cavendish.

"You're Still Hooked and Netflix Knows Why." 2016. The Netflix Media Center. September 21, 2016. https://media.netflix.com/en/press-releases/youre
-still-hooked-and-netflix-knows-why.

Yurcaba, Josephine. 2014. "This American Crime: Sarah Koenig on Her Hit Podcast 'Serial.'" *Rolling Stone,* October 24, 2014. https://www.rollingstone.com/
culture/features/sarah-koenig-on-serial-20141024.

Zafar, Mishal Ali. 2018. "How Many Episodes Is 'The Staircase'? This Newly
Updated Series Details Every Dramatic Turn in The Case." *Romper,* June
8, 2018. https://www.romper.com/p/how-many-episodes-is-the-staircase
-this-newly-updated-series-details-every-dramatic-turn-in-the-case-9341337.

Zeitchick, Steven. 2015. "Is 'The Jinx' a Threat to Traditional Feature

Documentaries?" *Los Angeles Times* March 18, 2015. https://www.latimes.com/entertainment/movies/moviesnow/la-et-mn-the-jinx-series-documentary-hbo-20150318-story.html.

Zelenko, Michael. 2014. "What's Next for Reddit's Amateur Serial Sleuths?" *Verge*, December 19, 2014. https://www.theverge.com/2014/12/19/7421469/whats-next-for-the-reddits-amateur-serial-sleuths.

Zizek, Slavoj. 2013. "Slavoj Zizek on 'The Act of Killing' and the Modern Trend of 'Privatizating Public Space." *New Statesman,* July 12, 2013. http://www.newstatesman.com/culture/2013/07/slavoj-zizek-act-killing-and-modern-trend-privatising-public-space.

Index

CPSIA information can be obtained
at www.ICGtesting.com
Printed in the USA
FSHW011058261019
63403FS